IMAGES
of America

NORTHFIELD

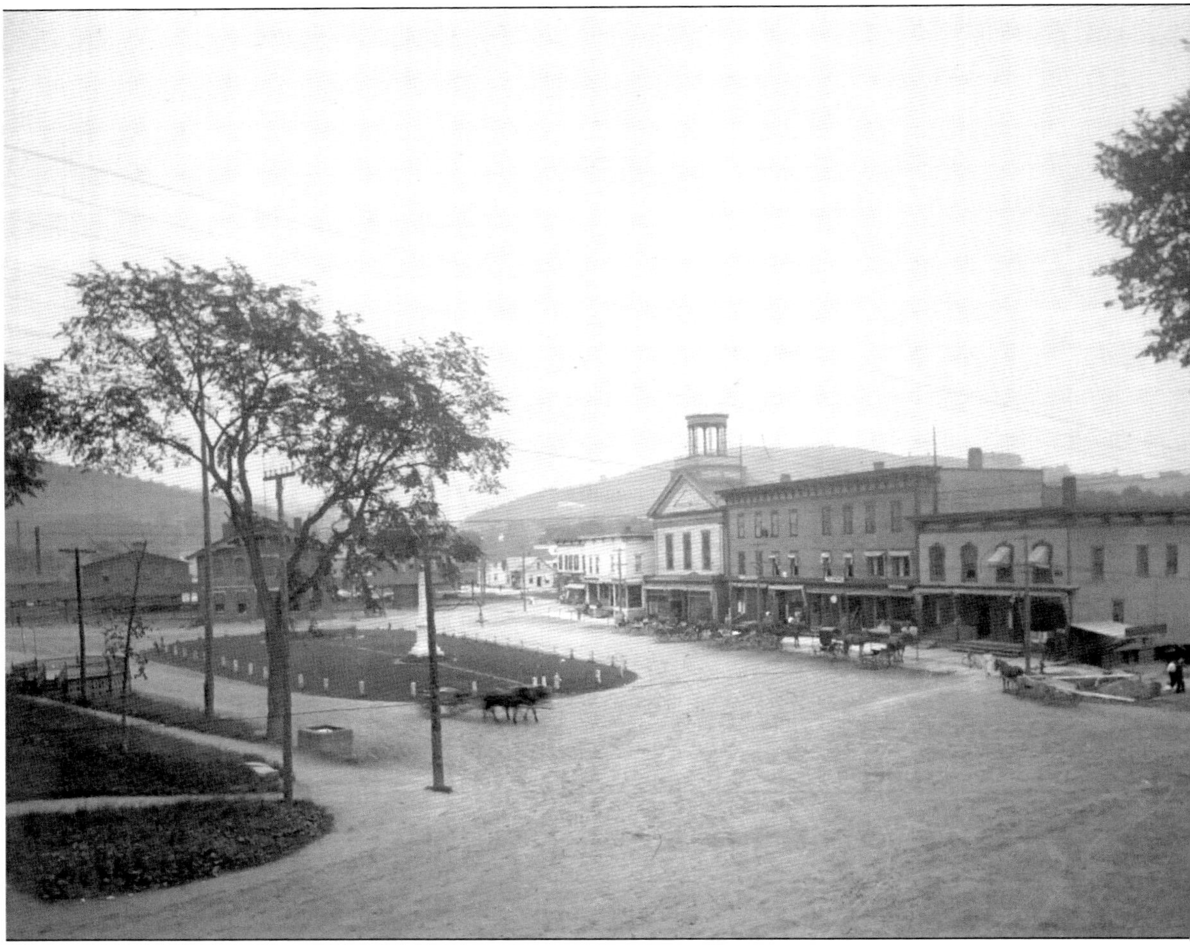

The essence of old Northfield is captured in this beautiful photograph of the Common, looking west. One sees the railroad station with its wings, the Civil War Monument in the center, the bandstand and watering trough on the left, and the Universalist Church and stores on the right. (Courtesy of the Northfield Historical Society.)

On the Cover: Woodbury Granite Company stone workers are shown in one of their stone sheds in the early 1900s. (Courtesy of the Northfield Historical Society.)

IMAGES
of America

NORTHFIELD

The Northfield Historical Society

ARCADIA
PUBLISHING

ISBN 978-1-4671-2076-0

Published by Arcadia Publishing
Charleston, South Carolina

Printed in the United States of America

Library of Congress Control Number: 2013942632

For all general information, please contact Arcadia Publishing:
Telephone 843-853-2070
Fax 843-853-0044
E-mail sales@arcadiapublishing.com
For customer service and orders:
Toll-Free 1-888-313-2665

Visit us on the Internet at www.arcadiapublishing.com

This book is dedicated to all in the Northfield community—past, present, and future. Without any of you, this book could not have been possible.

Contents

ACKNOWLEDGMENTS

The collaborative efforts of four members of the Northfield Historical Society have brought this book to life. Our appreciation goes out to these four members: Donald Boardman, Christopher Delmas, Linda deNeergaard, and Karen Halsted. This project began with a common interest in sharing with others their passion for the history, the land, and the people of Northfield. Many wonderful hours were spent pouring through the society's large and varied collection of images.

Previous books on the history of Northfield, notably *Green Mountain Heritage* and *Picture Northfield*, both largely written by the efforts of Julia McIntire and Richard Cleveland, were used extensively for information.

The work was made easier through the organization of images and artifacts by head cataloger Kay Schlueter, with the assistance of Ingrid Wilson and Joanna Caswell.

Unless otherwise noted, all photographs are courtesy of the Northfield Historical Society. Becky Merrilees and S.T. Morris did the drawings.

INTRODUCTION

When the town of Northfield was chartered in 1781, the frontier was growing, people were looking for places to expand, and no one had settled in Northfield. Even though it was chartered in 1781, the first person to settle in the area was Amos Robinson in 1785. Elijah Paine was offered 200 acres of land if he would build a sawmill and another 200 acres if he would build a gristmill. From there, numerous other families settled the town.

The 1790 census had nine families listed. The families of William Ashcroft, Isaiah Bacon, Aquilla Jones, Nathaniel Nicholas, Amos Robinson, Nathaniel Robinson, Eliphas Shipman, Stanton Richardson, and Ananias Tubbs are considered the founding families of Northfield.

The town started "at the North and most Westerly Angle" of Williamstown, which happens to be at the top of what is now called Mill Hill. The town grew down the mountain and into the valley below. It took the town a while to grow down into the valley because of having to clear the land to make it livable. By the early 1800s, the land and swamps were cleared enough along Sunny Brook and the Dog River and were ready for settlers, such as David Denny, to get mills started along the water sources throughout the valley. The area where Denny built the mills and other dwellings later became known as South Village. It also had other names, including Slab City and Upper Village. By 1828, South Village had at least seven mills and factories, along with a blacksmith shop, a chair factory, and a casket factory.

As the town grew northward from South Village, Center Village started to come alive with people. The first settler of Center Village was Joel Brown, who came to Northfield in 1800. His family stayed in the town for several generations and, at one point, ran the hotel in the Center. The Center Village was largely known to be the residential and social center for the town. This was because it sat a little ways off from the Dog River, meaning there was no good supply of waterpower, and, therefore, the area could not be useful to mills and such.

As America and the town flourished, the need for more industry became apparent. Thus, Factory Village was born. The woolen mill, built by Elijah Paine along the Dog River, was the beginning of this village. In 1812, it cost Paine $40,000 to build and equip this woolen mill. It was five stories high, and he constructed a dam beside it that lasted until 1924. Once fully functional, the factory employed 175–200 people. Charles Paine, the son of Elijah and later the 15th governor of Vermont, took over the business in 1823. Factory Village started out small but grew fairly quickly. In 1813, a schoolhouse and three houses were added to the village. In 1837, Charles Paine erected the Northfield House. It had over 100 rooms and a fishpond. Later, this area was also home to the stone sheds of Northfield. These sheds were used for the cutting of granite and slate from the area. Granite from Northfield is used in such buildings as Union Station in Washington, DC, as well as the Smithsonian Museum of Natural History. The stone industry really boomed when Charles Paine brought the Vermont Central Railroad through Northfield in 1846.

As the population of Northfield slowly grew north along the Dog River, another village began to take shape. This one was called "the Falls," even though the real name is Northfield Falls. The daughter of Aquilla Jones, Nancy, of one of the founding families, first settled Northfield Falls in 1804. In 1824, Capt. Abel Keyes built a flannel mill. By the mid-1830s, another flannel mill and a few other mills had been started by various people. The mill of note was started by James Gould, who became a prominent citizen of the Falls.

Each of these four villages had their own contributions to the makeup of the unique history of this town. Each one still has its own deep-set historical roots. Many of the businesses from the early eras have either been destroyed or have moved on to other areas of the town. The woolen mill business has moved but is still in operation. The dam built beside the woolen mill was destroyed in 1924 by one of the granite companies and replaced with concrete. It was then demolished in 1973, but parts of it can still be seen.

After the birth of these villages, there was a turning point in the history of the town. In 1846, the Vermont Central Railroad, with Charles Paine as president, announced it would build the railroad through Northfield. This decision changed the entire way industry was done in the town of Northfield. The board of directors also decided to locate the Vermont Central Engine House and Machine Shops in Northfield. They did this because the depot was located along the center of the line. Once the trains started to come through the town in 1848, the whole focus of the town changed. The people were now able to easily ship their goods all over the country with little to no hassle.

By the 1890s, a large influx of talented European immigrants came to work in Northfield's granite sheds. This began a long period of prosperity for the town. The outstanding work ethic of these men and their families helped Northfield thrive. The granite industry would remain the backbone of the town's industrial well-being for many, many years.

Today, even though the granite industry is gone, many of the descendants of these early families continue to enrich the town in many ways. Companies in town continue to produce quality products in the knitting and the wood products industries. Norwich University, through its faculty and student body, has become a vital part of the community. Their spirit and enthusiasm enhance the lives of not only the townspeople but also those from surrounding communities.

One

Mill Hill, South Village, and on to the Center

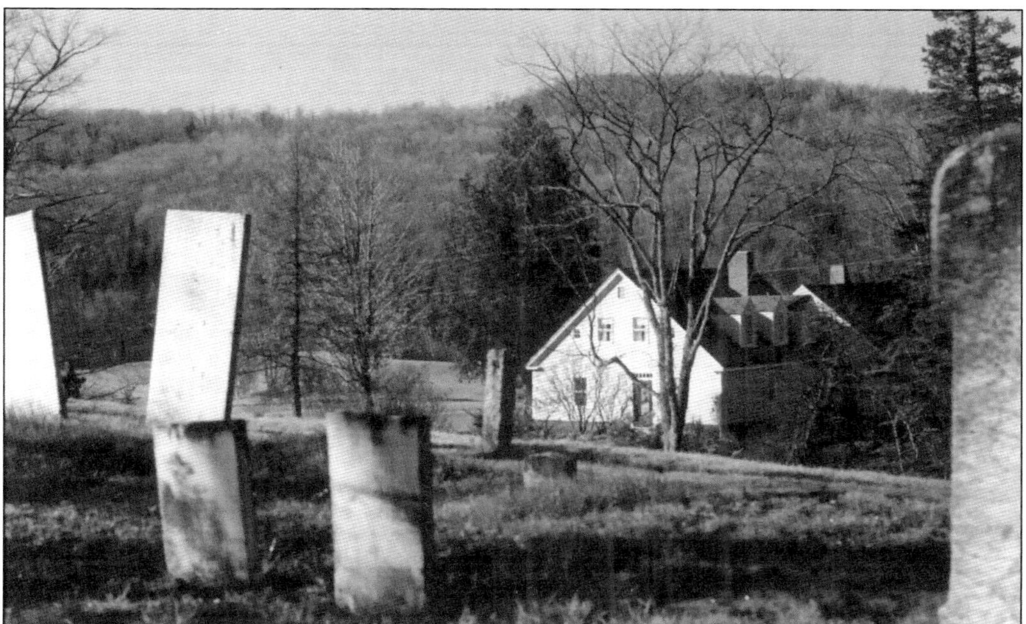

This photograph of Amos Robinson's farmhouse was taken from the Robinson Cemetery, nearby. Robinson was Northfield's first settler, arriving in May 1785. Even though Northfield was chartered in 1781, it was four years before Robinson came to clear the forested land and build his log cabin. The house is still standing on Robinson Road and is the oldest house in town.

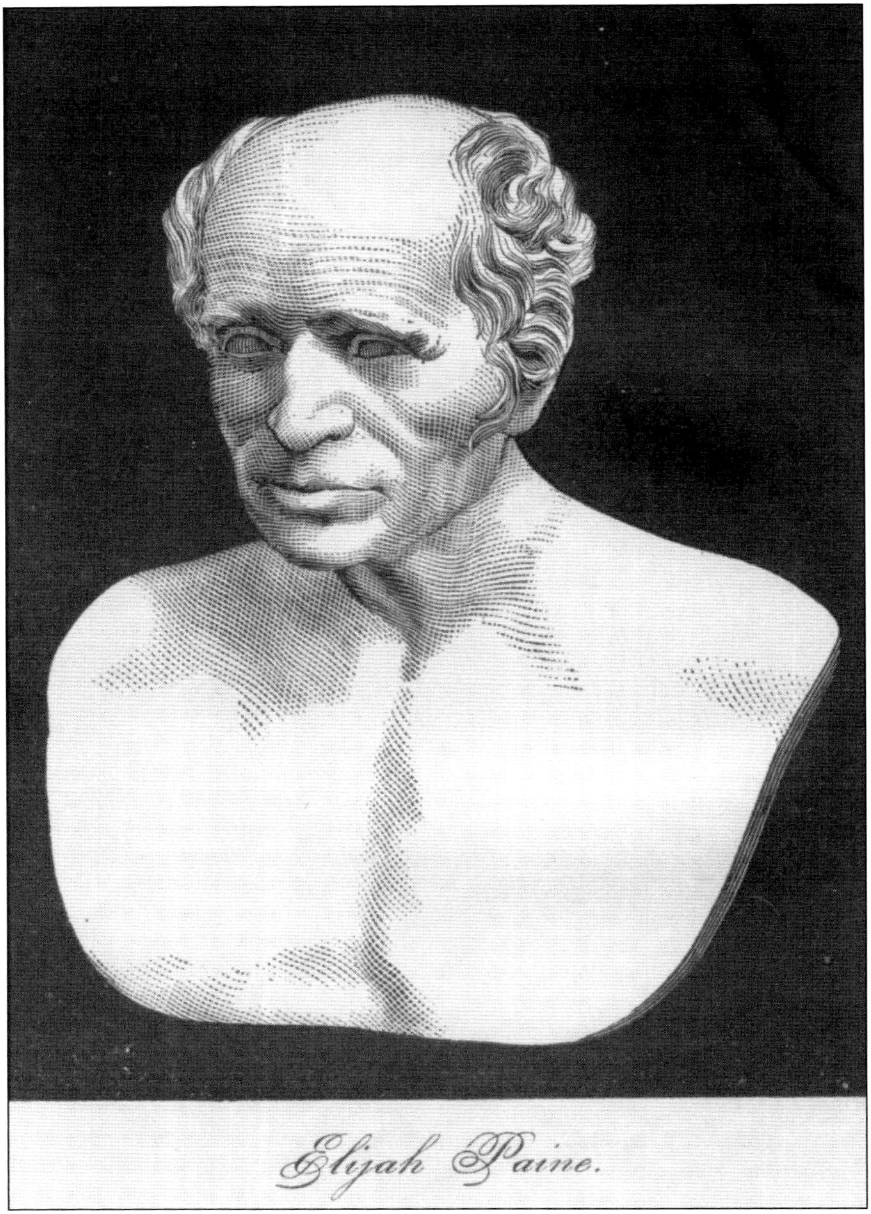

Elijah Paine was the patriarch and founder of Northfield and Williamstown. Born in Brooklyn, Connecticut, in 1757, he married Sarah Porter in 1790 and had seven children. He graduated from Harvard University, fought in the Revolutionary War, and became a personal friend of George Washington. He was given 400 acres to build a sawmill and a gristmill, which he did on Robinson Brook, on top of Mill Hill. One of the millstones lies in front of the Paine House today. Paine cleared the first land on Mill Hill. He was a scholar, lawyer, farmer, road maker, and pioneer in the manufacture of American cloth. Paine built the Paine Turnpike from Brookfield to Montpelier, which was completed in 1803 and was 22 miles long with three tollgates. It was part of the main route from Boston to Montreal. What is now Berlin Pond Road is the part of that road that lies in Northfield.

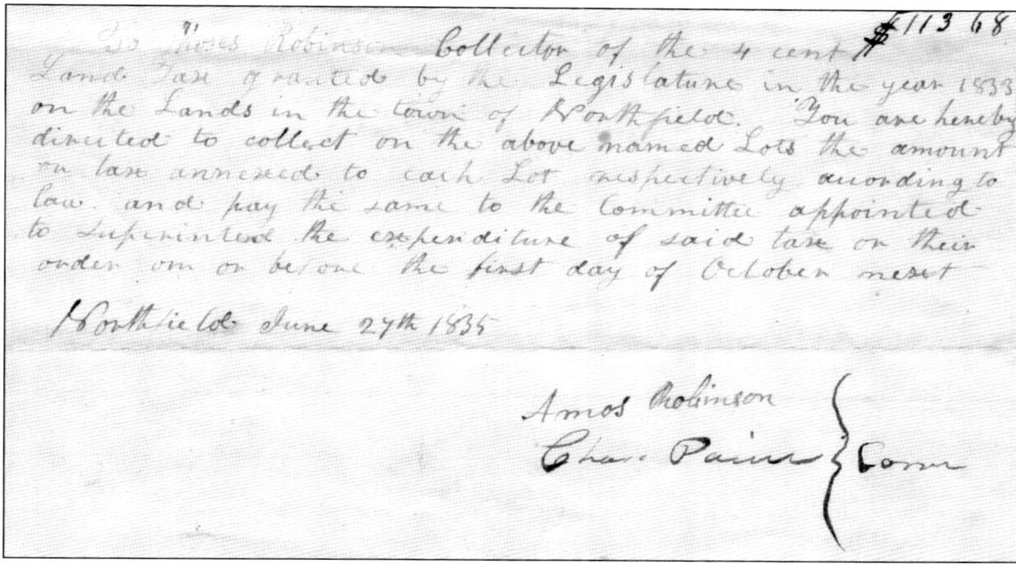

$113 68

To Moses Robinson Collector of the 4 cent Land Tax granted by the Legislature in the year 1833 on the Lands in the town of Northfield. You are hereby directed to collect on the above named Lots the amount on tax annexed to each Lot respectively according to law and pay the same to the Committee appointed to superintend the expenditure of said tax on their order on or before the first day of October next

Northfield June 27th 1835

Amos Robinson
Chas. Paine } Com

Moses Robinson was the town land tax collector in 1835. Charles Paine and Amos Robinson signed the document above, and Moses was to collect a 4¢ land tax from listed landholders in town. Below is a picture of an old cellar hole in Robinson pasture on Mill Hill. It may have been from Amos Robinson's log home, which he and his family lived in until their frame house was built. Many cellar holes, wells, and mill foundations still exist in this area. One can see the remains of Elijah Paine's sawmill and gristmill nearby on Robinson's Brook.

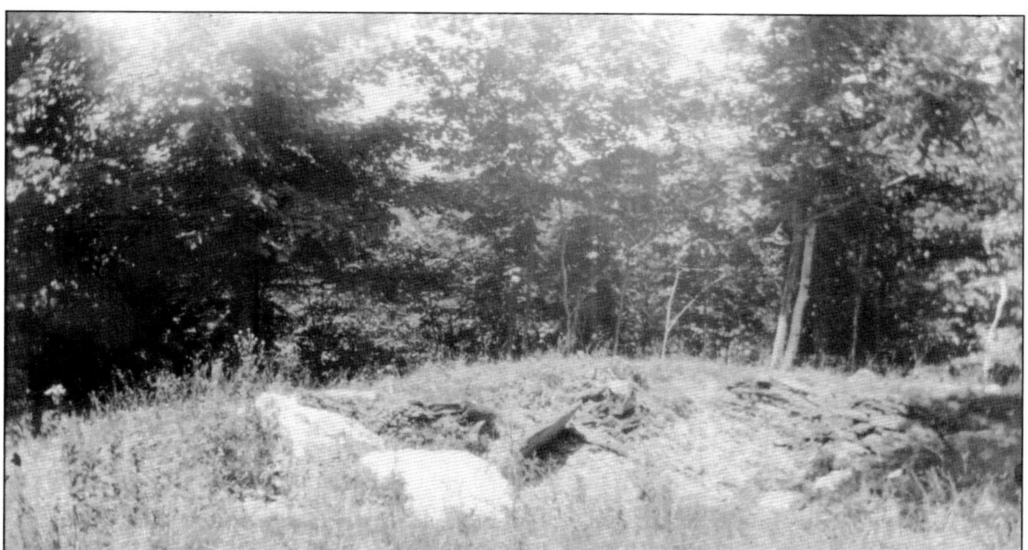

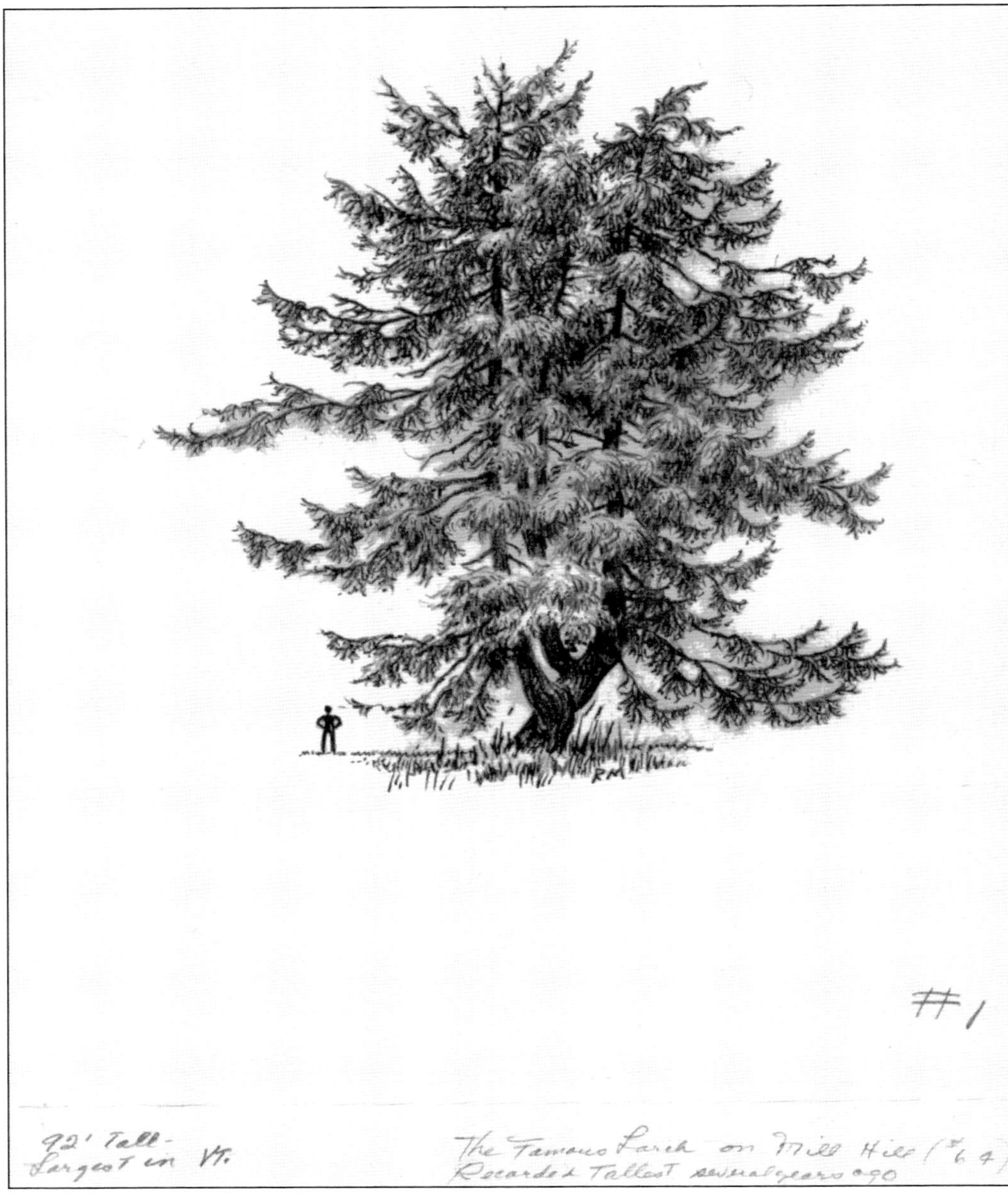

Depicted here is a European larch, which is commonly known as a tamarack tree. In 1980, the Green Mountain Division of the Society of American Foresters measured it; they were attempting to map and list the "big trees" of Vermont for the National Register of Historic Places. This tamarack came in as a national champion. It is the oldest known tamarack in the United States. Its circumference is 164 inches, its height is 86 feet, and it has a crown spread of 45 feet. Now ailing, it can be seen at the top of Mill Hill while traveling up Route 64 to Williamstown. (Drawing by Becky Merrilees.)

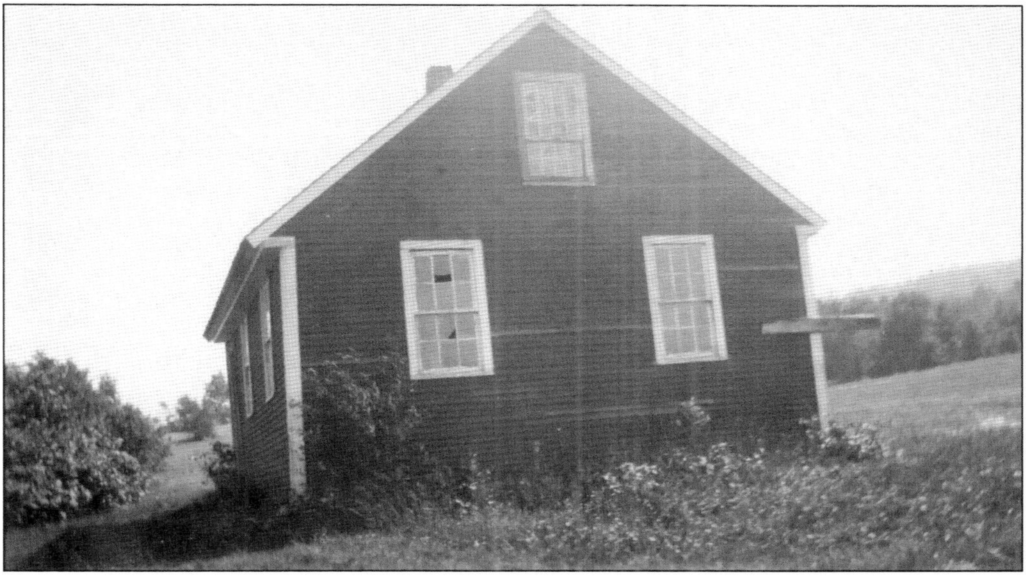

One of the first schools in Northfield, the Old Red Schoolhouse, or Robinson School, was located at the top of Mill Hill. It was one of the original one-room schoolhouses in town. It stood until the mid-1980s, when it was removed for the construction of the new road.

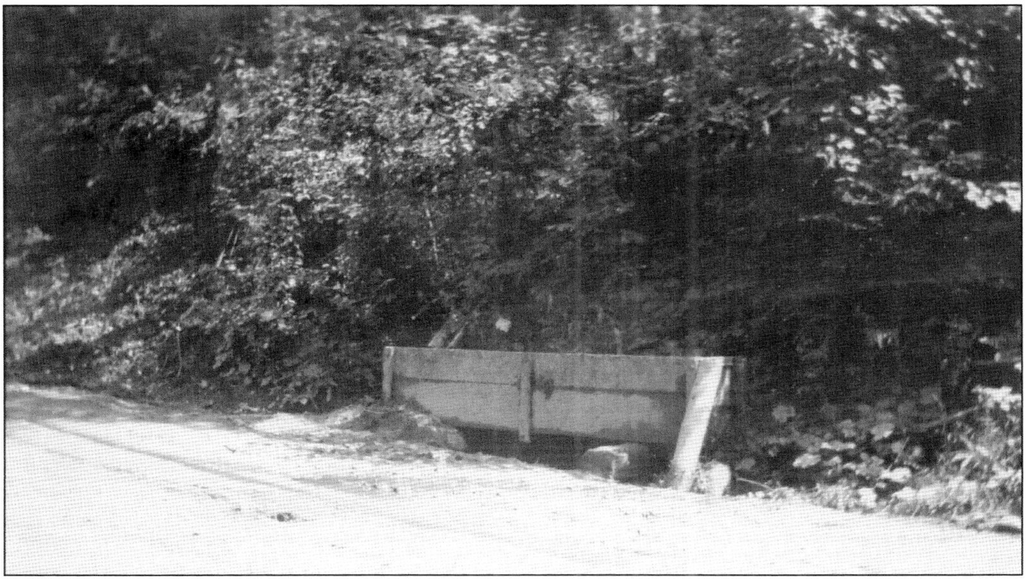

This watering trough was located on Old Mill Hill Road. It is such a steep and winding road that it would seem impossible to travel it with horses or oxen without a rest stop for water. In the mid-1980s, the construction of Route 64 replaced the road, which was considered dangerous.

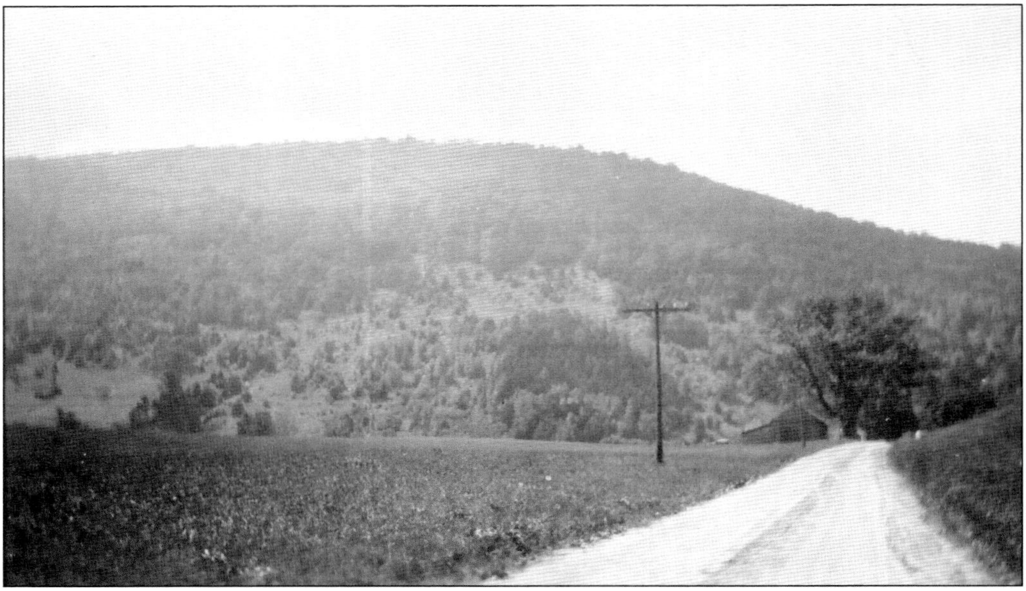

Traveling down Old Mill Hill Road to South Village are Winch Hill and the Denny farm, straight ahead. The Denny farm's barn can be seen in the background. The settlers gradually moved from the top of Mill Hill down the valley to the south, which later became known as South Village.

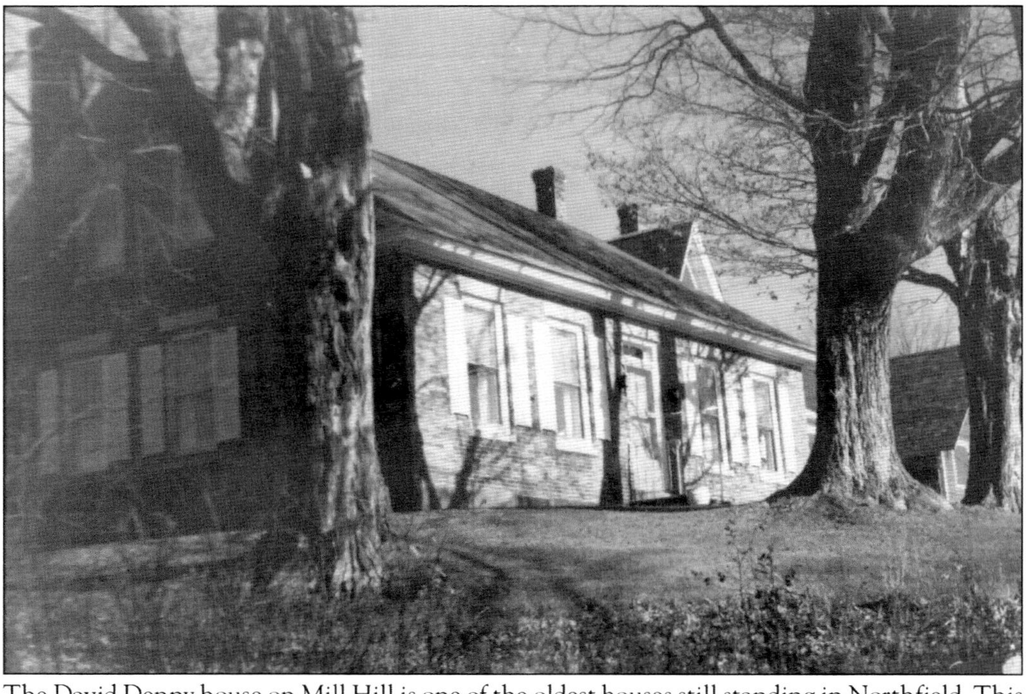

The David Denny house on Mill Hill is one of the oldest houses still standing in Northfield. This is one of the few houses in town that was built of brick before the Civil War. In the early 1900s, the Denny farm became famous for its butter, which was shipped by train to Boston.

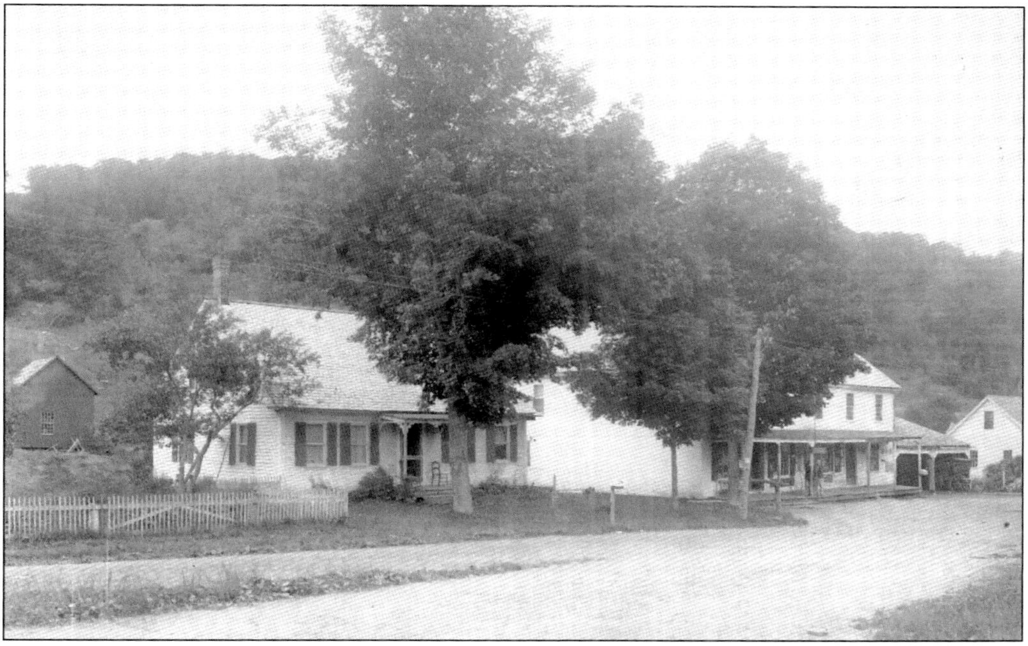

With the growth of South Village, a post office and general store was needed. The photograph above is of the Jones General Store and post office in the summer of 1885. In the early 1900s, it became the A.E. Cobleigh general store (below). Addie Cobleigh was the proprietor and also the postmistress for a time. Behind the man with a cat slung over his shoulder is a sled containing a large wooden barrel, perhaps of flour. Note the very fashionably dressed lady and the elegant horse-drawn sleigh to the right.

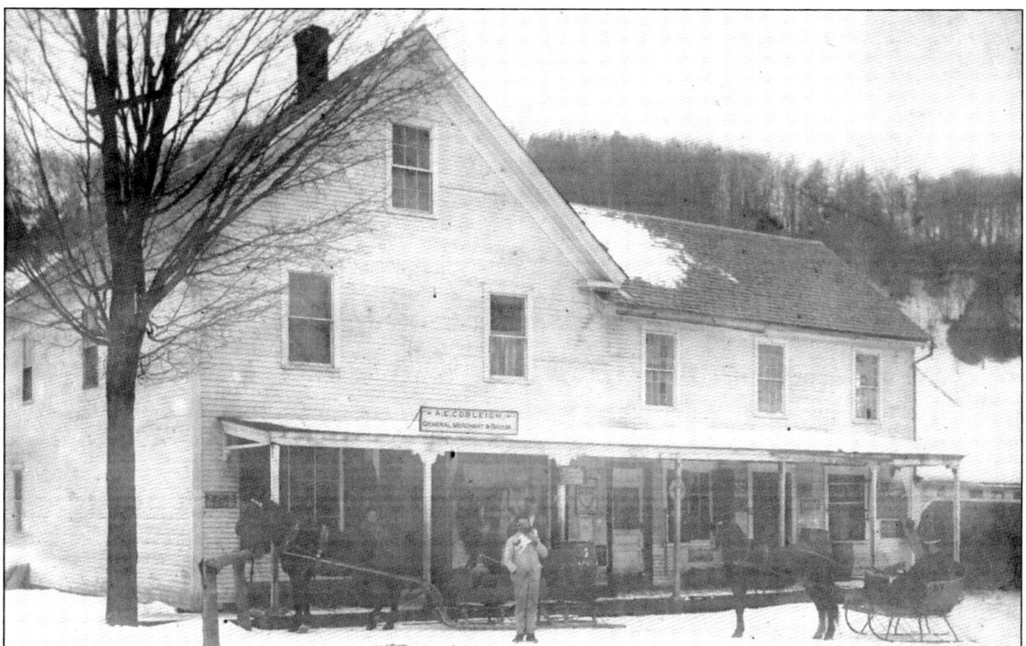

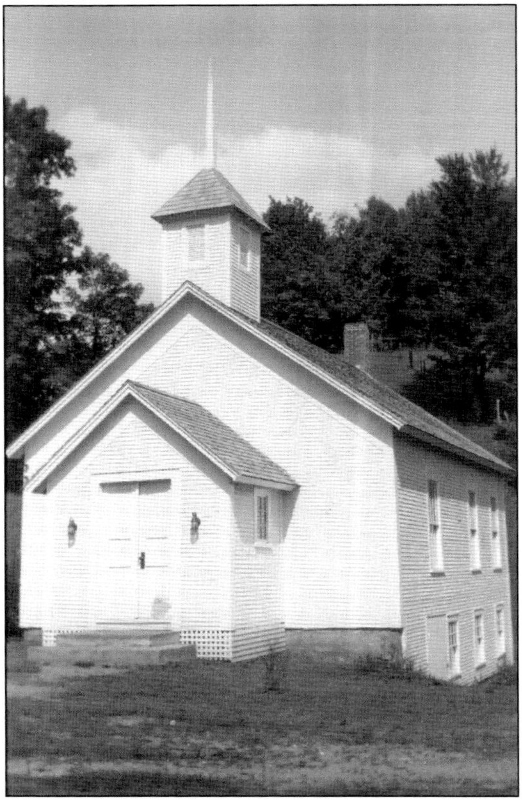

Rufus Covey built the Little White Church in 1941. An important part of South Village, the church still stands today. It started as an independent community church, emphasizing an evangelical Bible doctrine. Sundays were a day of rest and worship; businesses were closed so that families could gather together for a visit.

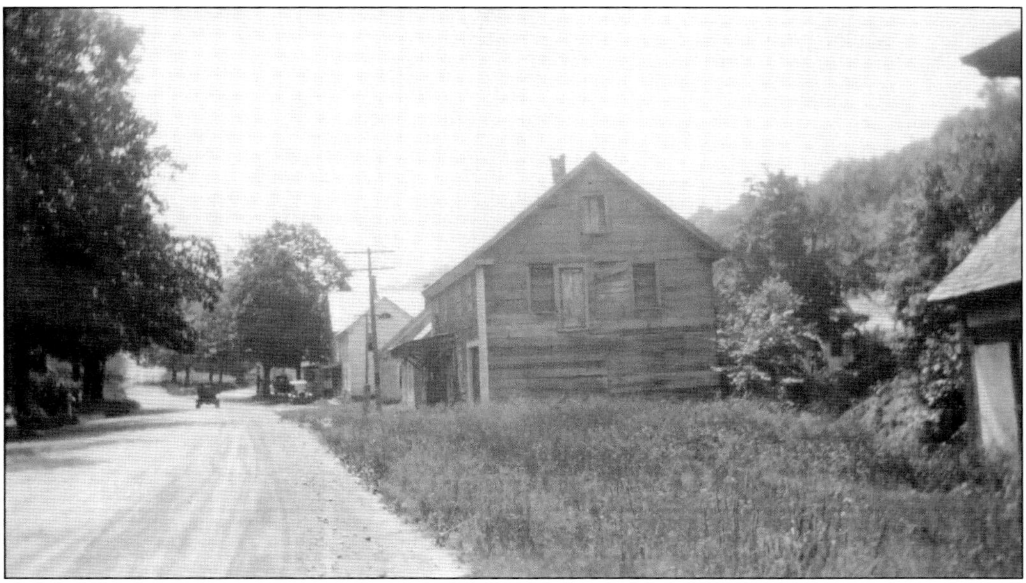

Here is a view of South Village in the 1920s. The village store is seen in the background, with Old Mill Hill Road on the left. The road to Randolph, which later became Route 12, meanders to the right through South Village, which is now primarily a cluster of homes, as most of the businesses have moved northward.

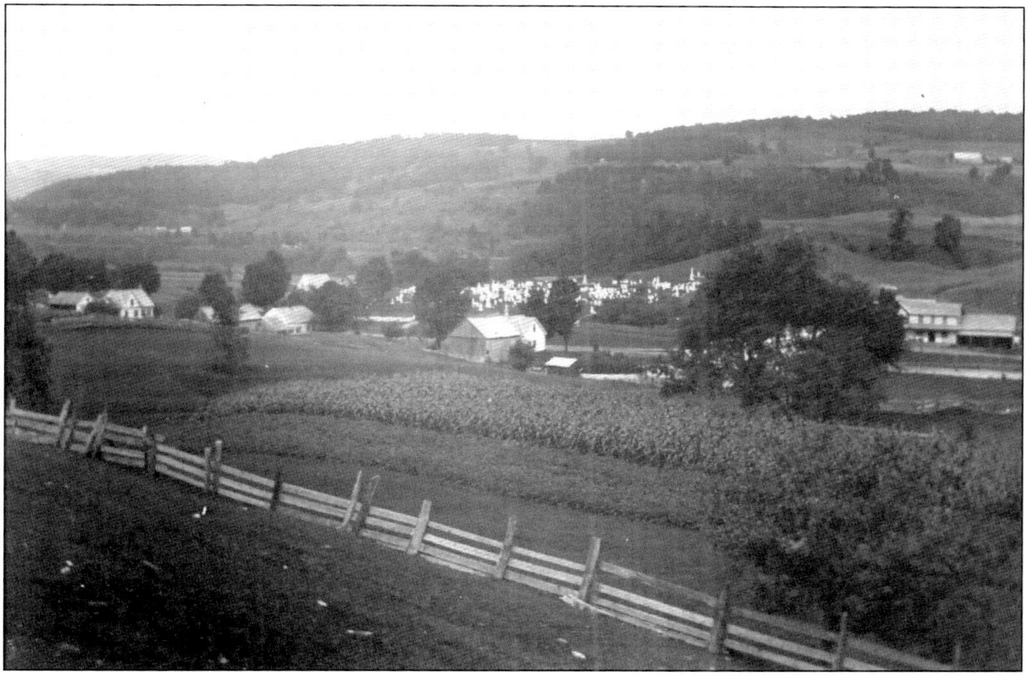

Here is a beautiful summer view of Center Village, looking west, in 1889. It was in 1800 when the first settler, Joel Brown, cleared land for a home. From the 1820s to the 1890s, Center Village included the area's first town hall, three churches, and several small shops. The area's first library and post office were also established here. Mount Hope Cemetery, also called Center Cemetery, is seen in the center, with its bright-white stone monuments.

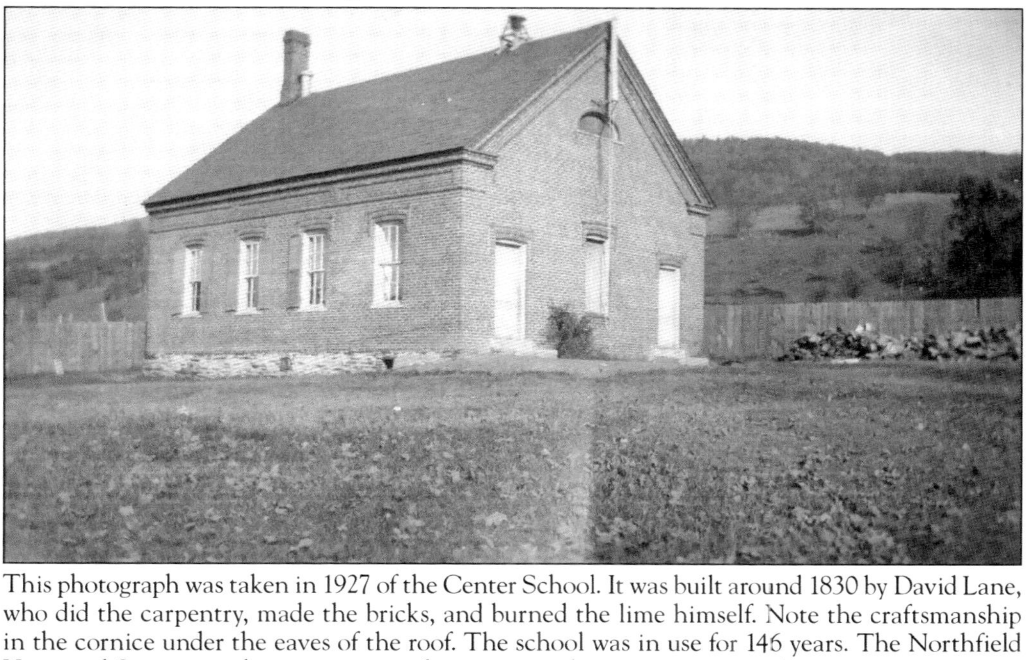

This photograph was taken in 1927 of the Center School. It was built around 1830 by David Lane, who did the carpentry, made the bricks, and burned the lime himself. Note the craftsmanship in the cornice under the eaves of the roof. The school was in use for 146 years. The Northfield Historical Society used it as a museum for a time, and it is now a private home.

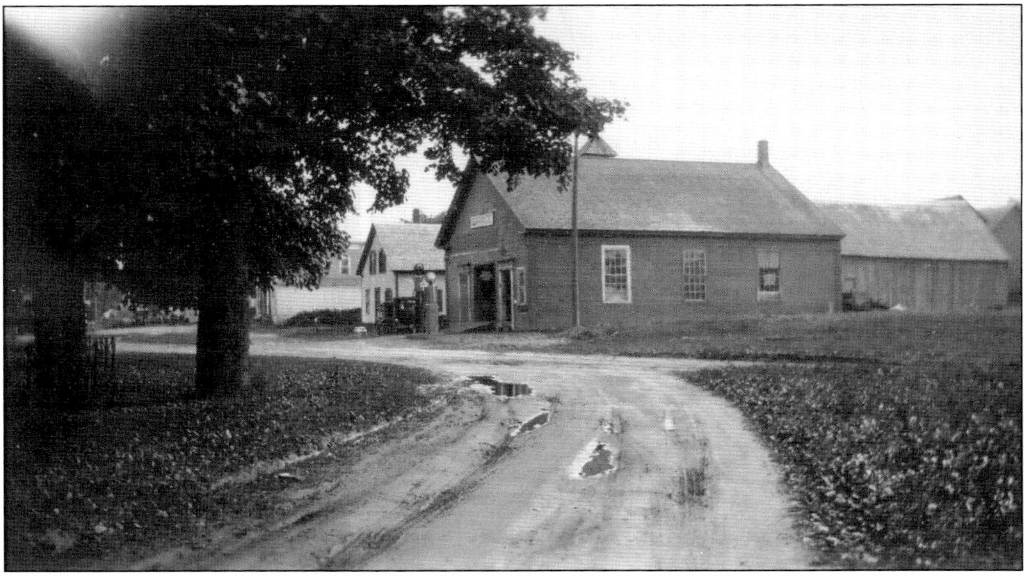

The old town hall is shown here in a 1928 photograph. It was the first town hall built in Northfield. The photograph shows that the building had been converted into a garage with gasoline pumps in the front. It still stands and is owned by Norwich University.

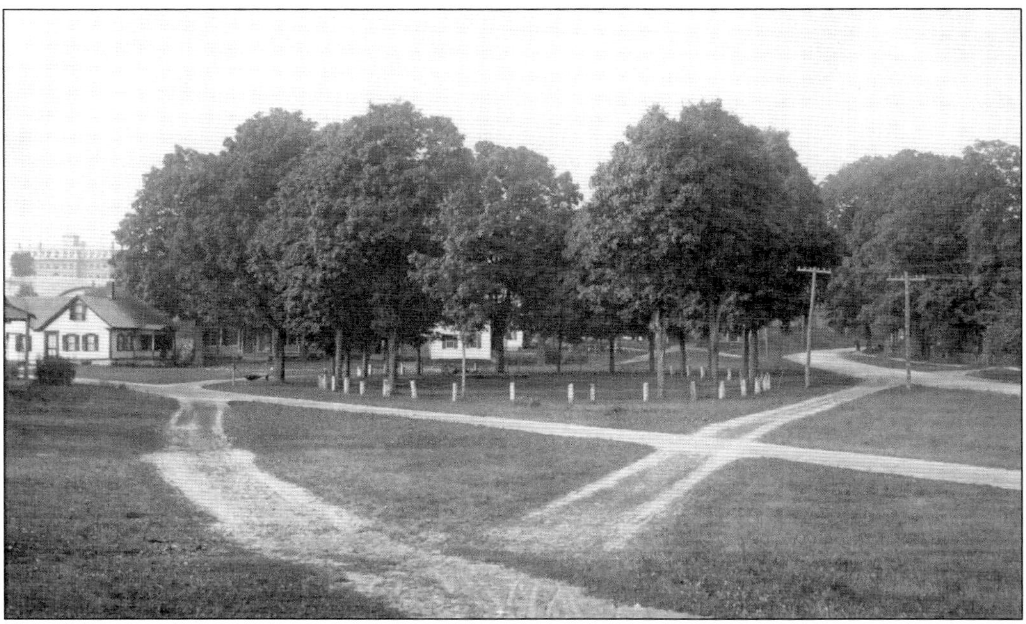

Center Park, shown here surrounded by granite posts and chains, once had a fountain with a deep reservoir. The water was used for fighting fires in the area. The park bench and hammock afforded folks a peaceful spot to stop and rest. Note Norwich University's Jackman Hall on the left in the background.

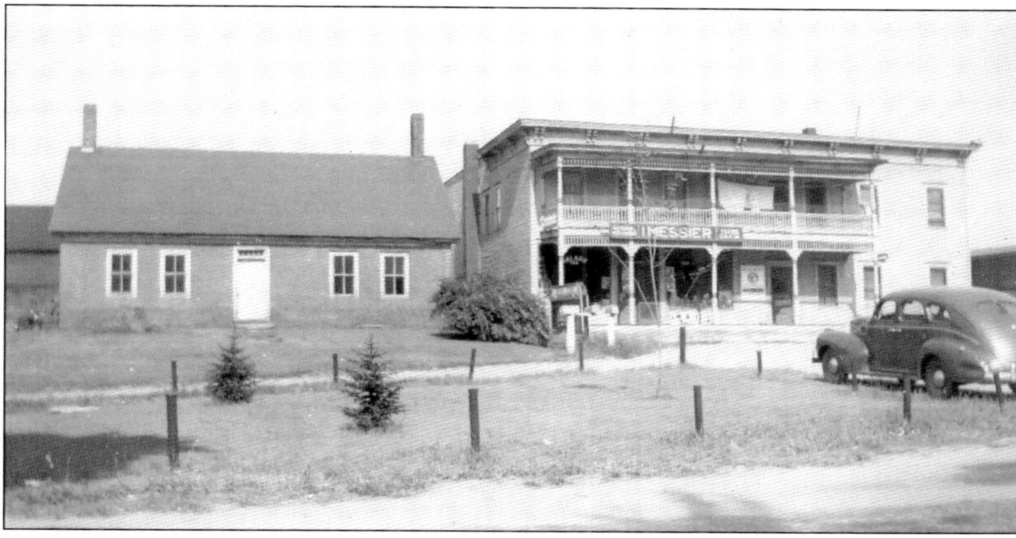

Mable Orderway's brick house and the Center Village store are shown here. Originally, it was John P. Davis's store, from 1850 to 1892. Davis was one of the largest wool merchants in central Vermont. It became Messier's store by the 1930s and continued to be a general store with apartments above it. Norwich University currently owns the property, and the store has been removed.

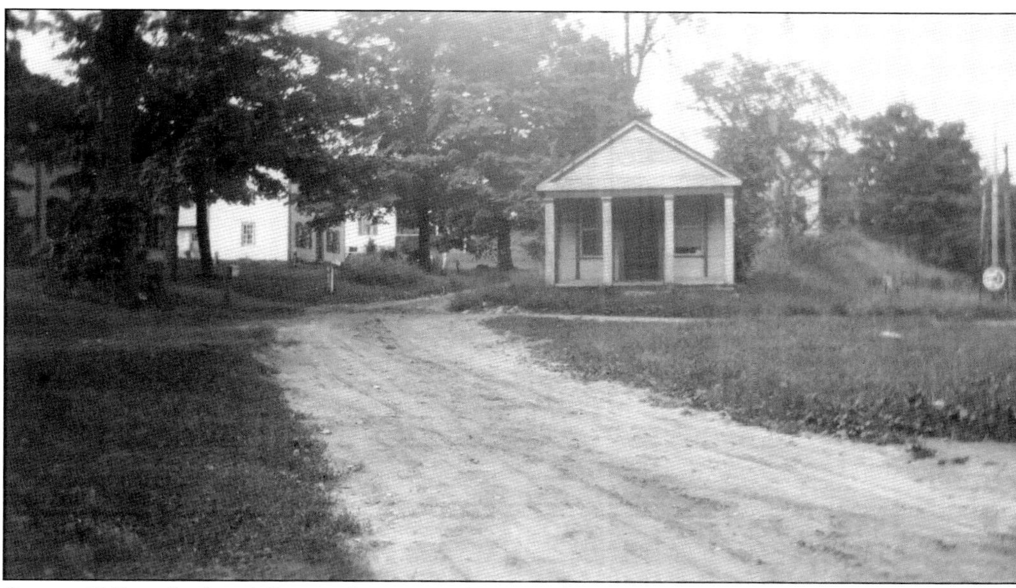

Center Village looks idyllic in this 1889 photograph. The country lane borders the fenced-in cornfield opposite the little, brick schoolhouse. The Universalist church in the center of the photograph faces several farms scattered atop Dole Hill. The village also contained a tavern, seen on the far left, a livery stable, a village hall, and Henry Jones's farmhouse.

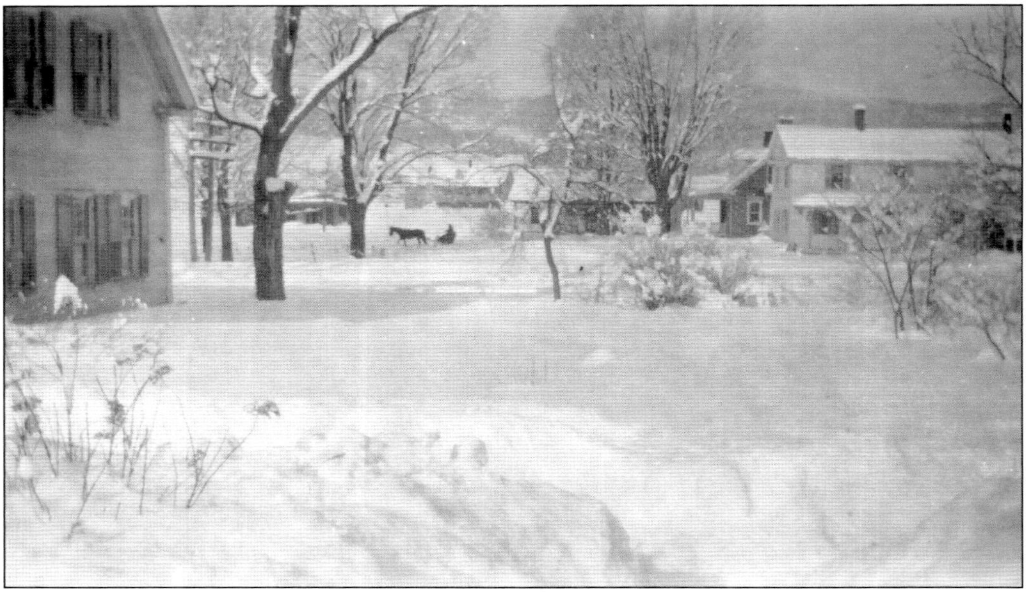

A very heavy snowfall has turned the Center Village into a scene from a Currier and Ives Christmas card. One hardy individual is seen dashing through the snow behind Center Park in his one-horse open sleigh even before the snow rollers have had an opportunity to make their accustomed rounds.

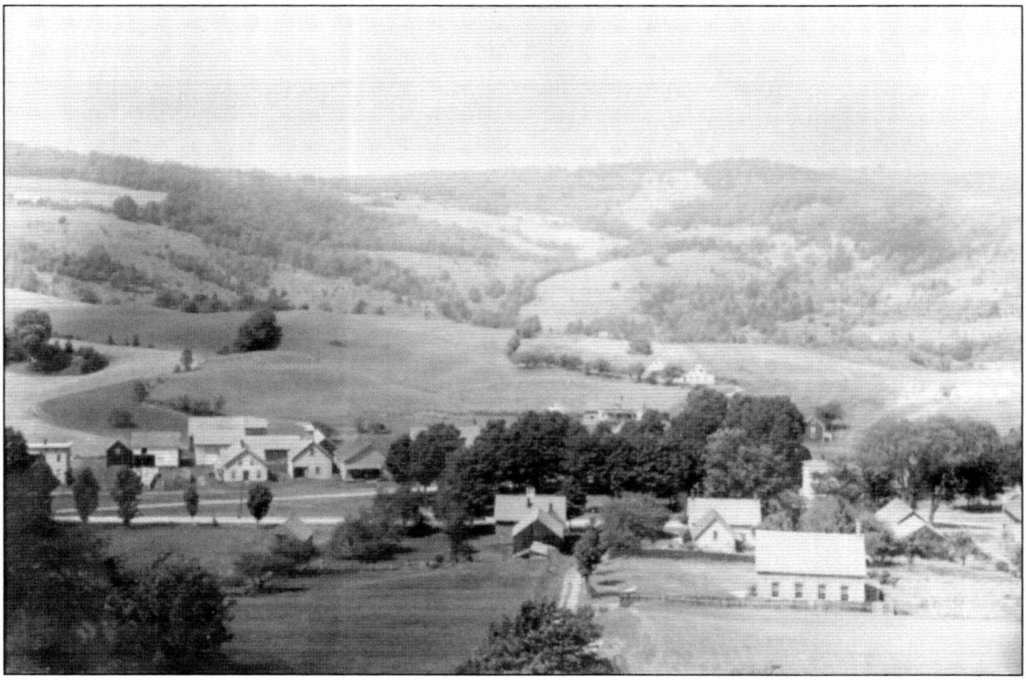

This photograph shows the Center Village as it appeared in 1920, with Messier's store to the far left in the flat-roofed building. The Universalist church is now gone from the Center. The Dole farm, in the left background, is now the Norwich University Cemetery. Today, new Norwich buildings stand on the rolling hills to the right of the photograph.

Two

Around the Common and Down to the Falls

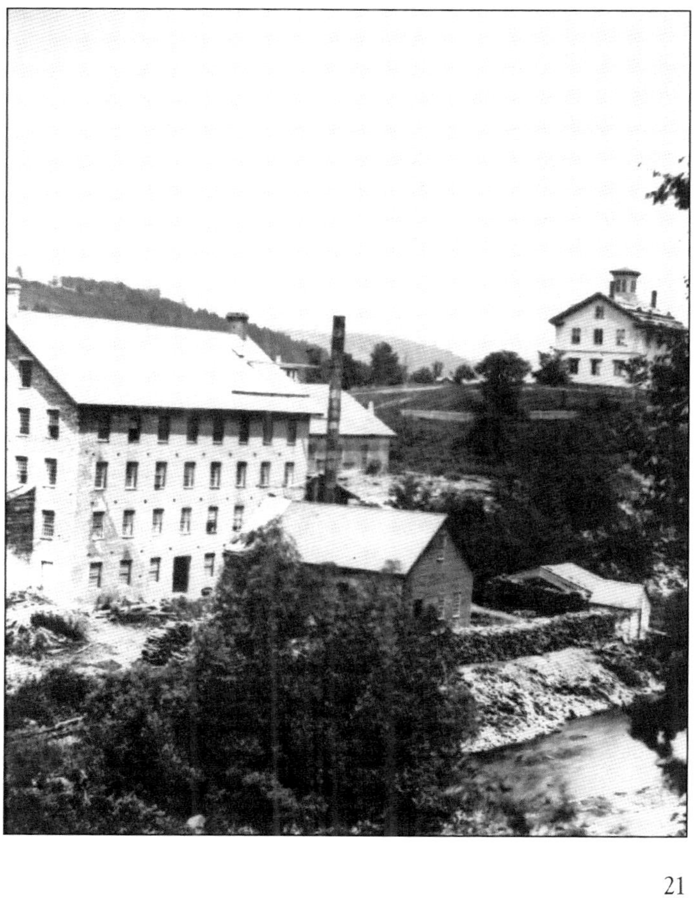

Today, the Village Common is the heart of Northfield, but when Elijah Paine saw it in the early 1800s, it was just forested land a mile north of the Center Village with a broad river and waterfall running through it. His vision to build a woolen mill and a wooden dam became a reality in 1812. A fire eventually destroyed the mill in 1895, after it had stood for 83 years.

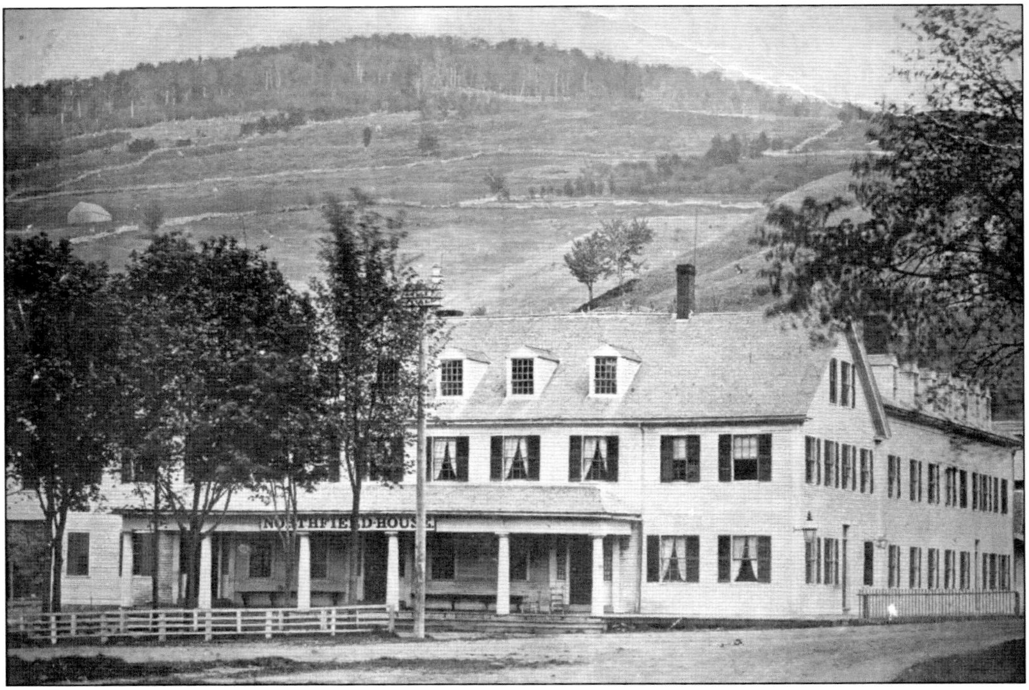

The small village continued to steadily grow with homes, mills, factories, and a hotel. Charles Paine built this hotel, the Northfield House, in 1837. As president of the Vermont Central Railroad, he brought the train to town in 1847. Travelers from the train needing a place to stay enjoyed the 100-room hotel.

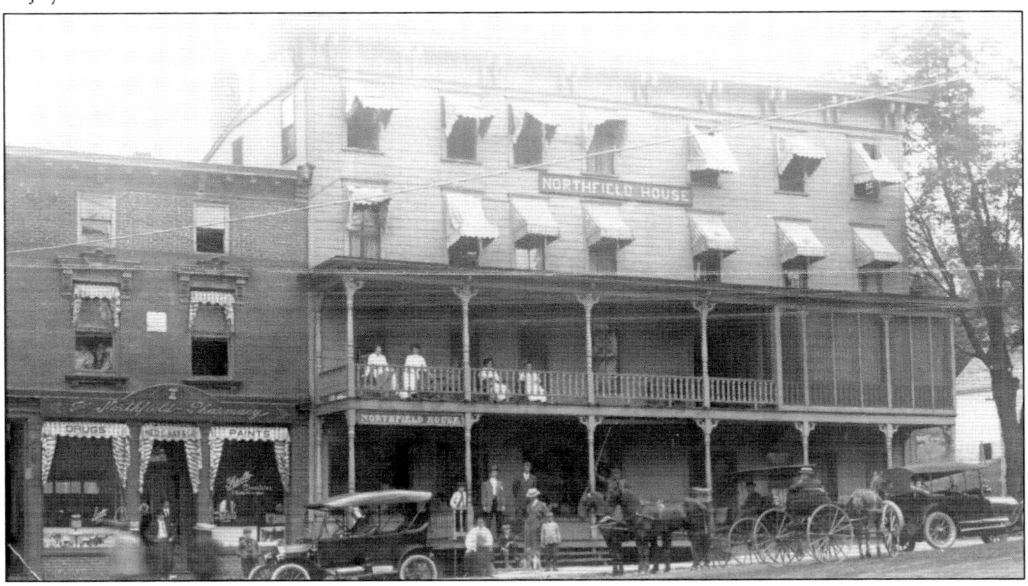

The second Northfield House, built in 1880 on the east side of the Common, was one of the most popular places for dances in central Vermont. As many as 200 couples would attend, and dinner would be served at midnight. In winter, a large sleigh would collect village residents and bring them to the hotel.

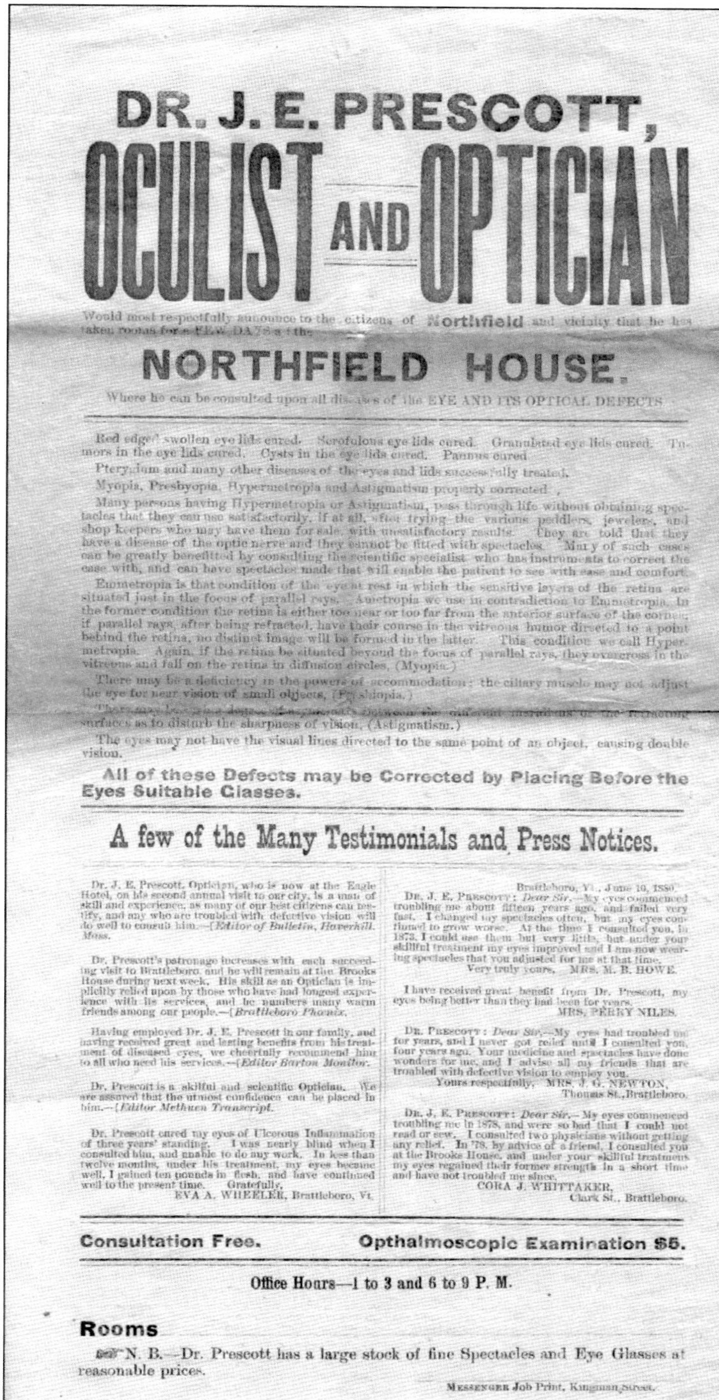

DR. J. E. PRESCOTT,

OCULIST AND OPTICIAN

Would most respectfully announce to the citizens of Northfield and vicinity that he has taken rooms for a FEW DAYS at the

NORTHFIELD HOUSE.

Where he can be consulted upon all diseases of the EYE AND ITS OPTICAL DEFECTS

Red edged swollen eye lids cured. Scrofulous eye lids cured. Granulated eye lids cured. Tumors in the eye lids cured. Cysts in the eye lids cured. Pannus cured

Pterygium and many other diseases of the eyes and lids successfully treated.

Myopia, Presbyopia, Hypermetropia and Astigmatism properly corrected.

Many persons having Hypermetropia or Astigmatism, pass through life without obtaining spectacles that they can use satisfactorily, if at all, after trying the various peddlers, jewelers, and shop keepers who may have them for sale, with unsatisfactory results. They are told that they have a disease of the optic nerve and they cannot be fitted with spectacles. Many of such cases can be greatly benefitted by consulting the scientific specialist who has instruments to correct the case with, and can have spectacles made that will enable the patient to see with ease and comfort.

Emmetropia is that condition of the eye at rest in which the sensitive layers of the retina are situated just in the focus of parallel rays. Ametropia we use in contradiction to Emmetropia. In the former condition the retina is either too near or too far from the anterior surface of the cornea; if parallel rays, after being refracted, have their course in the vitreous humor directed to a point behind the retina, no distinct image will be formed in the latter. This condition we call Hypermetropia. Again, if the retina be situated beyond the focus of parallel rays, they overcross in the vitreous and fall on the retina in diffusion circles, (Myopia.)

There may be a deficiency in the powers of accommodation; the ciliary muscle may not adjust the eye for near vision of small objects, (Presbiopia.)

There may be [illegible] degree of [illegible] between the different meridians of the refracting surfaces as to disturb the sharpness of vision, (Astigmatism.)

The eyes may not have the visual lines directed to the same point of an object, causing double vision.

All of these Defects may be Corrected by Placing Before the Eyes Suitable Glasses.

A few of the Many Testimonials and Press Notices.

Dr. J. E. Prescott, Optician, who is now at the Eagle Hotel, on his second annual visit to our city, is a man of skill and experience, as many of our best citizens can testify, and any who are troubled with defective vision will do well to consult him.—[*Editor of Bulletin, Haverhill, Mass.*

Dr. Prescott's patronage increases with each succeeding visit to Brattleboro, and he will remain at the Brooks House during next week. His skill as an Optician is implicitly relied upon by those who have had longest experience with his services, and he numbers many warm friends among our people.—[*Brattleboro Phœnix.*

Having employed Dr. J. E. Prescott in our family, and having received great and lasting benefits from his treatment of diseased eyes, we cheerfully recommend him to all who need his services.—[*Editor Barton Monitor.*

Dr. Prescott is a skilful and scientific Optician. We are assured that the utmost confidence can be placed in him.—[*Editor Methuen Transcript.*

Dr. Prescott cured my eyes of Ulcerous Inflammation of three years' standing. I was nearly blind when I consulted him, and unable to do any work. In less than twelve months, under his treatment, my eyes became well, I gained ten pounds in flesh, and have continued well to the present time. Gratefully,
EVA A. WHEELER, Brattleboro, Vt.

Brattleboro, Vt., June 10, 1880.
DR. J. E. PRESCOTT: *Dear Sir*,—My eyes commenced troubling me about fifteen years ago, and failed very fast. I changed my spectacles often, but my eyes continued to grow worse. At the time I consulted you, in 1873, I could use them but very little, but under your skillful treatment my eyes improved and I am now wearing spectacles that you adjusted for me at that time.
Very truly yours, MRS. M. B. HOWE.

I have received great benefit from Dr. Prescott, my eyes being better than they had been for years.
MRS. PERRY NILES.

DR. PRESCOTT: *Dear Sir*,—My eyes had troubled me for years, and I never got relief until I consulted you, four years ago. Your medicine and spectacles have done wonders for me, and I advise all my friends that are troubled with defective vision to employ you.
Yours respectfully, MRS. J. G. NEWTON,
Thomas St., Brattleboro.

DR. J. E. PRESCOTT: *Dear Sir*,—My eyes commenced troubling me in 1878, and were so bad that I could not read or sew. I consulted two physicians without getting any relief. In '78, by advice of a friend, I consulted you at the Brooks House, and under your skillful treatment my eyes regained their former strength in a short time and have not troubled me since.
CORA J. WHITTAKER,
Clark St., Brattleboro.

Consultation Free. **Opthalmoscopic Examination $5.**

Office Hours—1 to 3 and 6 to 9 P. M.

Rooms

N. B.—Dr. Prescott has a large stock of fine Spectacles and Eye Glasses at reasonable prices.

MESSENGER Job Print, Kingman Street.

This advertisement announces to the citizens of Northfield that Dr. J.E. Prescott has temporarily taken up residence in the Northfield House. Consultations were free, and ophthalmoscopic examinations were $5.

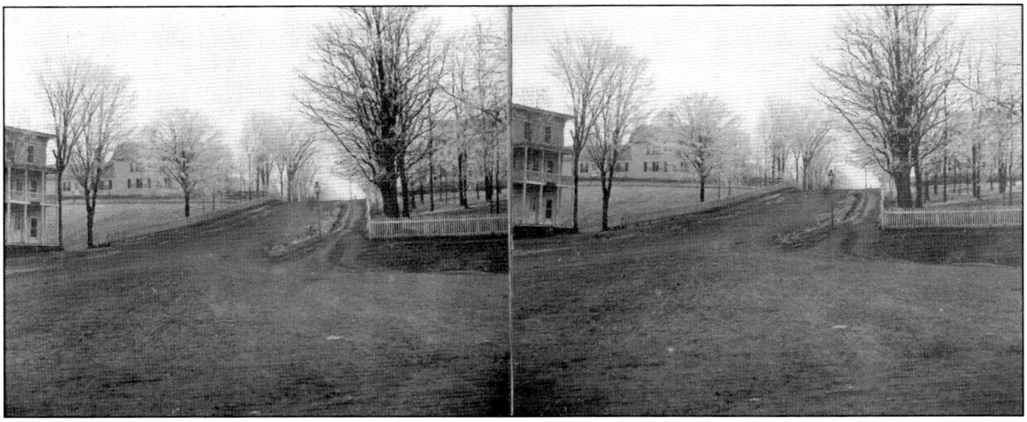

Looking south along Main Street is Charles Paine's house (center background), standing where the Brown Public Library is today. In the lower left, one can see part of the Northfield House. From his home, Governor Paine could look across the street to the Congregational church he built, north to the Northfield House he built, up the hill to the school he helped establish, and across the square to the mill his father built and the Vermont Central railroad buildings his father established. Factory Village had now become known as Depot Village, and, for a short time, it was known as Painesville. As seen in the advertisement below, from the *Northfield News* in the early 1900s, businesses were multifunctional. This one sold household goods and did some undertaking on the side.

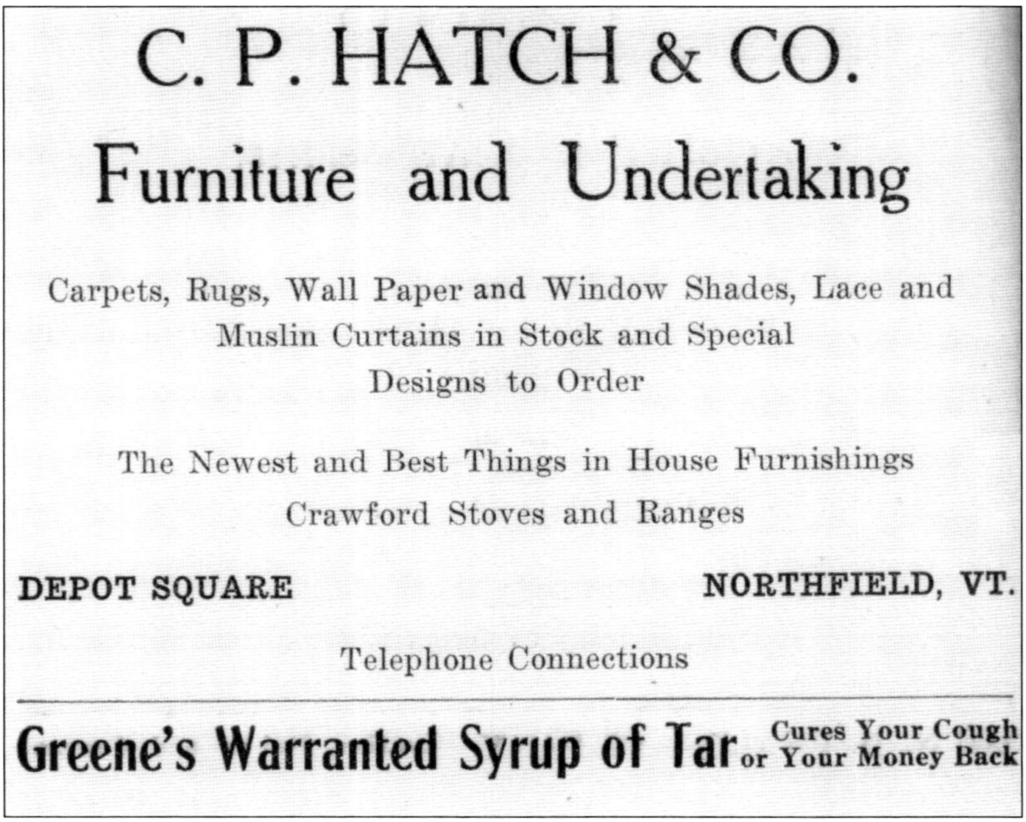

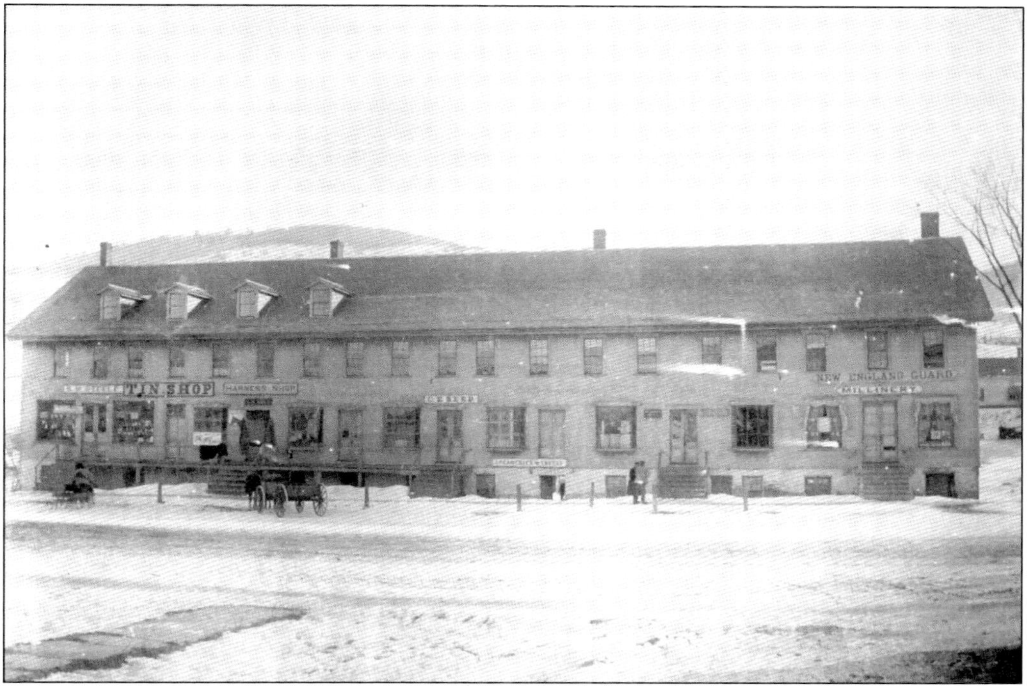

The Paine Block was a two-story wooden structure built leading north from the square. Built in 1850, the original structure burned in 1856 but was immediately rebuilt. Northfield's first library, dedicated in 1896, was housed in the Paine Block, as were a variety of businesses. Dr. William B. Mayo bought the Paine Block, placed it on rollers, and moved it to face south on East Street.

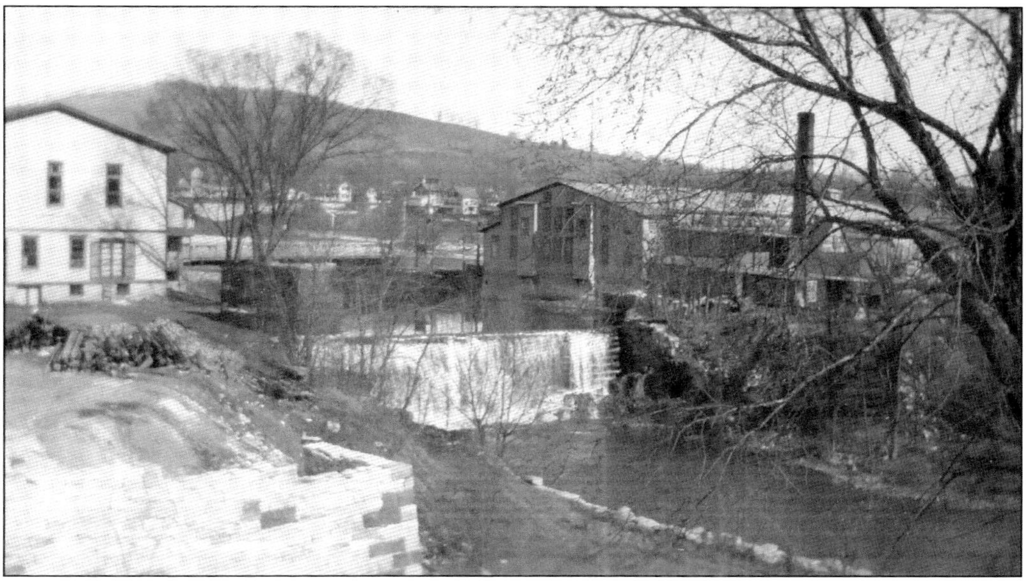

Dr. Mayo next built the Armory Block (left) on North Main Street. The west-facing building opened with an orchestral concert, dancing, and festivities. Years later, it became known as the Guesthouse, with a small building beside it known as the Guesthouse Dining Room. It is pictured here with the Cross Brothers Granite Company's shed (right).

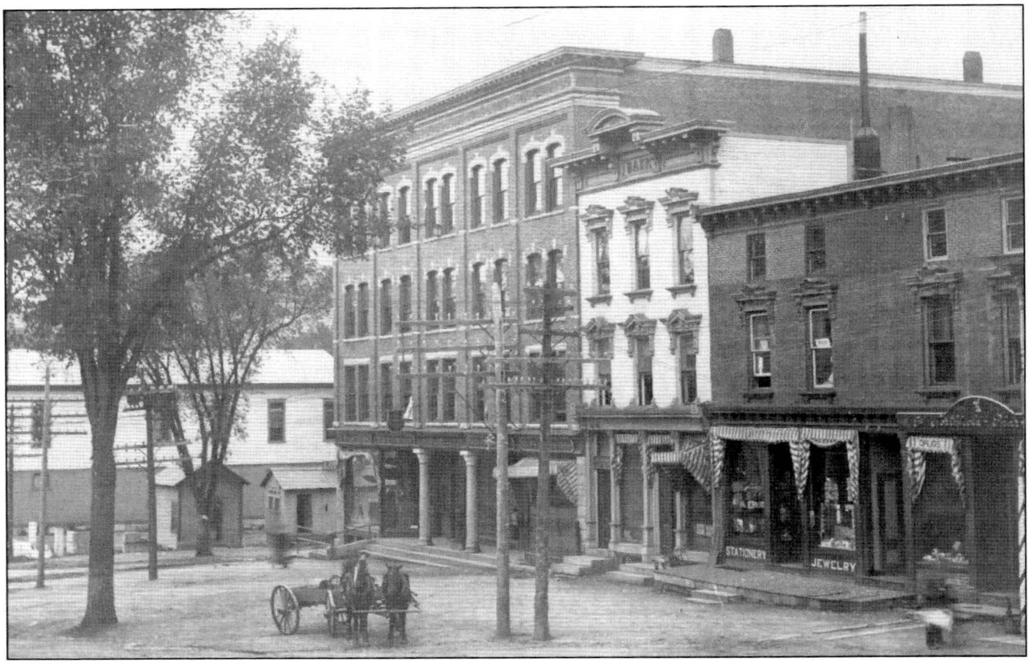

The Mayo Block was Dr. Mayo's largest construction on the Village Common. Built in 1900 on the east side of the Common, it was a four-story brick building on the site of the first Northfield House. With granite trim and full plate-glass windows, there were businesses on the first floor, offices on the second, tenants on the third, and the Masons and other fraternal orders on the fourth.

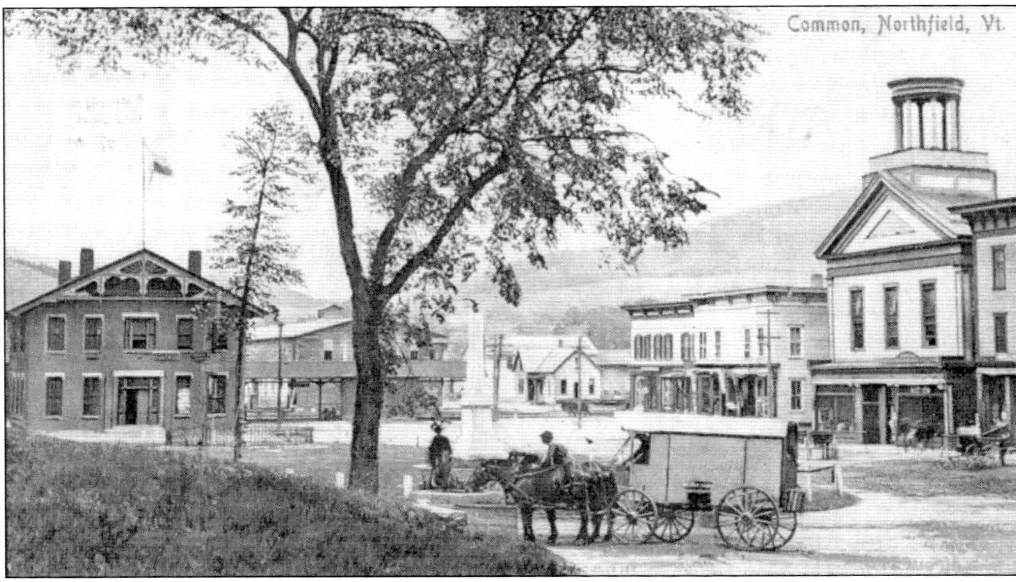

By 1890, Northfield had many businesses in town. The Common had become the new center of activity. There were lawyers, dressmakers, slaters, nurses, and more. With the opening of the first granite shed, Northfield grew and prospered. A common site in the village was peddlers selling their wares. A meat cart, a bakery cart from Montpelier, a scissors grinder, and a tin peddler all traveled the streets.

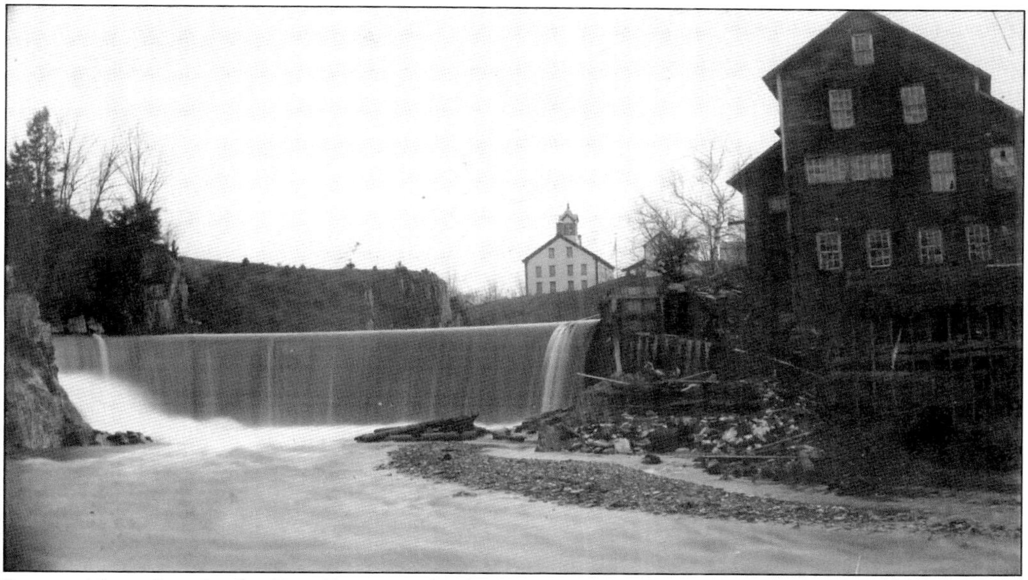

Pictured here beside the Dog River, with the Gray Building in the background, is the electric light station. Streetlights were turned on for the first time on June 25, 1895. There was quite a celebration as the cornet band paraded through town. The electric plant produced enough electricity for lighting but not enough for industrial use.

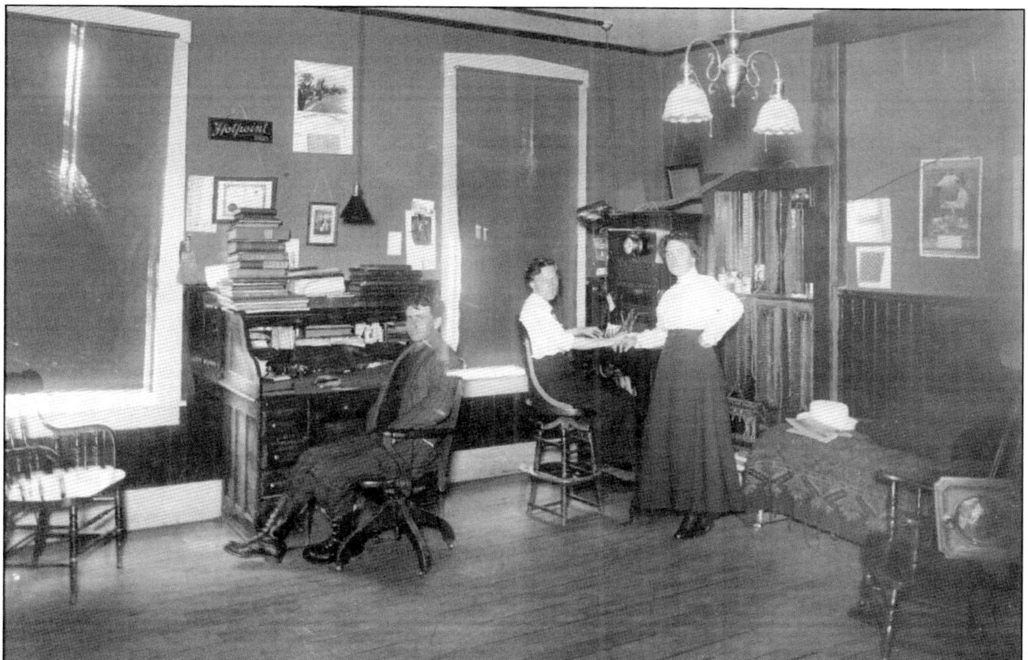

In 1895, there were only 10 telephones connected in Northfield. The service charge was 50¢ a month, and installation cost $15. Just 12 years later, there were 180 phones connected. There were no private lines, and "listening in" was a great way to get all the news around town. This is the business office of the Northfield Telephone Company around 1910.

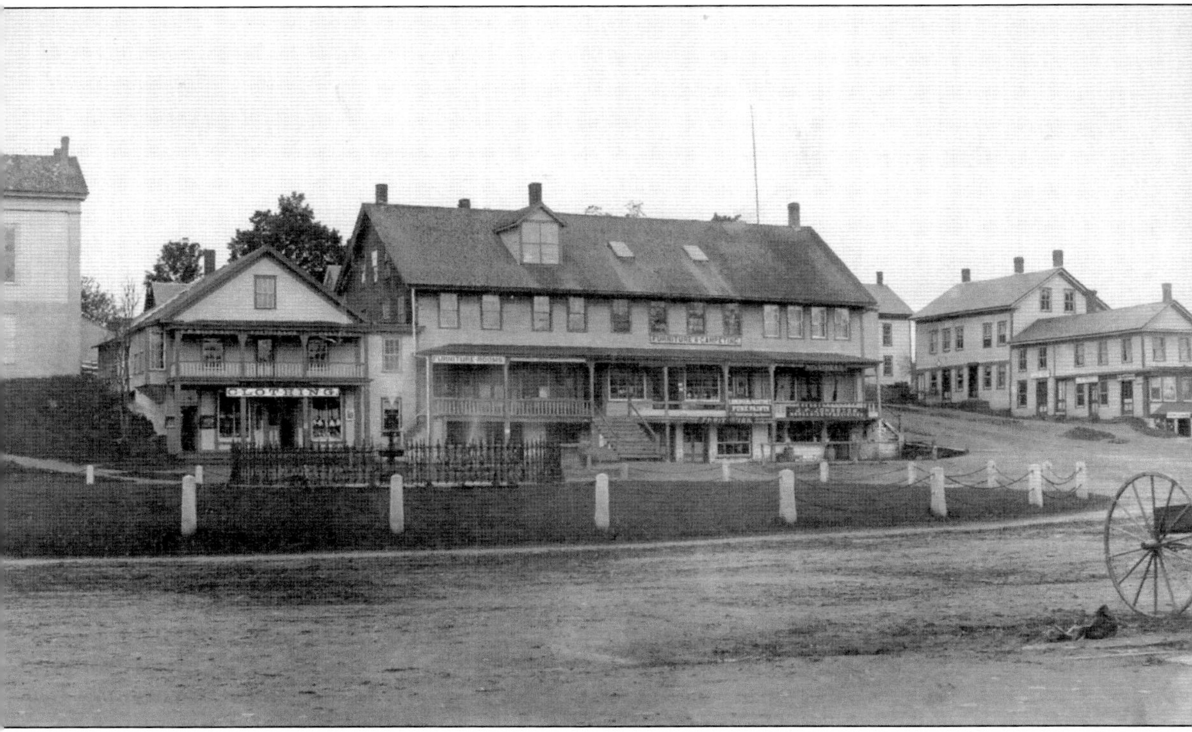

This 1898 photograph shows the west end of the Common and the end of Central Street. Reuben McIntosh's photography studio was above the building on the left. The Donahue Block and the old creamery building are also shown.

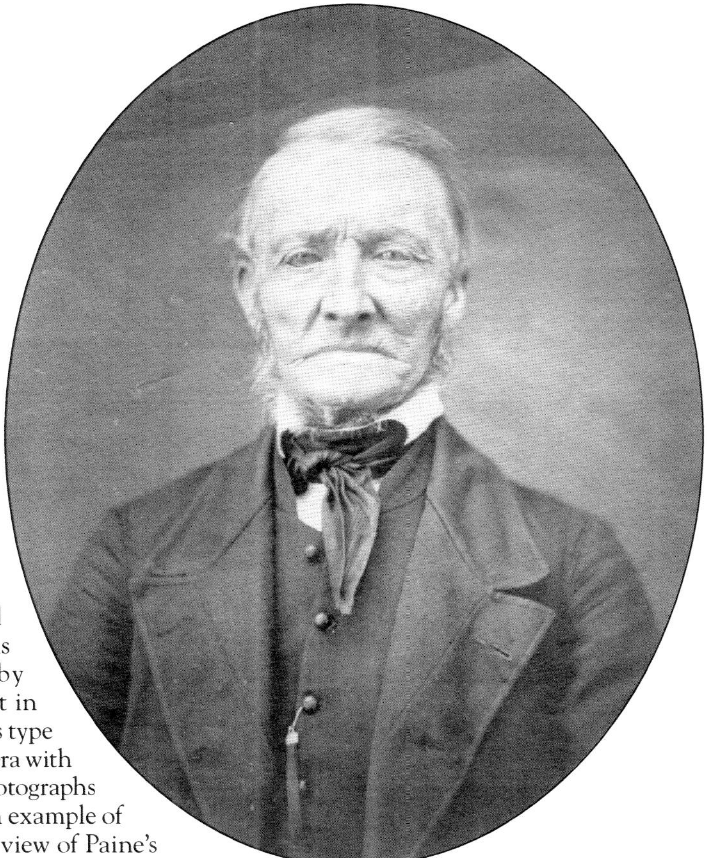

Reuben McIntosh was born in 1823 and raised to be a farmer, but he spent his life taking pictures. He had a photograph gallery on wheels, looking like a gypsy wagon, with a darkroom and a studio pulled by horses. He also had a permanent studio on the Village Common and took hundreds of photographs of Northfield and nearby towns. He became a specialist in stereopticon photography. This type of photography required a camera with two special lenses that took photographs of slightly different angles. An example of his work is shown below in a view of Paine's log dam, the iron bridge, and the Arch Bridge.

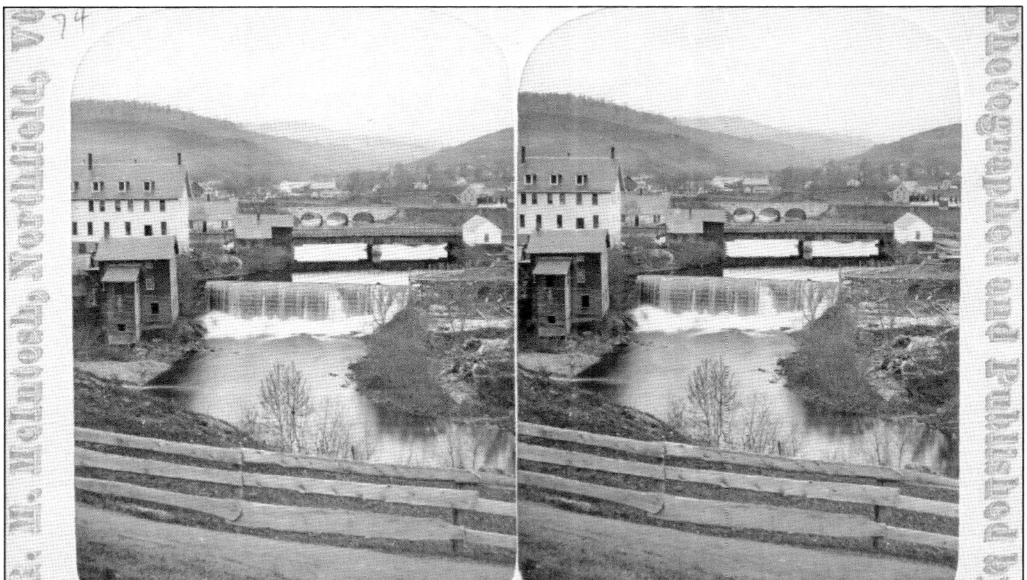

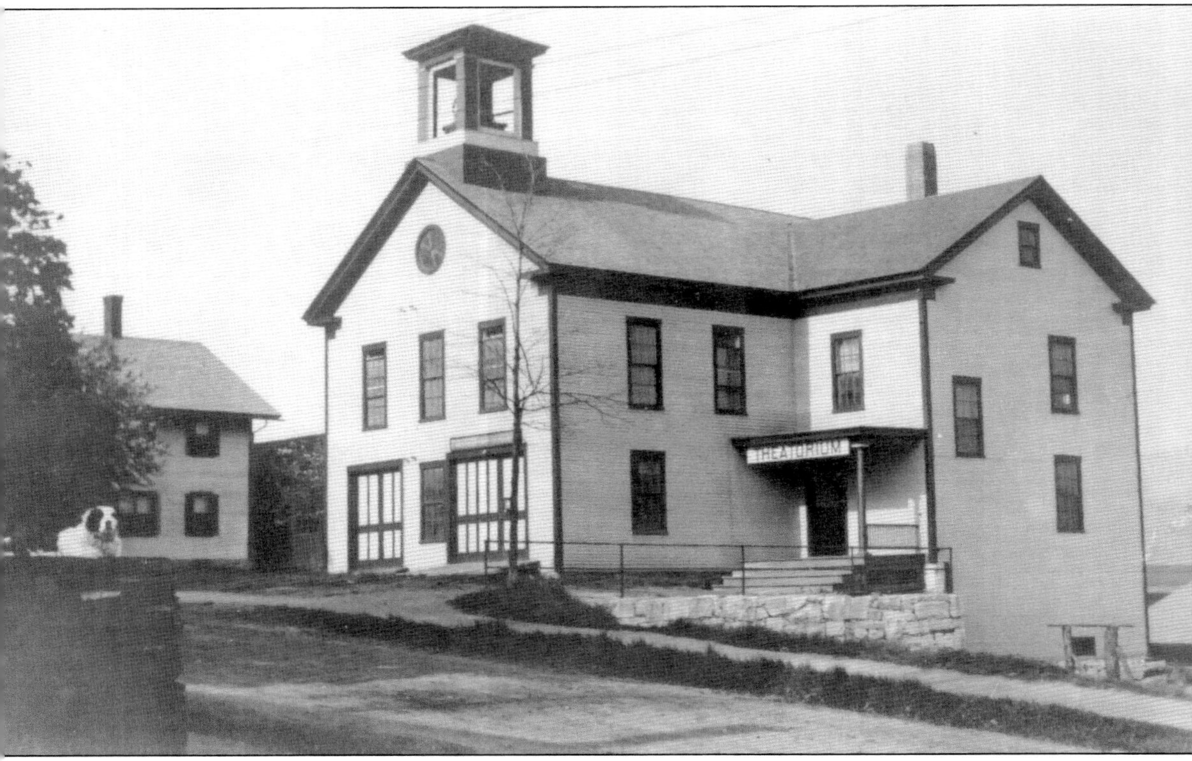

This historic building, known as the village hall, was built in 1867 and still stands today. It has been used for village meetings, and, for a long period of time, it was home to the Torrent and Water Witch volunteer fire companies. The hand-drawn Water Witch fire engine was kept on the first floor. The doors were kept open so if someone saw a fire break out, he could run in and ring the fire bell, which was later replaced by a siren. The first movies in Northfield were shown here, and the infamous Marsh murder trial of the 1890s was also held here, where the townspeople listened to the scandalous testimony. Perhaps the most intriguing rooms in the building are the two windowless jail cells in the basement.

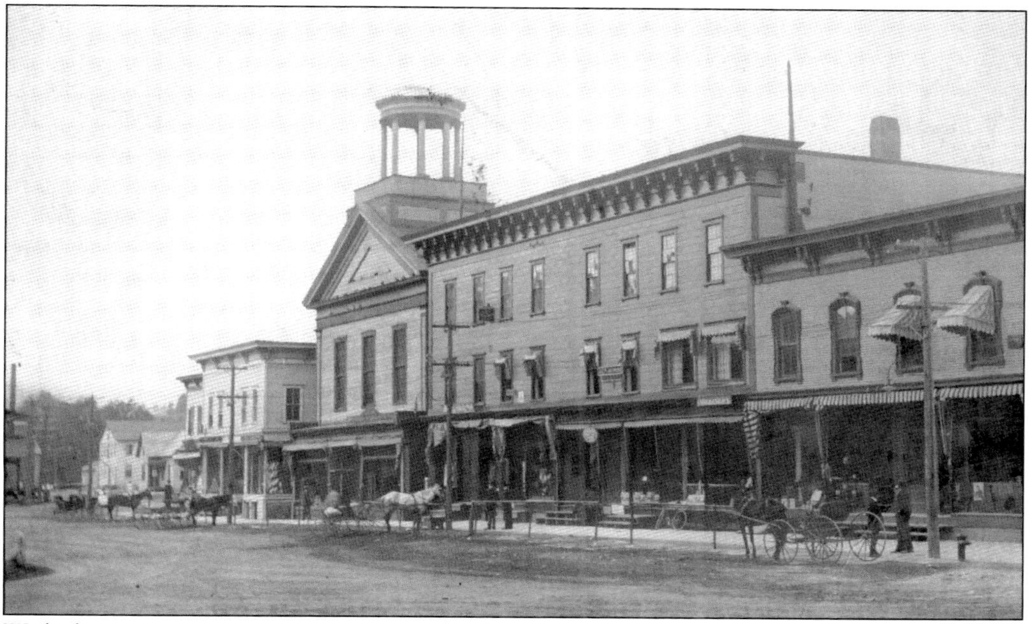

With the train arriving in town in 1848, the downtown was now considered to be Depot Village, not Factory Village. Many more businesses were now located around Depot Square, with new homes constantly springing up along Main Street. As shown in this photograph, travel was done by horse and wagon. The eastern side of the Common had electricity, as shown by the poles and wires running down the street. Note the location of the first Northfield Pharmacy. Another mode of transportation was the bicycle, as seen by the one leaning against the store.

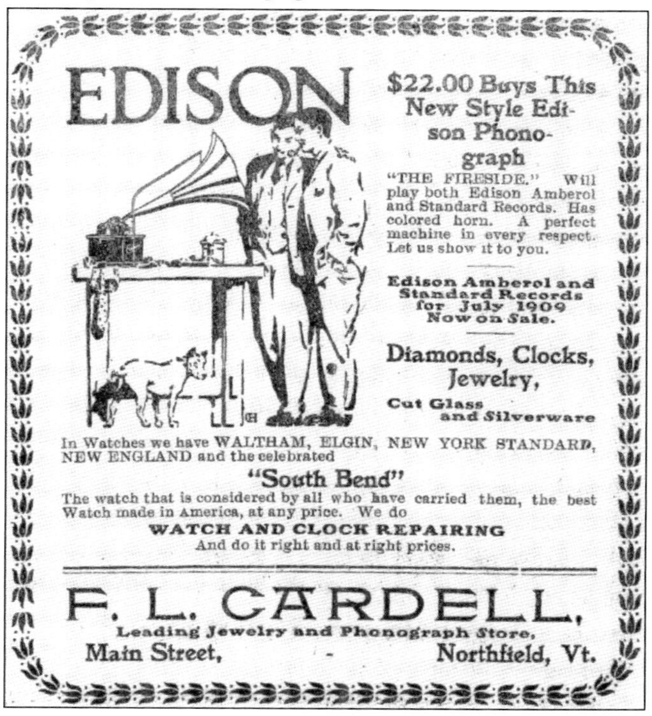

This F.L. Cardell advertisement promotes one of the latest home entertainment systems of the era. People treasured these phonographs for generations.

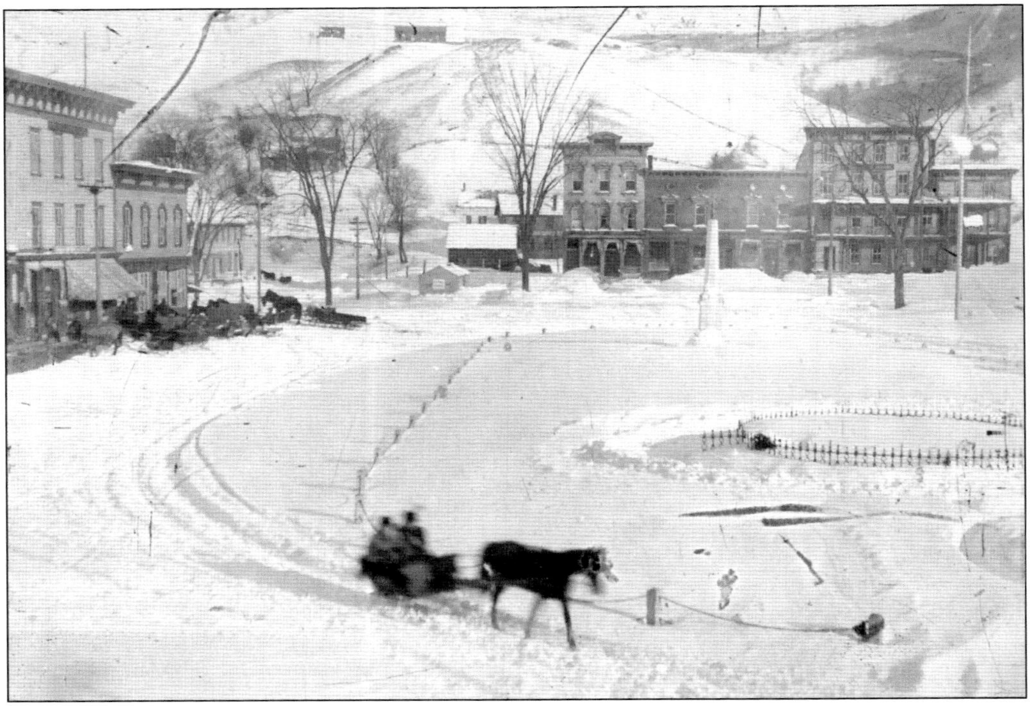

Winter was a costly time for towns, as roads had to be kept open for travel. Sleighs and wagons needed to be equipped with runners to get through the snow. In these early-1900s photographs, even the Common looks difficult to navigate. Snowing bridges was a practice of bringing snow onto the covered bridges so that sleighs and wagons equipped with runners could glide through.

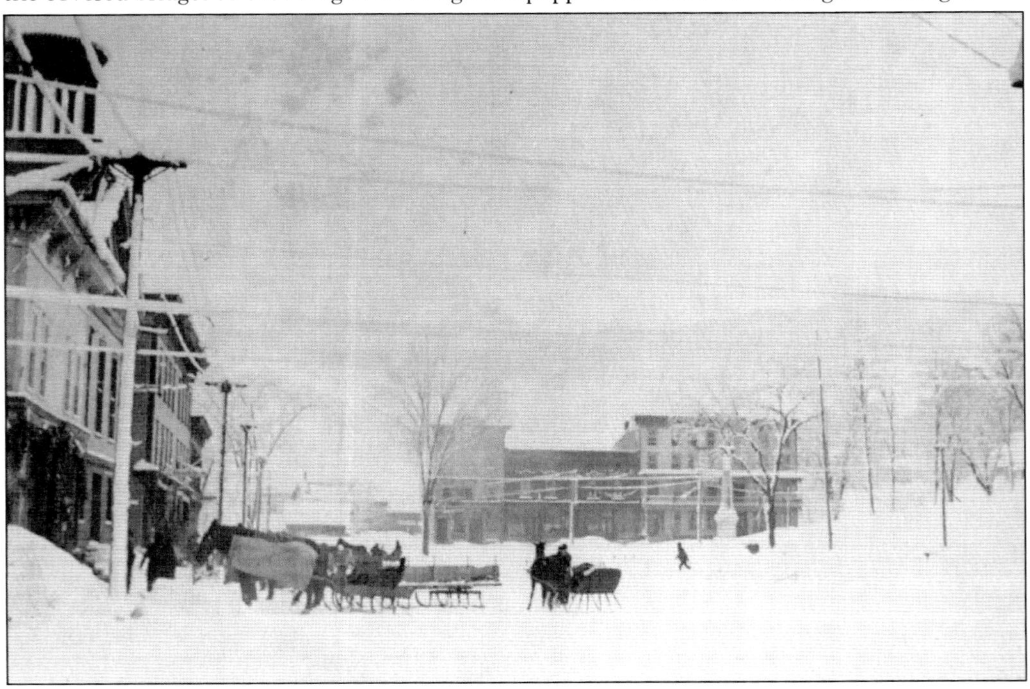

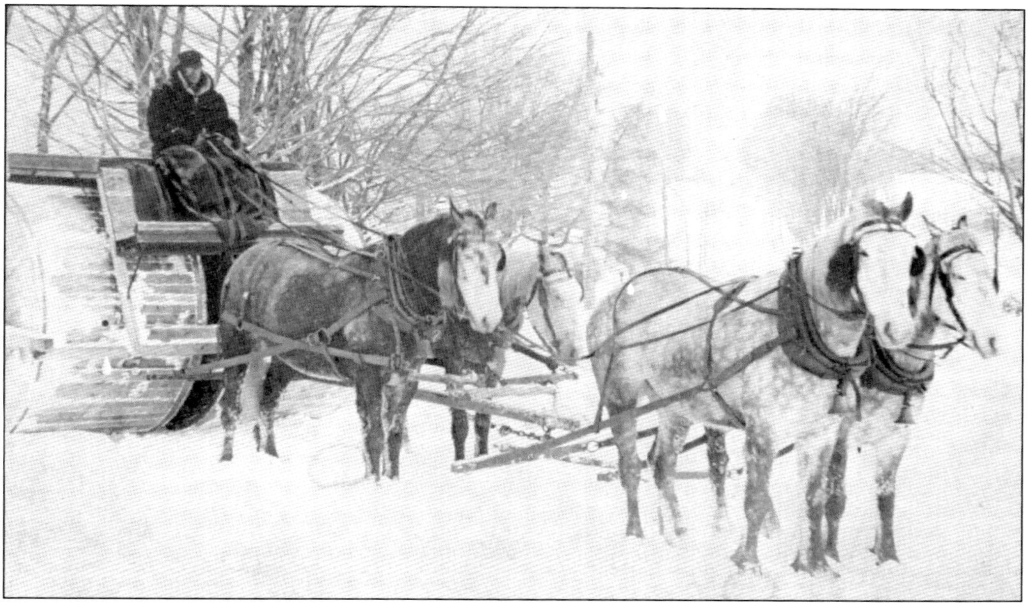

To keep roads open in winter, snow rollers drawn by horses were used. Six horses were needed for snow depths of more than six inches. Men with shovels were sent ahead of the roller to break a path. This method packed the snow hard enough for sleighs and wagons with runners to travel smoothly. Clarence Tracy is pictured here on the snow roller.

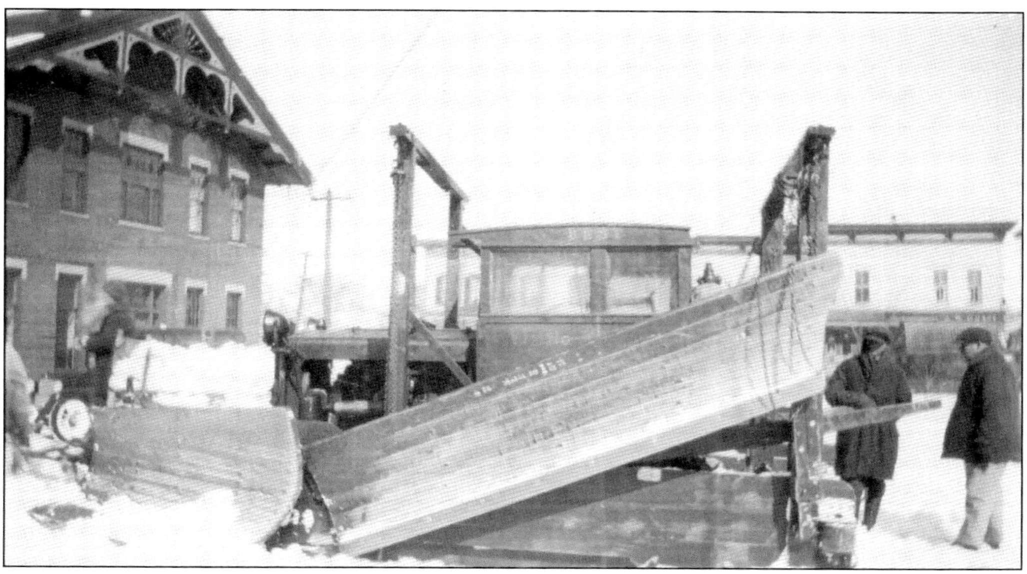

As the years went by and more automobiles began to appear in town, large wooden snowplows were used to clear the snow from the town streets and roads. A wooden horse-drawn snowplow driven by a town favorite, Dexter Macy, was used to clear the sidewalks. Macy always kept horses and could be depended upon for any difficult job needing to be done.

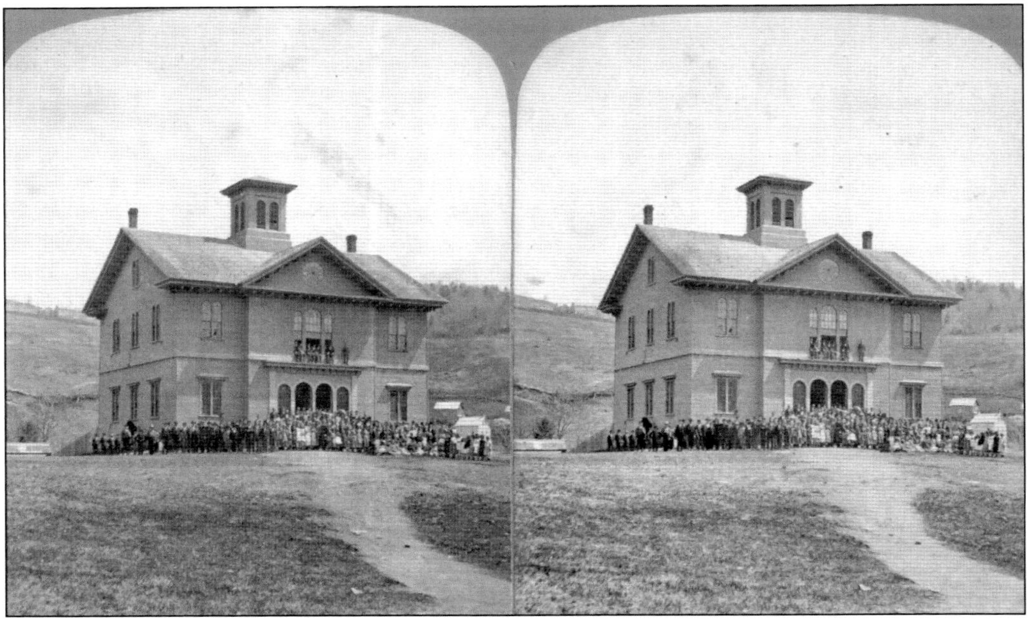

Northfield Academy stood where the Gray Building now stands. It was chartered in 1846 by the Vermont Legislature. A group of local citizens raised $2,400 to construct the building. It was dedicated in 1851. In 1870, the Depot Village School District established the school as a graded school and high school. On opening day, they had 331 students. The building was lost to a fire in 1876.

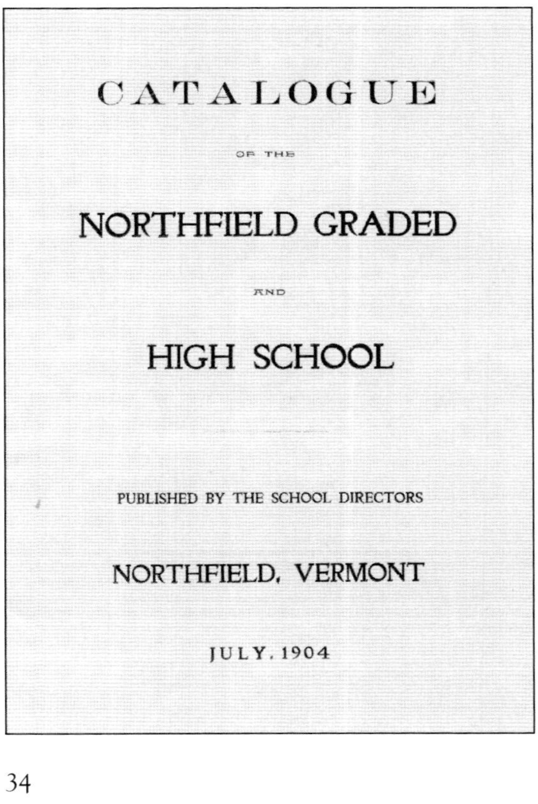

CATALOGUE

OF THE

NORTHFIELD GRADED

AND

HIGH SCHOOL

PUBLISHED BY THE SCHOOL DIRECTORS

NORTHFIELD, VERMONT

JULY, 1904

This is the cover of the 1904 catalogue for the Northfield Graded and High School. This would be where students could find their courses of study from first grade all the way through high school. Also, the booklet would give the rules and regulations for the year.

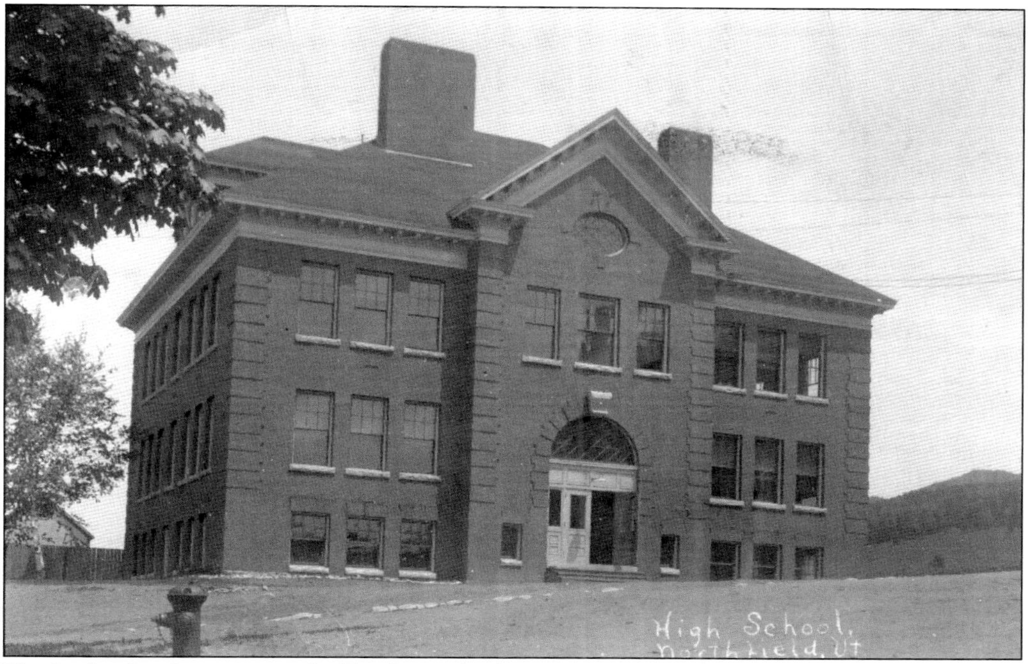

The high school, constructed of brick, was built in 1905 and cost $21,861. It was built beside the wooden graded school. Problems with the design and the weight of the slated roof plagued the building and raised concerns about student safety. The building was declared unsafe just 65 years after construction and was closed permanently.

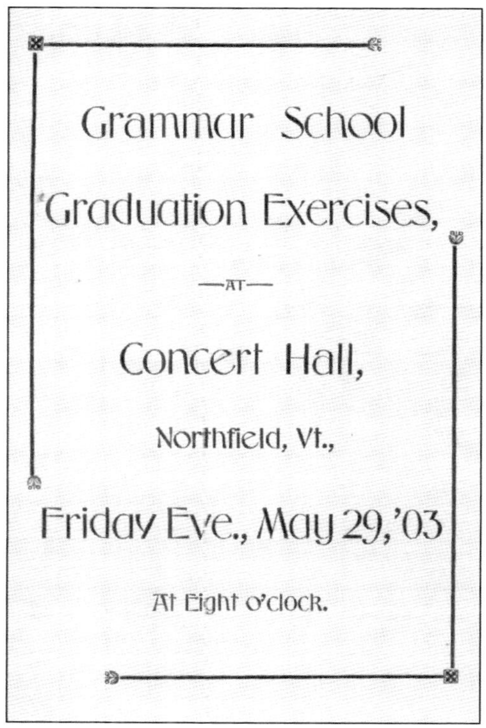
Grammar School

Graduation Exercises,

—AT—

Concert Hall,

Northfield, Vt.,

Friday Eve., May 29,'03

At Eight O'clock.

This is a pamphlet cover for the eighth-grade graduation exercises for the Northfield Grammar School. These graduation exercises still happen each year.

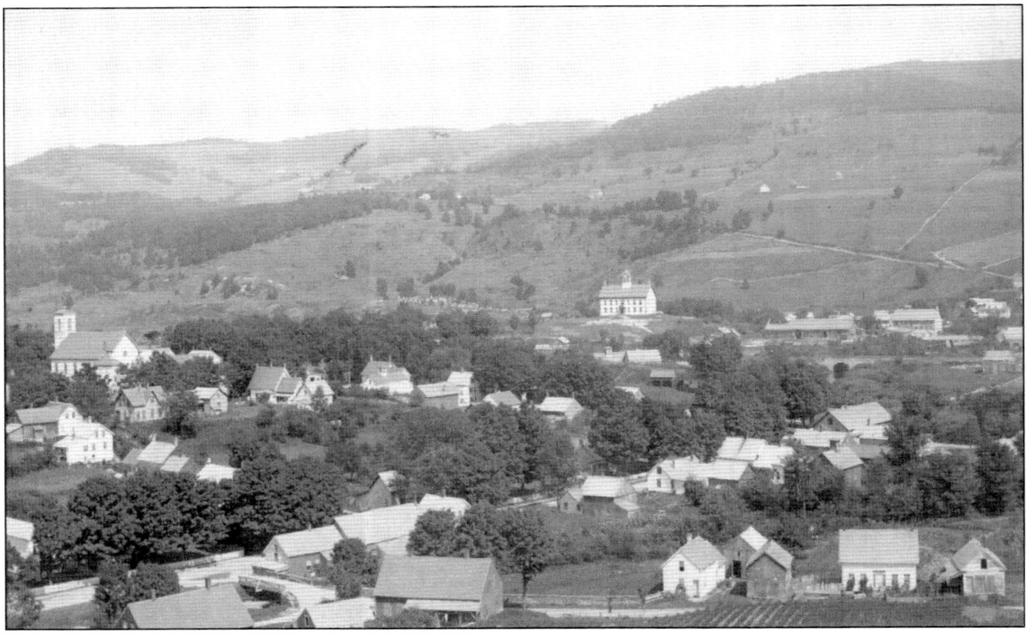

Perhaps the most iconic building in Northfield, the Gray Building, was erected in 1876 to replace the Northfield Academy. It was the most up-to-date building of its day, initially housing high school students and later elementary school students. There were weighted pulleys in the attic that would allow a wall to be raised so two small classrooms could become one large assembly room. There was a large bell in the cupola that called generations of students to class. Today, the Gray Building continues to proudly stand over the village, as it did on the day it was built. Newly renovated, it now serves the town as a community center.

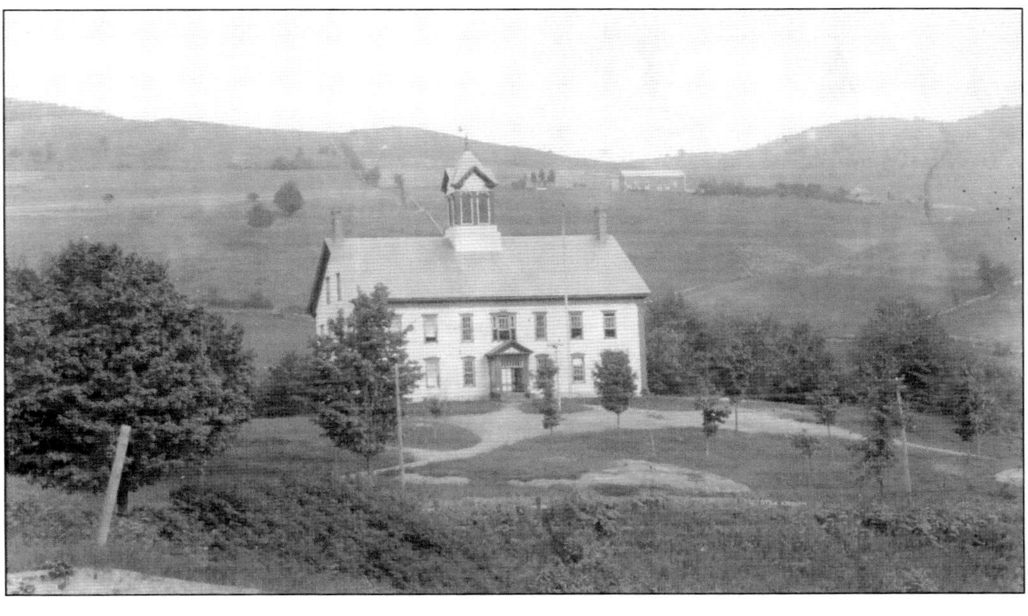

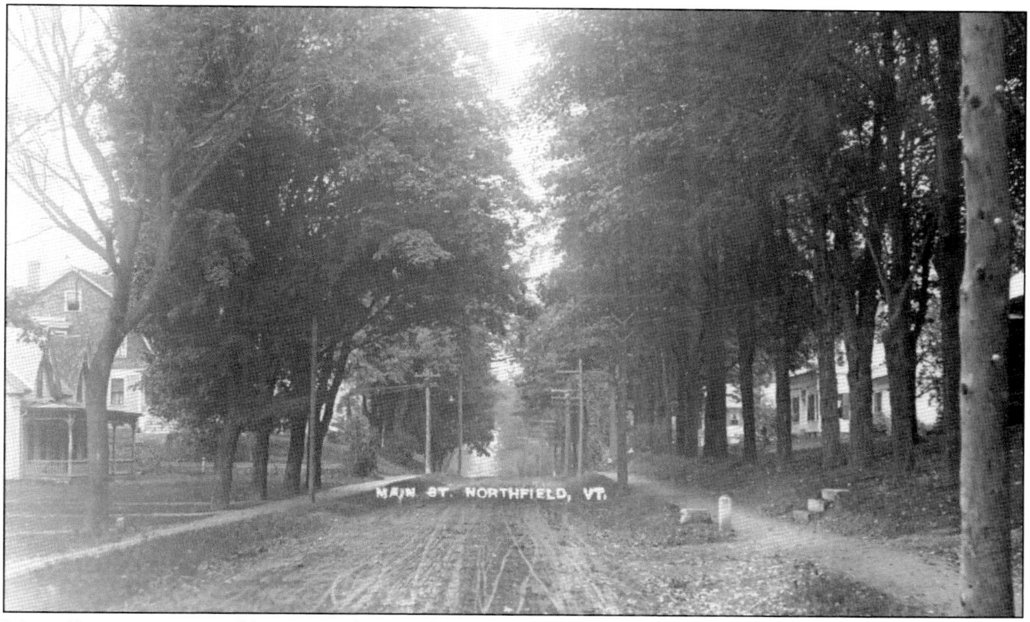

Main Street is pictured here as a dirt road. Unfortunately, the many beautiful elm trees that lined both sides of the street would fall victim to Dutch elm disease, but, for many years before that, they added a special grace and welcome shade along this major thoroughfare.

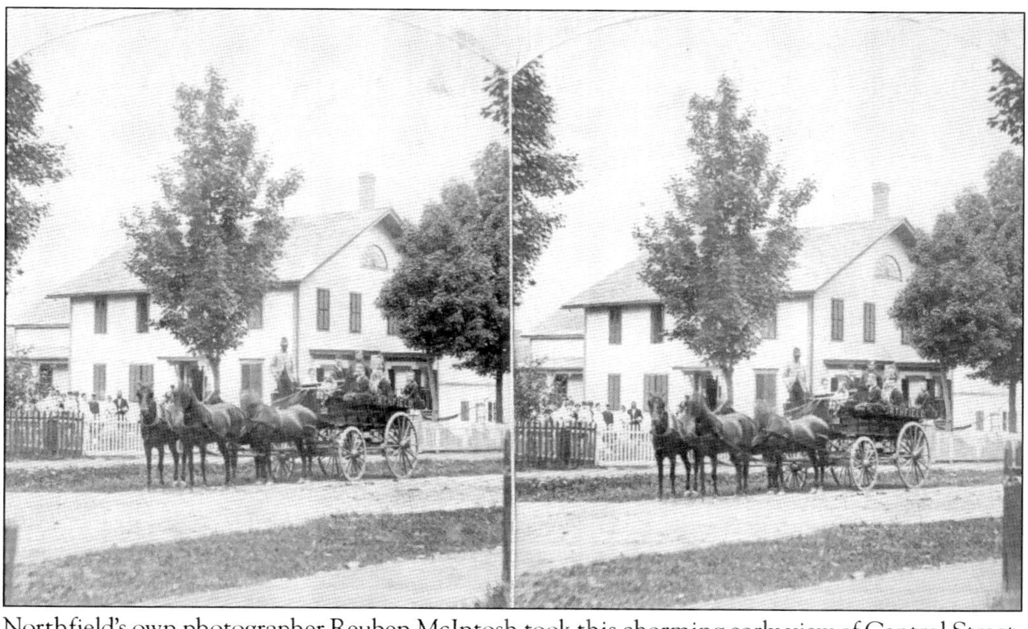

Northfield's own photographer Reuben McIntosh took this charming early view of Central Street. Beautiful elm trees also line both sides of this street. On lower Central Street were two large apartment buildings housing Vermont Central Railroad workers. Northfield's village hall, which also housed a volunteer fire department, was located on the end of the street.

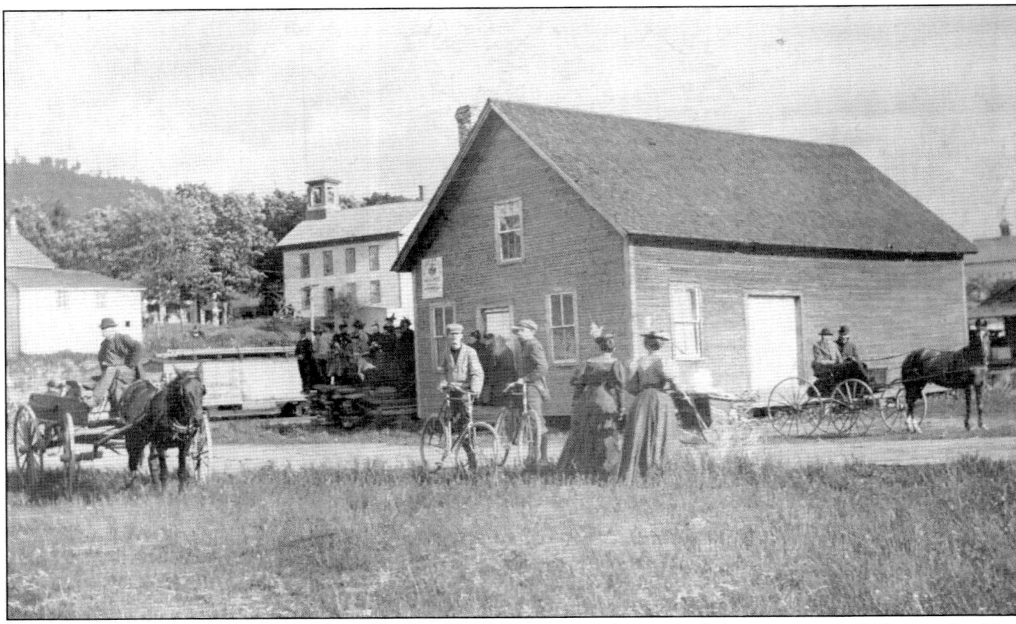

Just 1.5 miles north from Depot Village, the Falls was aptly named for two waterfalls on the Dog River, one above the confluence of Cox Brook and one below. The Falls was the last of the four villages to be settled along the Dog River valley. The first house was built in 1828, and, 12 years later, there were 17 homes.

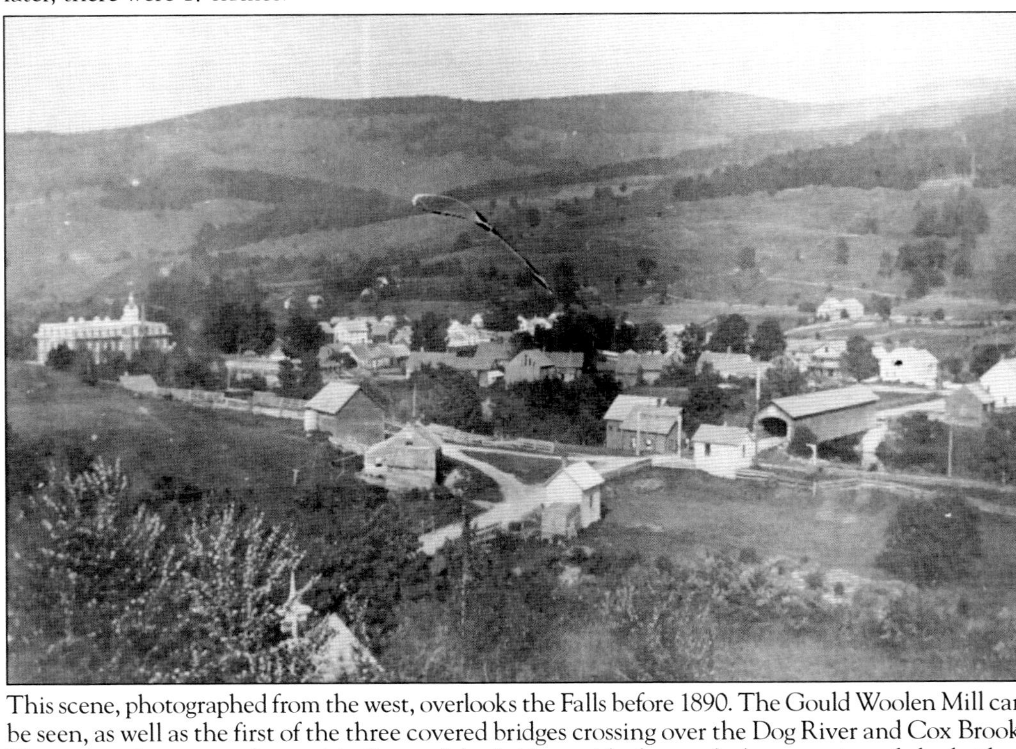

This scene, photographed from the west, overlooks the Falls before 1890. The Gould Woolen Mill can be seen, as well as the first of the three covered bridges crossing over the Dog River and Cox Brook. The railroad station is located in front of the bridge, with the tracks between it and the bridge.

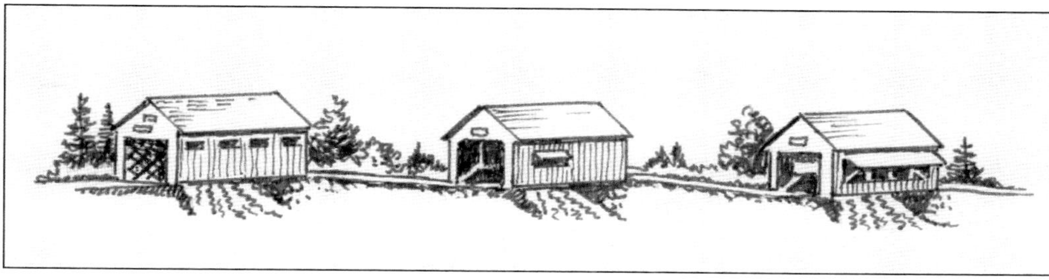

Northfield is the proud home of six covered bridges, three of which are in the Falls. In the National Register of Historic Places are the Town Lattice Station Bridge, built in 1872; the Queen Post Newell Bridge, built in the 1870s; and the Queen Post Upper Bridge, also built in the 1870s. These bridges are unusual because they are located so close together. The bridges bring visitors from across the country and around the world to photograph them or capture them in oil or watercolor. Because of this, the town has added steel beams and made necessary improvements for safety due to the increased traffic. (Drawing by Becky Merrilees.)

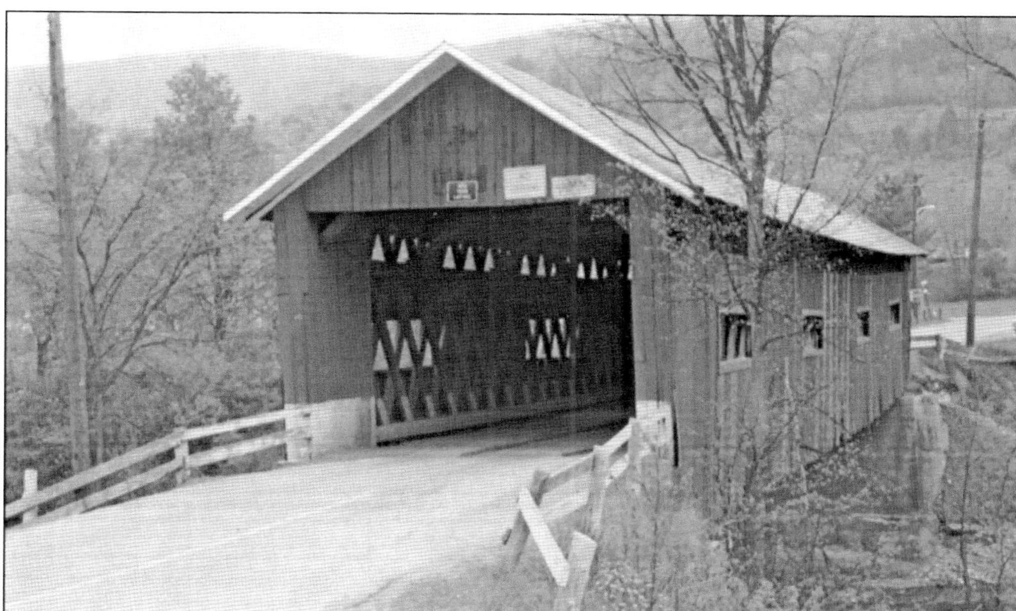

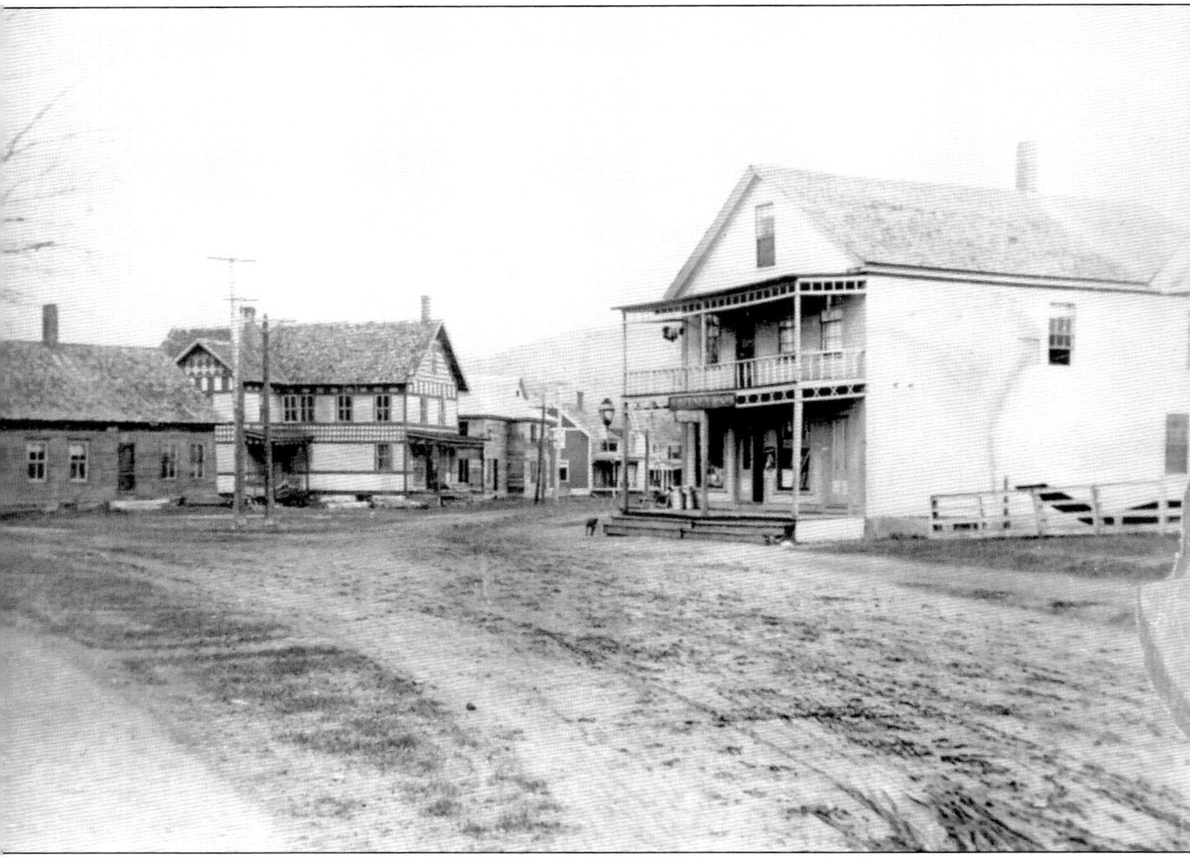

This early-1900 photograph of the Falls shows the Whitney & Company general store on the east side of Main Street. Horace H. Whitney was the owner of the store at the time, but, in 1918, Mr. and Mrs. John W. Ford came from Randolph, Vermont, to run the business. He was the manager, and she was the clerk of the store. In this typical general store, one could buy grain, groceries, footwear, rubber boots, bananas, barbwire fencing, and Montpelier Crackers, just to name a few of the items on the shelves. The owner never allowed tobacco to be sold in the store. It went out of business in 1935 when Col. Gerald Cross bought the property from Dr. Bert Allen. It then contained three apartments, and the former store became Colonel Cross's woodworking shop.

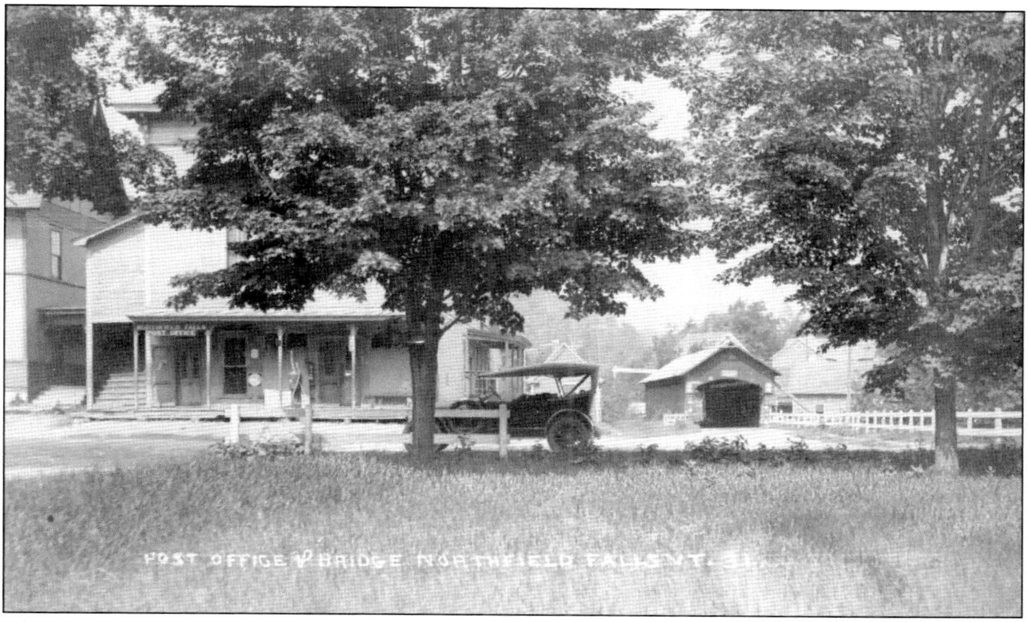

This early photograph of Main Street in the Falls is of the 1892 Cross Block, which contained the first post office and a general store with an early gasoline pump in front. Note the Ford Model T parked in the shade of the tree in the foreground. In the background is the first of the three covered bridges, the Station Bridge, for which the Falls is famous. To the left of the general store is Northfield Falls Elementary School, which housed students in first through eighth grades. In the 1920s, the school building was moved with rollers up the hill to its present location and extensively remodeled.

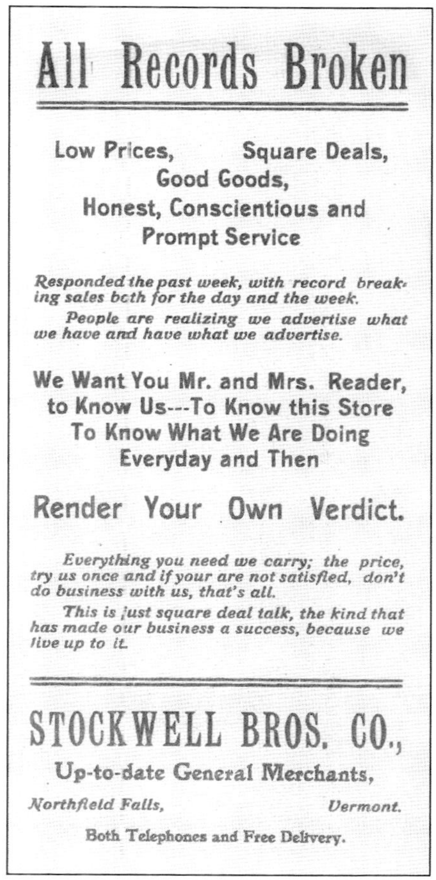

All Records Broken

Low Prices, Square Deals, Good Goods, Honest, Conscientious and Prompt Service

Responded the past week, with record breaking sales both for the day and the week.

People are realizing we advertise what we have and have what we advertise.

We Want You Mr. and Mrs. Reader, to Know Us---To Know this Store To Know What We Are Doing Everyday and Then

Render Your Own Verdict.

Everything you need we carry; the price, try us once and if your are not satisfied, don't do business with us, that's all.

This is just square deal talk, the kind that has made our business a success, because we live up to it.

STOCKWELL BROS. CO.,

Up-to-date General Merchants,

Northfield Falls, Vermont.

Both Telephones and Free Delivery.

This early-1900s advertisement for Stockwell Bros. Co. of Northfield Falls is very upbeat. Note that customers could phone in their list of groceries and the store would deliver them for free.

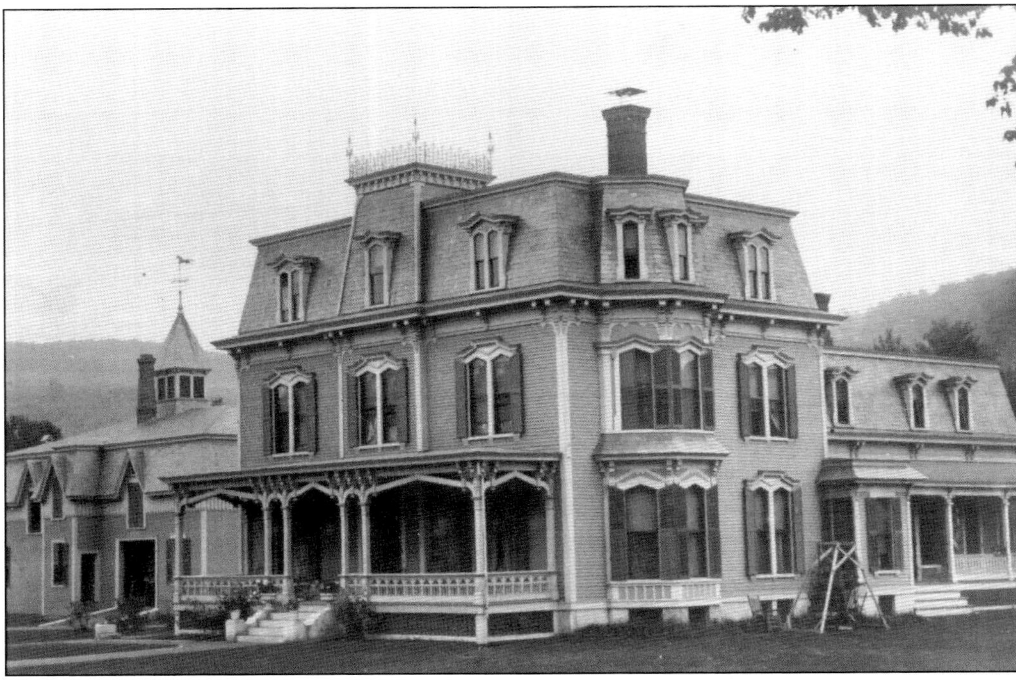

The Gould family became the largest employer and owned the most houses in the Falls. For a time in the mid-1800s, the Falls was known as Gouldsville due to their influence and generosity. Many houses they owned along Mill Street were used to house mill workers. Joseph and Mary Gould built the beautiful Victorian mansion above and lived there for many years. Built after the Civil War, this home was certainly a departure from the architectural styles of other Northfield homes. Behind the house was a small footbridge over the Dog River (below) to an island where the Goulds would run their horses.

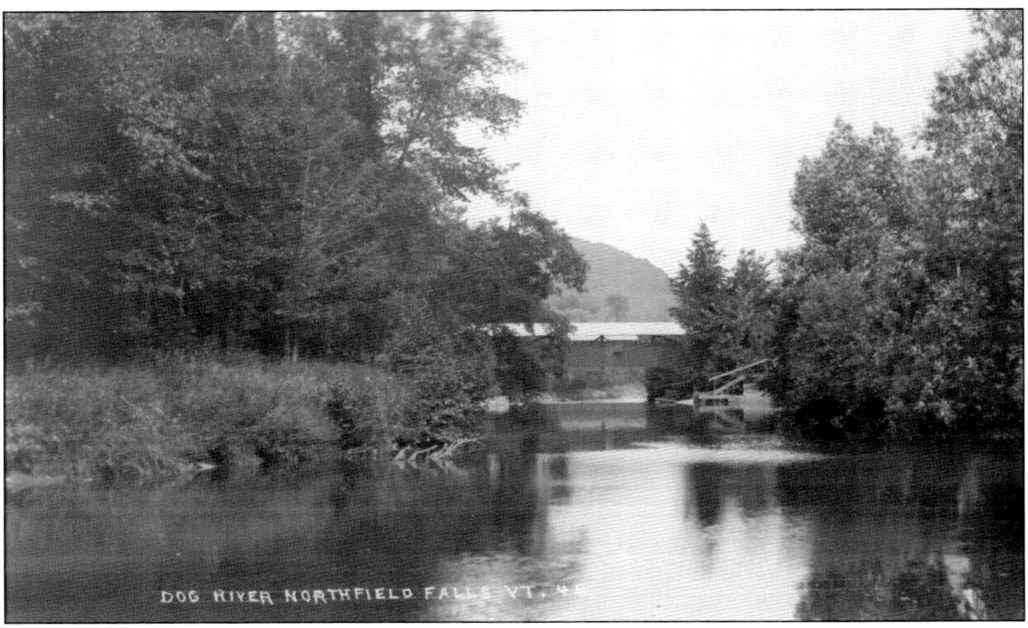

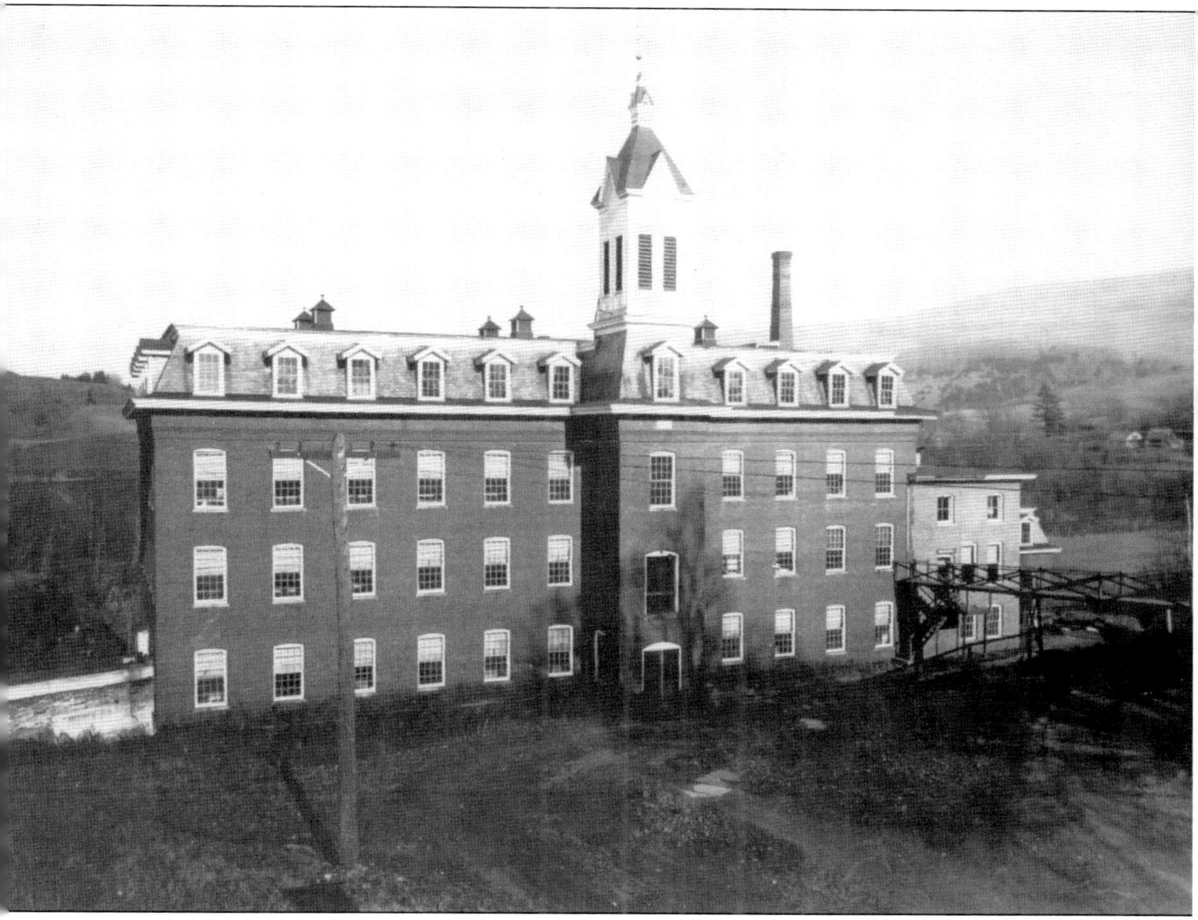

Once again, in the Falls, the Dog River played an important role in the location of mills. As Elijah Paine built his mill near the river, so did James Gould and his partners in the Falls. Initially built of wood in 1833, it was rebuilt in brick following a disastrous fire in 1873. Rebuilt in the French Second Empire style, it was four stories high and 110 feet long. At its peak, it employed a very large workforce, with whole families working in the mill. Working long days for a wage of under $1 a day in 1900, in winter, workers came and left work in the darkness. The mill produced white flannel for its 100 years of operation. The Gould family owned the mill until 1900, when they sold it to Charles M. Davis, a local lawyer, who ran the mill for another 30 years. It eventually burned down in 1931.

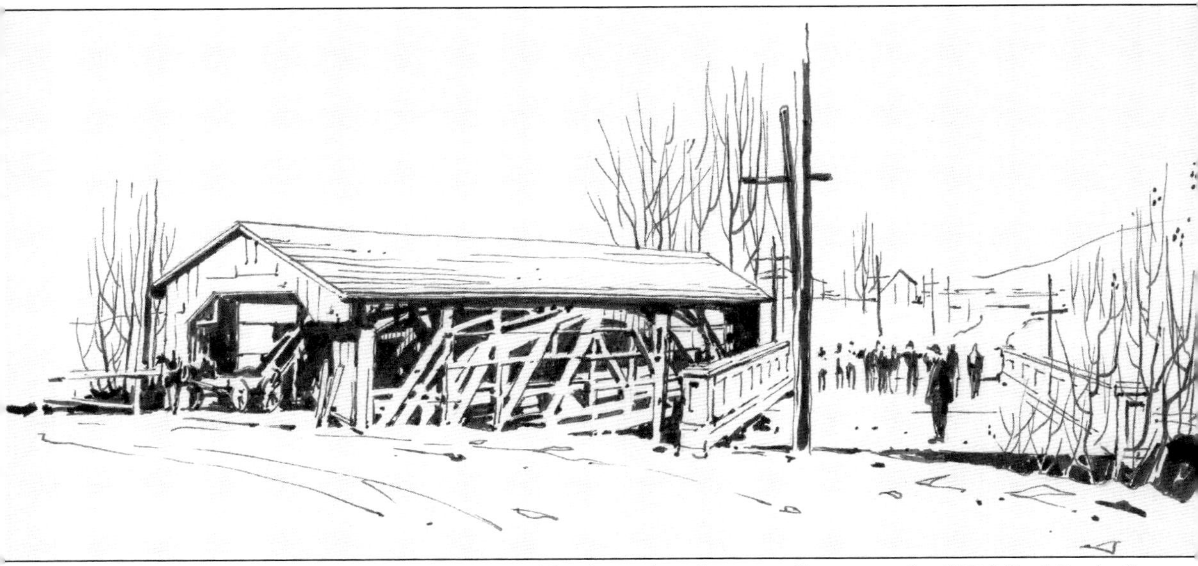

As Northfield is known for its covered bridges, this drawing illustrates the "Old Red Bridge" being replaced by a new cement bridge on North Main Street, leading to the Falls. The bridge was considered to be unsafe, and the town fathers called a special meeting in 1914, when it was decided that a new bridge was needed. The sharp curve onto the old covered bridge was difficult to navigate, especially with the increasing volume of automobile and truck traffic. The new bridge was constructed of steel and concrete at a cost of $8,000. The old bridge was auctioned off to J.P. Rabidou, a local builder, for $60. This change from the old wooden covered bridge to the new, safer, modern bridge could be seen as leaving the horse-and-buggy mode of transportation in the past and moving into the era of the automobile. (Drawing by S.T. Morris.)

Three

Busy Farms and Booming Mills

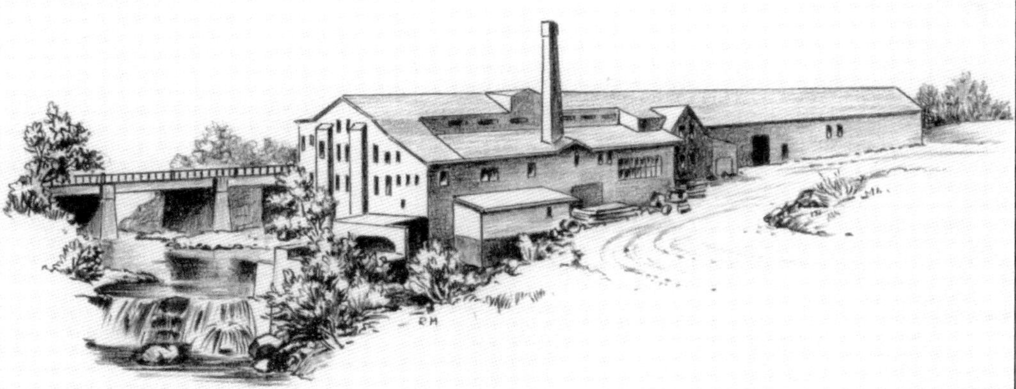

Cetrangolo's Granite Works

The coming of the granite industry, beginning in the 1890s, would dramatically change the town of Northfield. Having very little granite to quarry in town, it was the railroad bringing the stone to town that created a new industry. This drawing by Becky Merrilees depicts the Cetrangolo's granite shed, one of many sheds that was built and prospered.

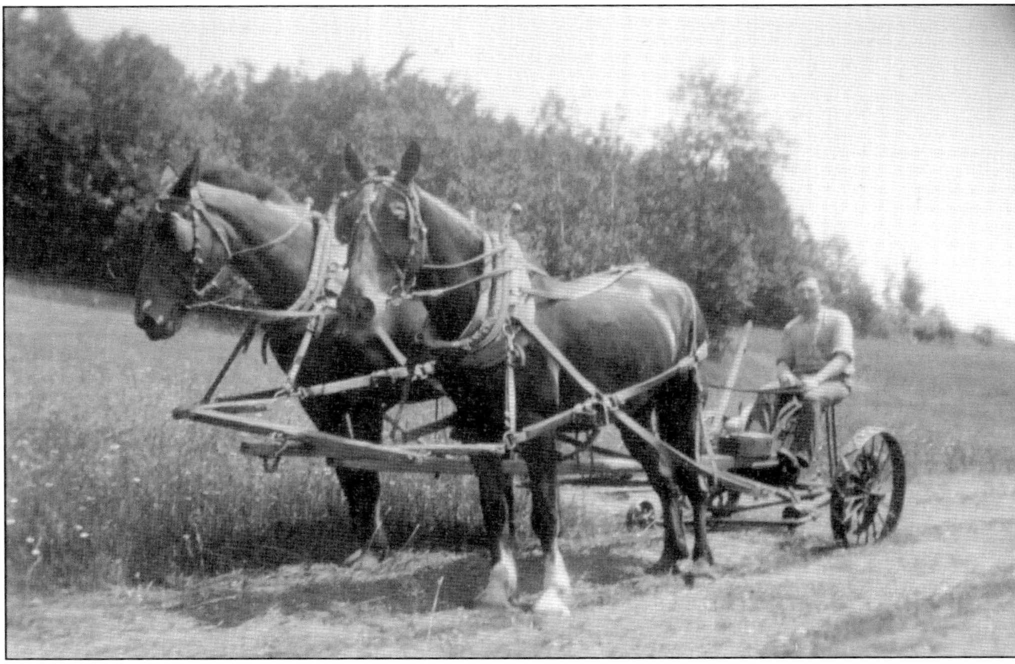

Work on the family farm was never-ending and was tied to the rhythm of the seasons. Here, Sumner Boardman is mowing hay on the family farm in 1916. The "mowing bee," a popular event, occurred when 20–25 men got together with scythes and worked in unison to cut the hay.

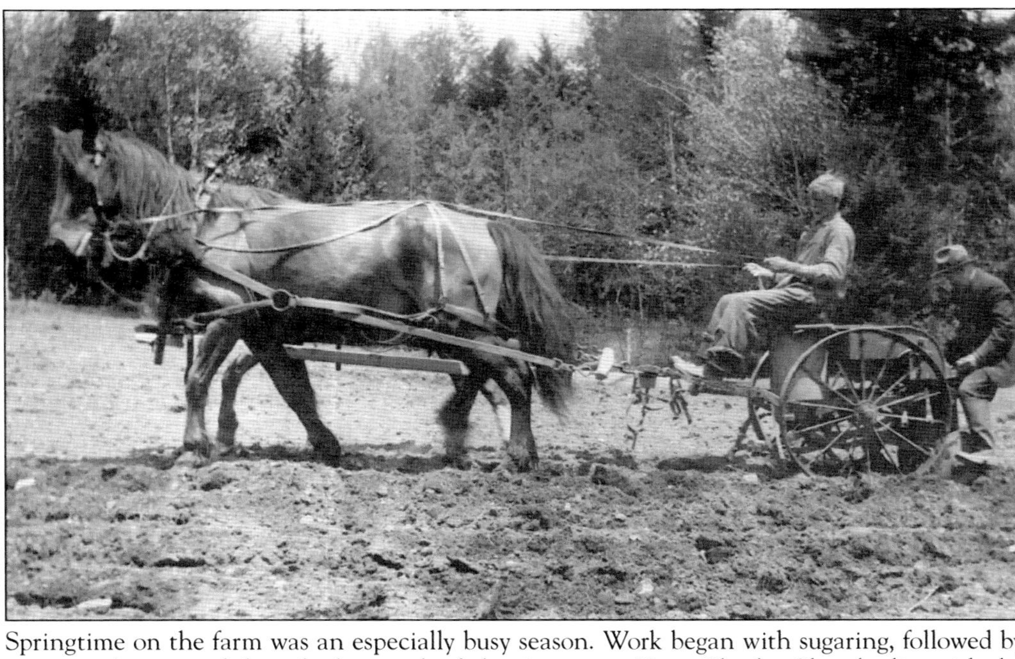

Springtime on the farm was an especially busy season. Work began with sugaring, followed by repairing fences, and then the busy task of planting crops. Here, Charles Chamberlin, with the help of his neighbor, is most likely planting seed potatoes. Extra crops such as potatoes could be sold to local merchants or traded for commodities such as flour, sugar, or coffee.

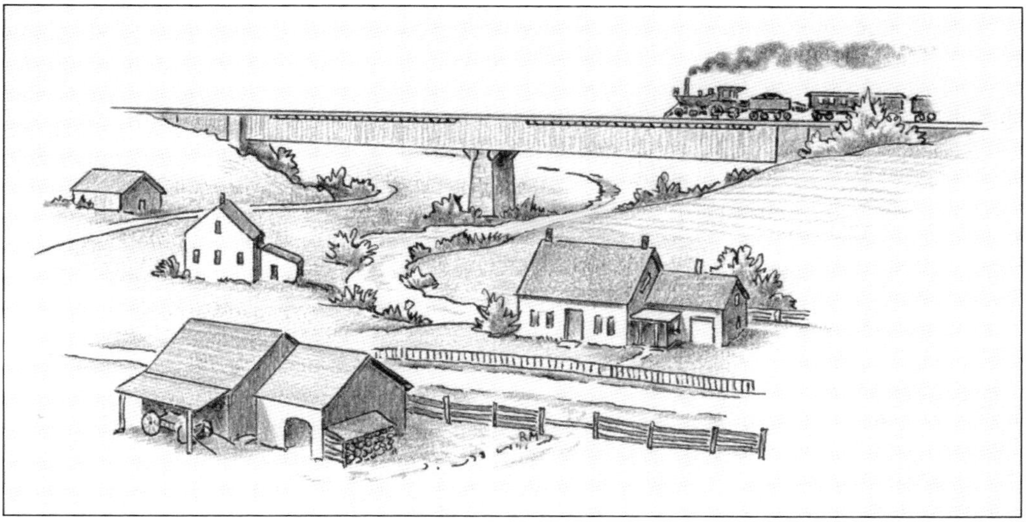

Pictured here is Becky Merrilees's drawing of the Tracy farm as it appeared in the late 1800s. One sees the gentle curve of the Dog River and the main road leading south to Roxbury. Above the road and river is the old wooden Harlow Bridge, with a train crossing over.

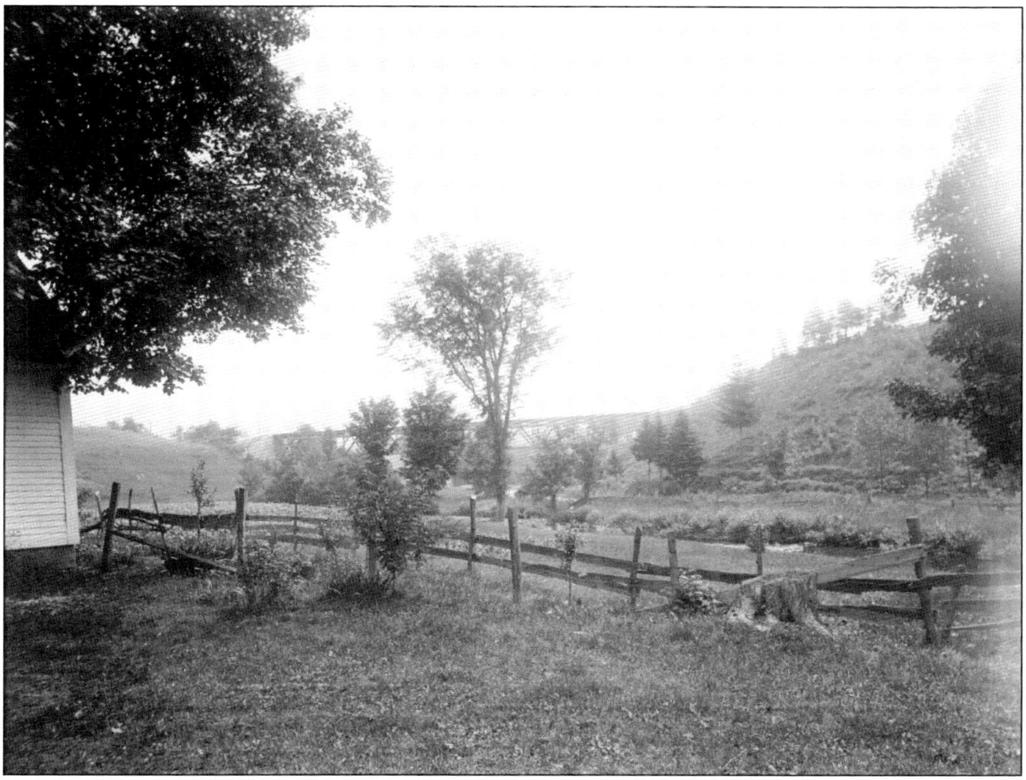

The beauty of rural Northfield is clearly evident in this outstanding view looking eastward from the farm located near the Stony Brook Bridge. The new, steel Harlow Bridge, which replaced the old wooden structure, is seen; interestingly enough, the bridge still rests on the original piers. The lovely wine-glass elm in the center of the photograph is sadly gone.

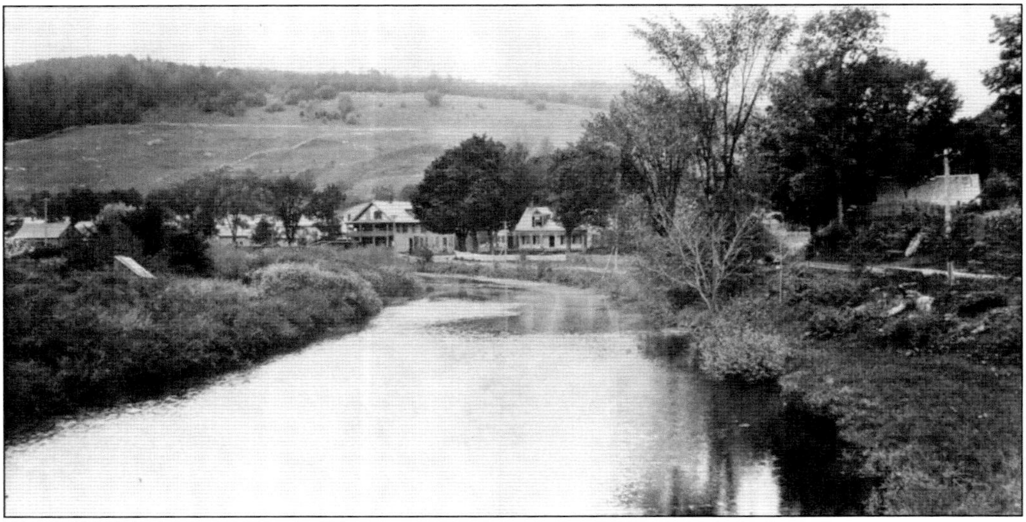

Northfield's vital waterway is the Dog River. It provided the power for the early mills and also generated the electricity for Northfield's first power plant. Here, its placid waters flow along Water Street, passing the Kerr store and the Carpenter home.

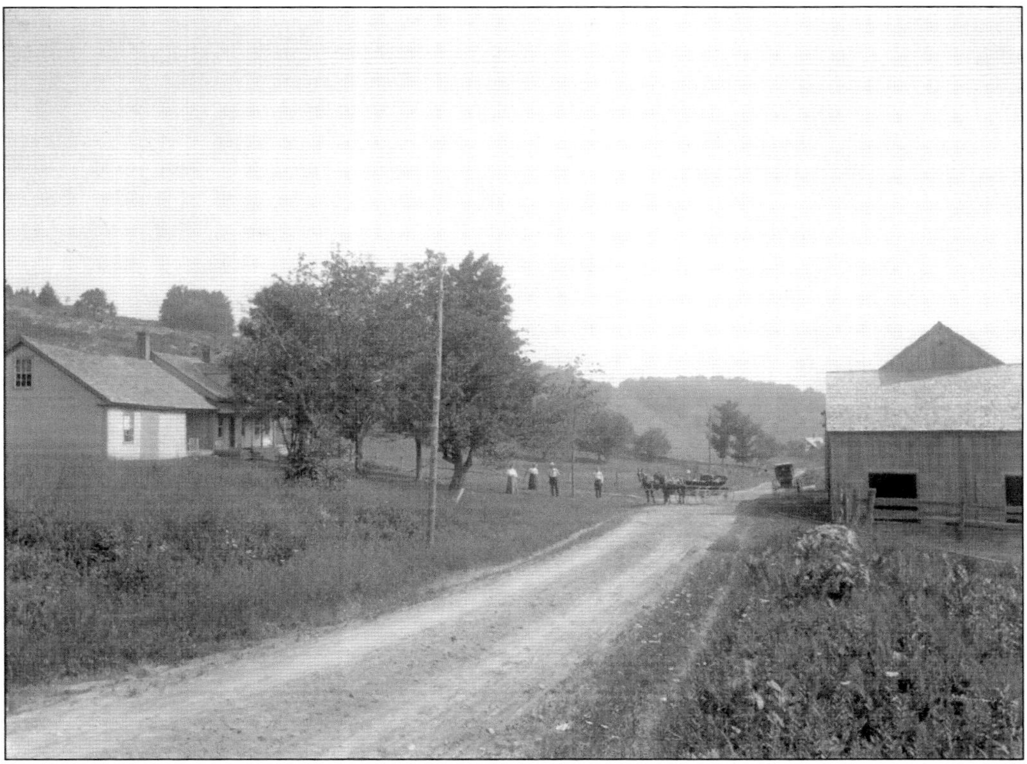

Hattie Mayo, Georgianna Mayo Holton, Charles Lyman Holton, and Edward Mayo Holton, in no particular order, are standing on the lawn of their beautiful West Hill homestead on a summer morning in 1908. The well-kept buildings, neatly trimmed lawn, and horse-and-buggies show the pride the family took in their homestead.

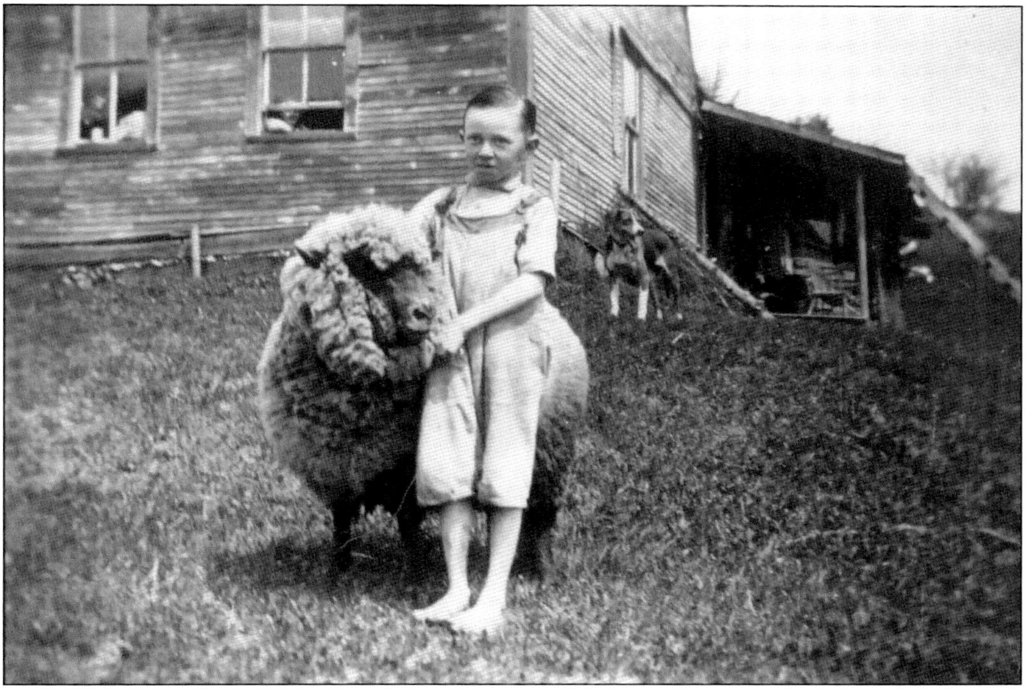

Children on early farms soon learned the value of hard work. Their contributions to the family included helping to harvest crops, chopping and piling wood, raking hay, shoveling snow, and tending the animals. These animals often became their pets. Howard Boardman is pictured here in 1918 with a pet sheep.

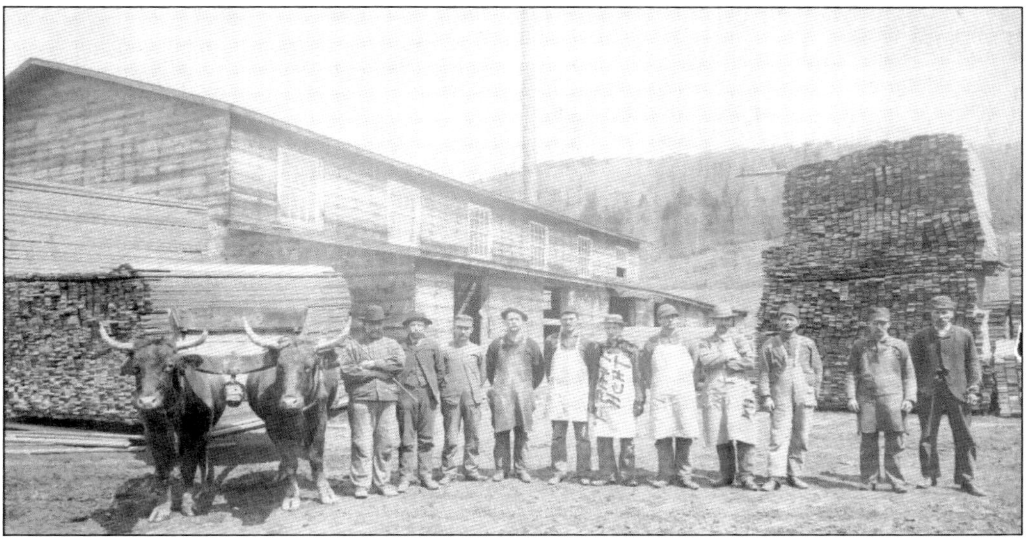

Oxen were used both on farms and at the mills. They were better in the woods than horses and were used to bring in hay and wood. Oxen were used in town through the 1920s. Oxen pulls at the fair were popular events, with owners taking great pride in their animals, which normally had bells and decorations hanging from their yokes.

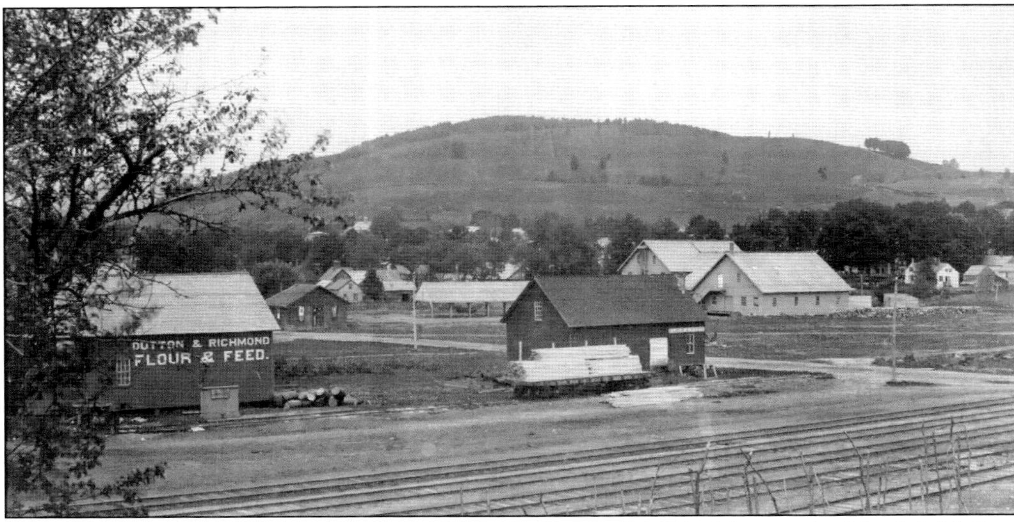

Pictured here behind the Dutton & Richmond Flour & Feed Building is the Northfield Corn Company, established in 1894. The husking shed, storehouse, and processing plant with its outside elevator are shown. This company was located on the former site of the Central Vermont roundhouse. The first corn-packing season ended with a production of 300,000 cans of corn. The company paid 5¢ a bushel for husking the corn, a job well suited for children. The bushels of husked corn went up on the elevator to be shelled and then to the third floor for the cutting machines. With such a successful enterprise canning corn, the company began canning apples.

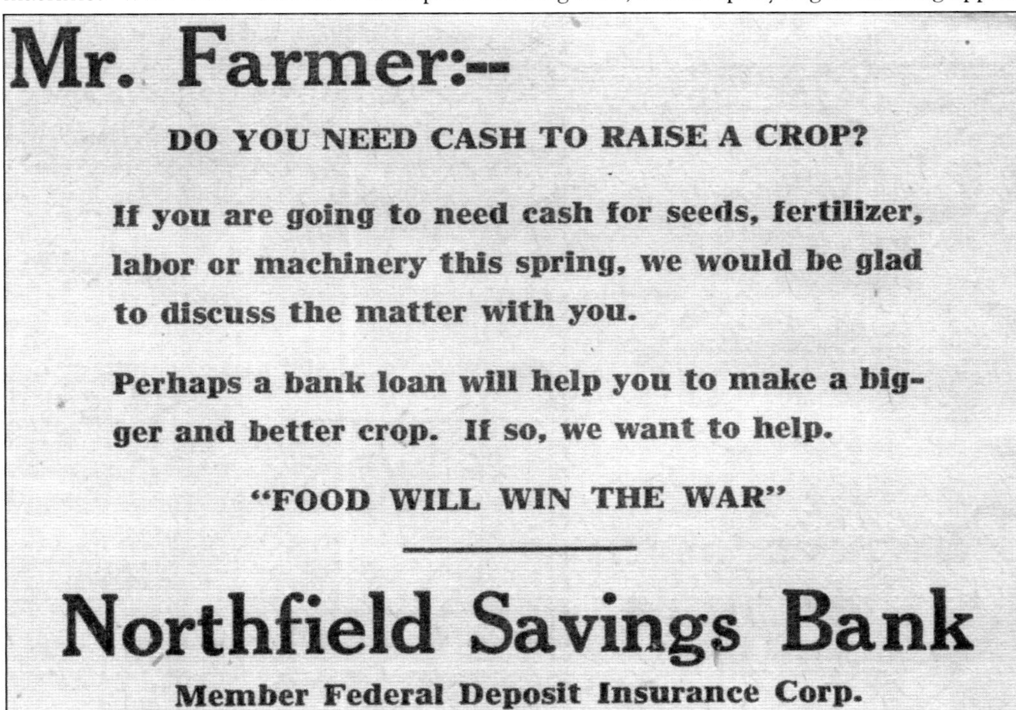

Rev. Edward Bournes and a group of community leaders founded the Northfield Savings Bank in 1867. The bank's first home was in the J.C.B. Thayer Tailoring and Clothing store.

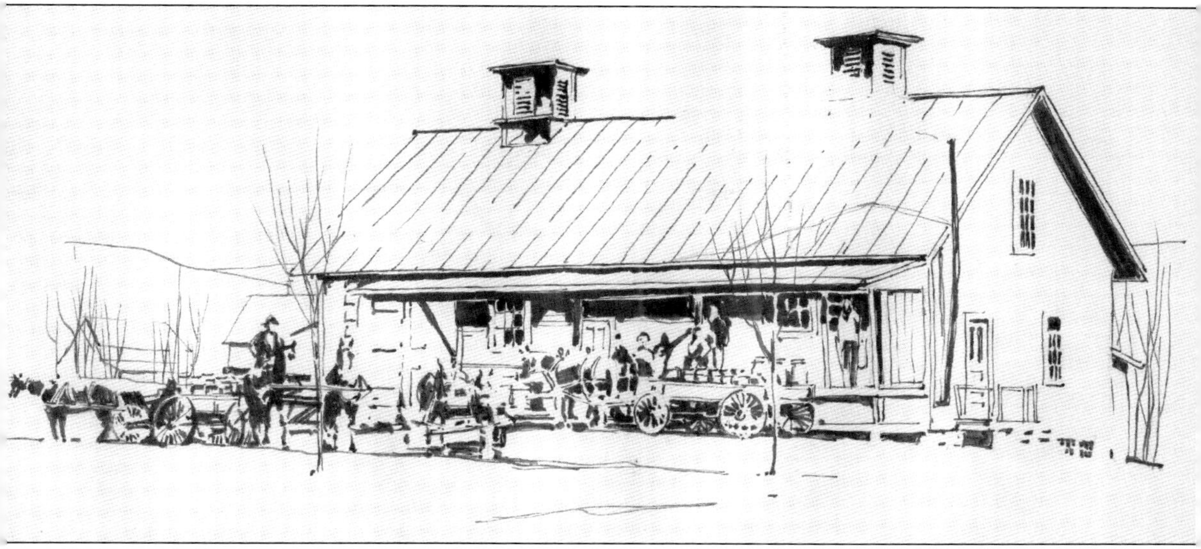

William Mullen established the creamery in 1894. The plant was able to produce 800 pounds of butter each day that was shipped as far away as Massachusetts. The plant continued to do well and, by the 1920s, was receiving 10,000 pounds of milk and 1,000 pounds of cream each day. Skim milk was made into Dutch cheese. A new plant was built closer to the railroad in 1920; however, it was heavily damaged in the 1927 flood, and the company went into bankruptcy. The flood, also causing the Nantana Woolen Mill to go into bankruptcy, led to some hard economic times for the town of Northfield. The creamery would eventually be sold to the Granite City Creamery Association in 1928. The building still stands today near the railroad tracks and has become an attractive family home. (Drawing by S.T. Morris.)

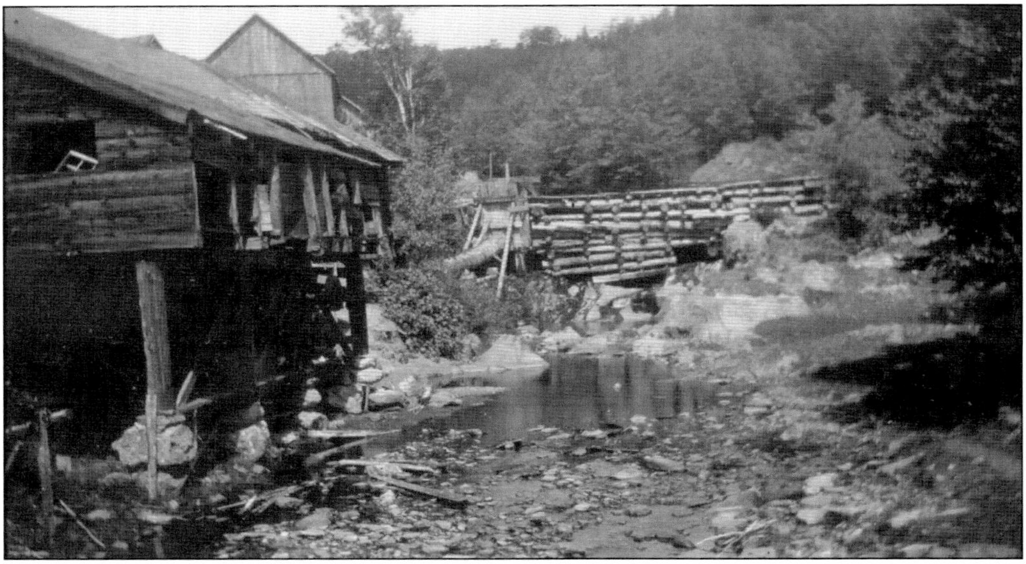

George Glidden bought this sawmill from William and Charles Benson the day after the Civil War ended. The water-powered mill made shingles, matchboards, and butter tubs, and also provided lumber needed by local farmers. In the springtime, the yard beside the mill would be piled high with logs brought by men to be sawed into a variety of timber and boards.

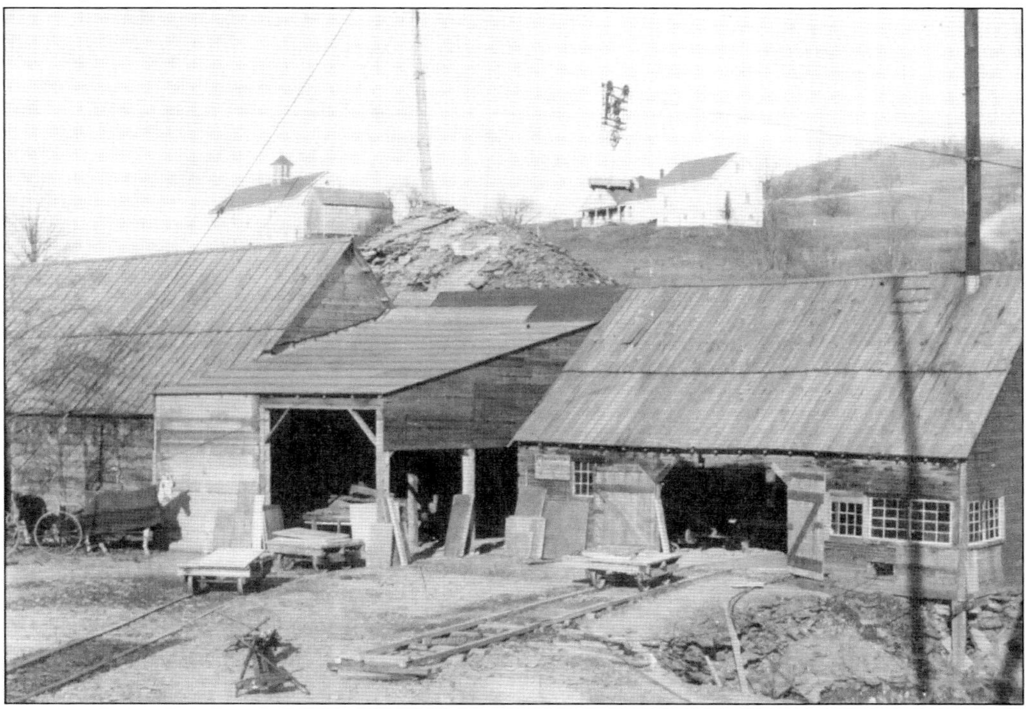

The Northfield Formation of slate is found on the eastern side of the Dog River; the soft slate is a beautiful blue-gray color. Early slate quarrying occurred when slate was dug up and used for tombstones. The slate tombstones have actually held up better to weathering than the more fashionable marble used later.

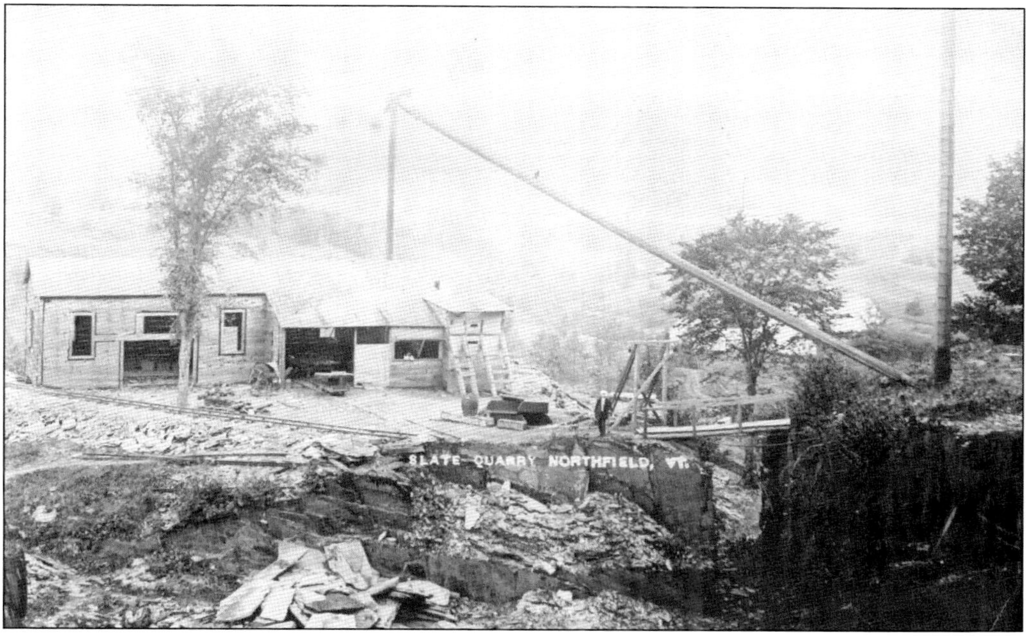

The slate industry began in earnest in the 1860s and thrived for about 30 years. The slate was primarily used for roofing. Slate was brought down from the quarries by mule teams, cut into approximate sizes, and then split into roofing shapes. The slate industry brought many Welsh immigrants to Northfield, as they were skilled in working with it.

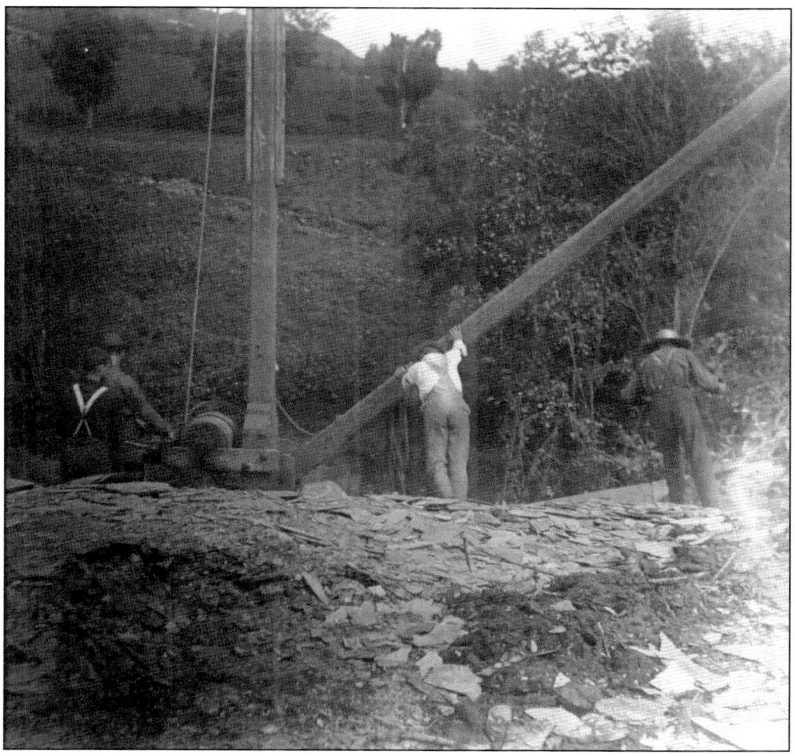

Mounds of waste slate can still be seen today where the old slate quarries used to be. Once employing 100–200 men, the slate industry ceased operation by the early 1890s and never again revived. This slate formation that runs through town is thought to be the largest contiguous deposit of slate in the United States.

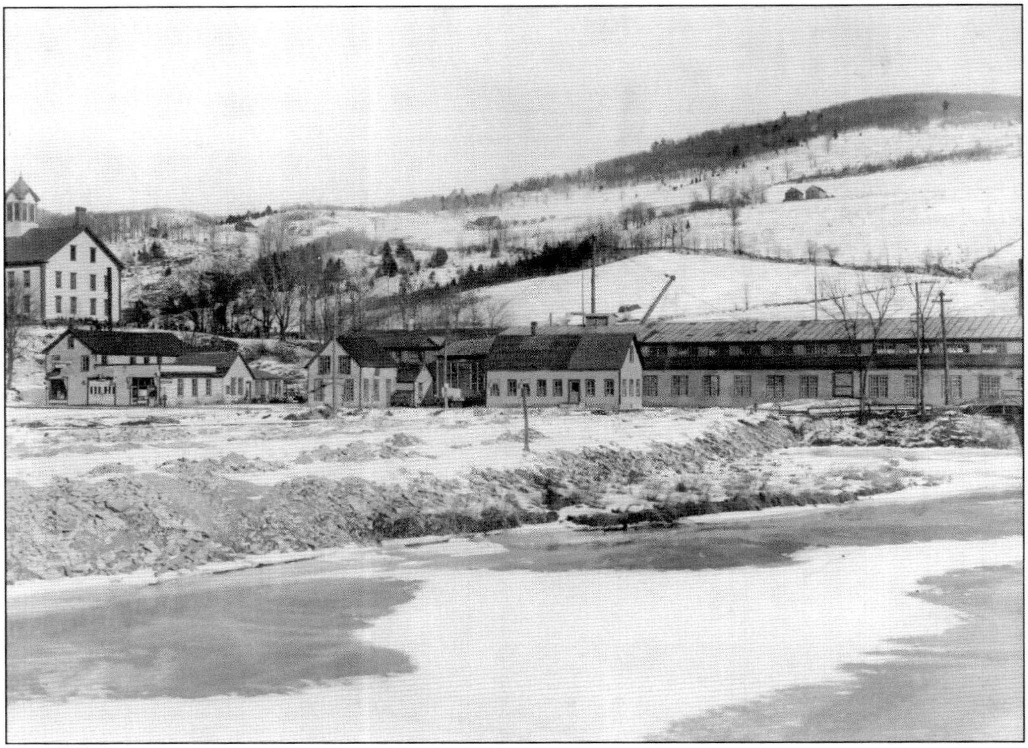

Northfield's poor economy in the late 1800s led some local men to build a spur track, erect a small half-moon working shed, and build a derrick in order to bring granite in from Barre. In 1891, the five Cross brothers built a plant on the old Paine factory yard and became one of the largest cutting companies in town. Pictured are some of the Cross Brothers Granite Company sheds.

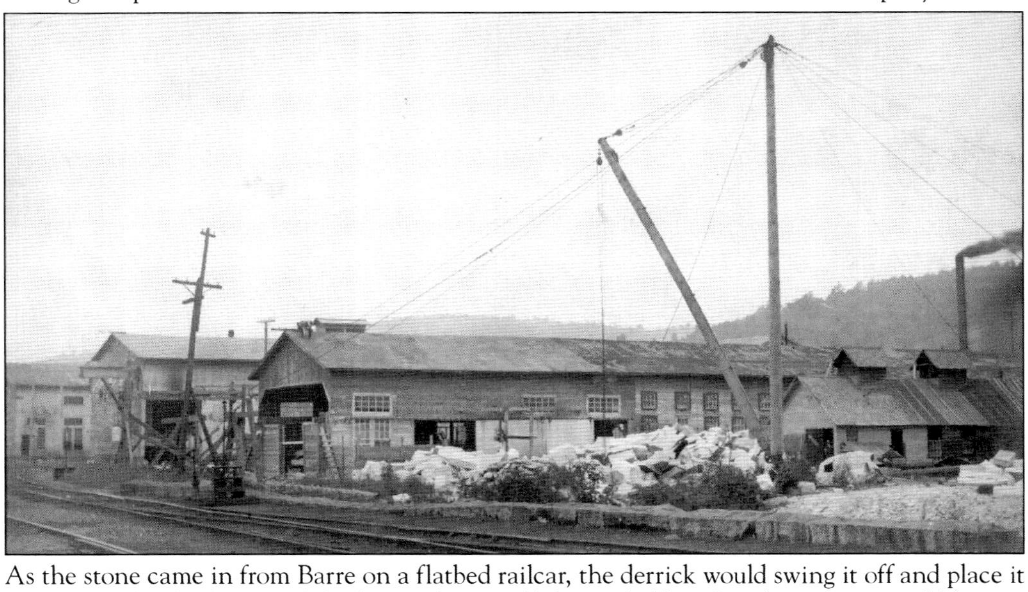

As the stone came in from Barre on a flatbed railcar, the derrick would swing it off and place it in front of the shed. Several sheds together would form a half circle. The granite would be cut, chipped, and shaped, and then loaded again on the flatbed cars.

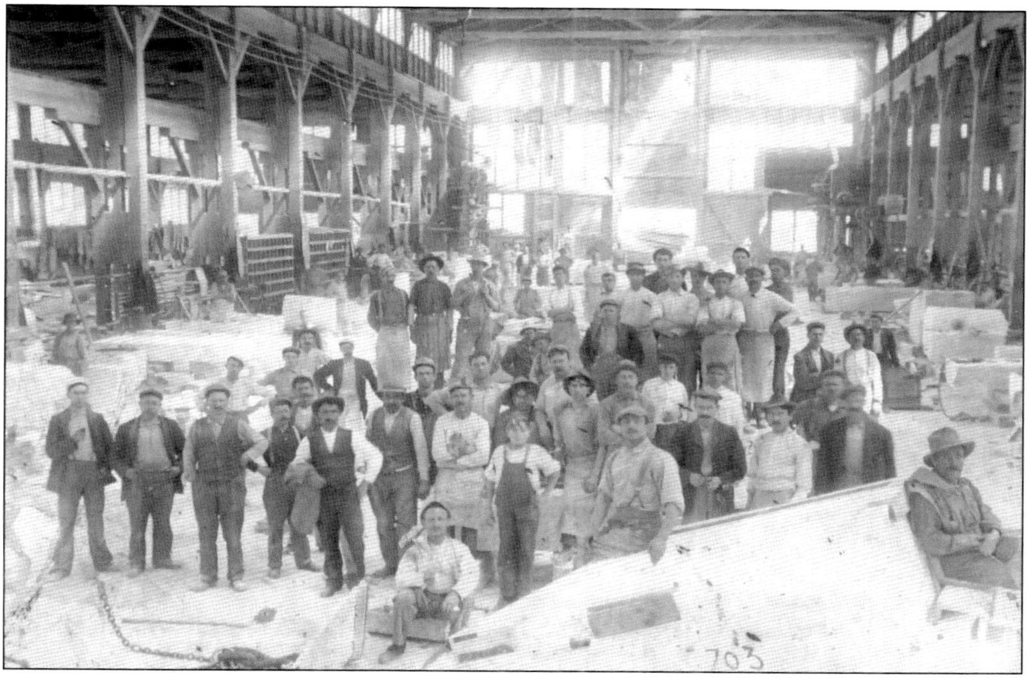

Many young stonecutters and skilled carvers came from Italy, Spain, and Scotland to work in the sheds. Work was arduous, with no safety devices or medical insurance. An average worker's pay in 1895 was about 29¢ a day. Most of these men died young from silicosis, which they got from breathing in the fine dust raised in working with granite.

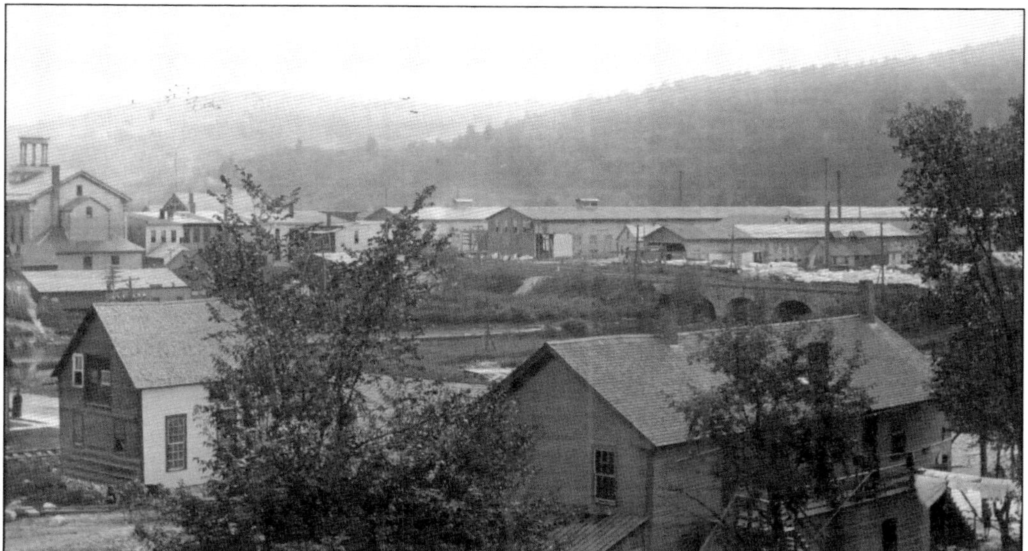

In 1914, nearly 1,000 flatbed railcars loaded with finished granite left Northfield. There were at least 18 independent granite companies that did business in town and employed hundreds of workers. Granite that was cut and carved in these sheds can be seen throughout the country. Union Station in Washington, DC, the Franklin & Marshall Building in Chicago, and the Flatiron Building in New York City are a few examples.

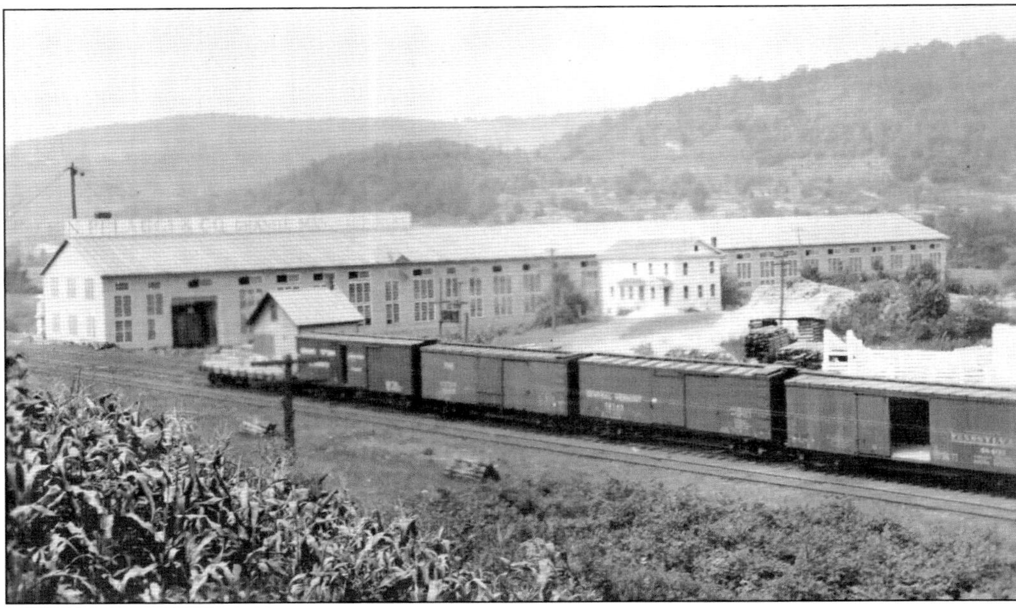

Eventually, as businesses grew, the sheds grew bigger and covered more land. The Pelaggi plant, pictured here, grew to take up four acres in the area where the senior housing and fire station is today. The importance of the granite industry cannot be understated. It brought new economic life to an ailing town and lasted for 106 years, ending with the closing of Cetrangolo Finishing Works in 1997.

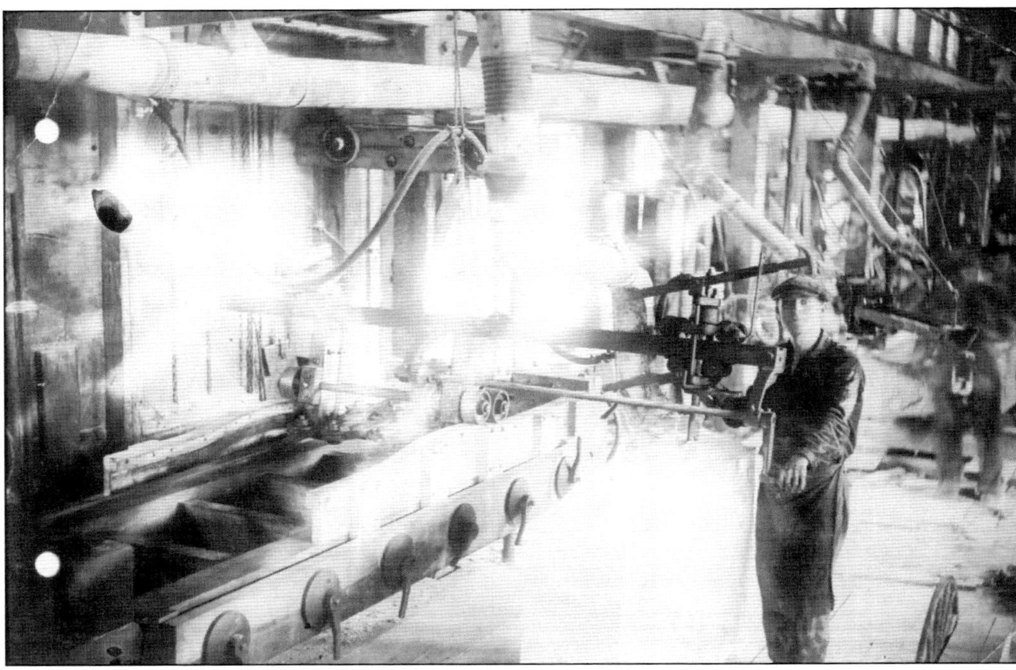

The inside of a granite finishing shed is shown here with the worker operating a cutting machine. In the late 1890s, a worker in the sheds would work 10 hours a day, six days a week. Taking home just $22 a week was a norm for these workers, many of whom had large families.

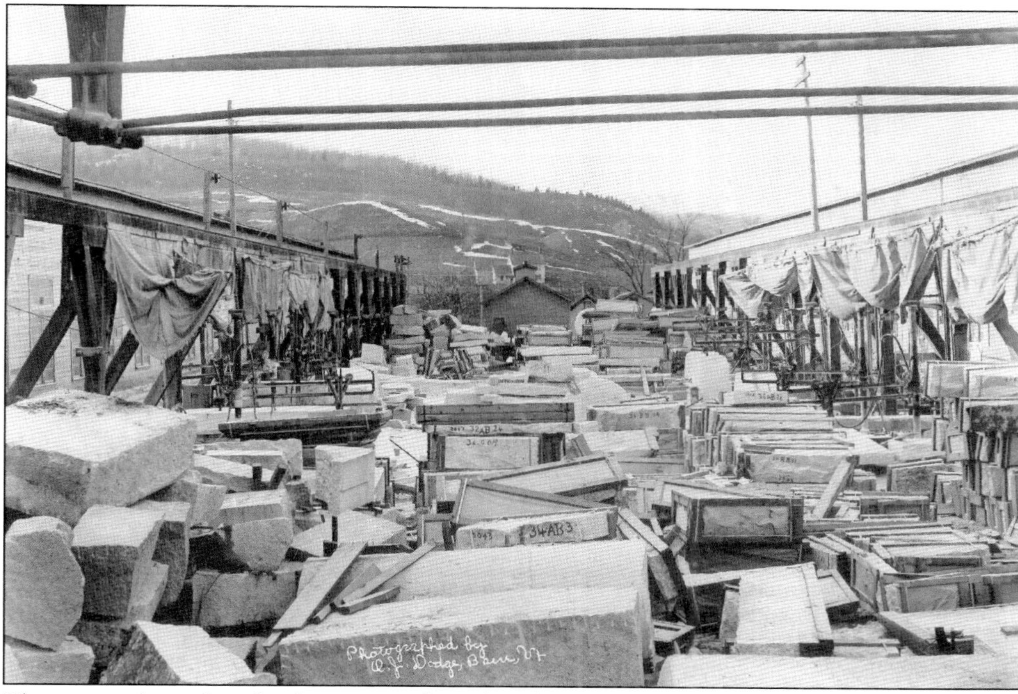

The granite shown here has been cut and numbered and waits to be chipped, shaped, and polished. Large blocks of granite came in on flatbed railcars; a large derrick would swing the granite off the cars and place it in front of the stone shed. The sheds were wedge-shaped buildings with the longest side in the back. Several sheds together would form a half circle.

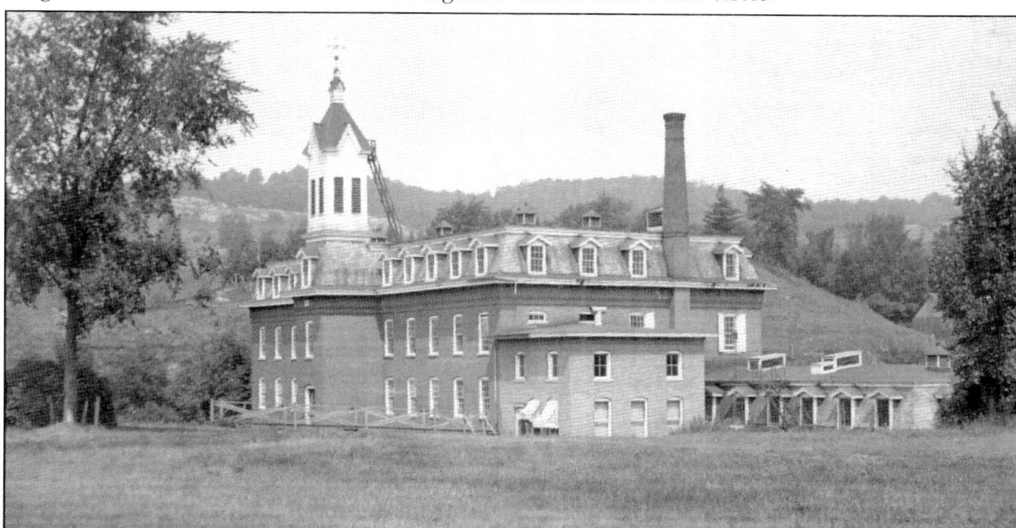

Woolen mills have long been a part of the town's history. From Elijah Paine's first woolen mill to Cabot Hosiery today, woolen mills have been an important part of the economy. The Gould mill in the Falls, later owned by Charles M. Davis, produced such high-quality goods that, in 1928, Comdr. (later Rear Adm.) Richard E. Byrd ordered wool from the mill for his men to wear on their expedition to the South Pole.

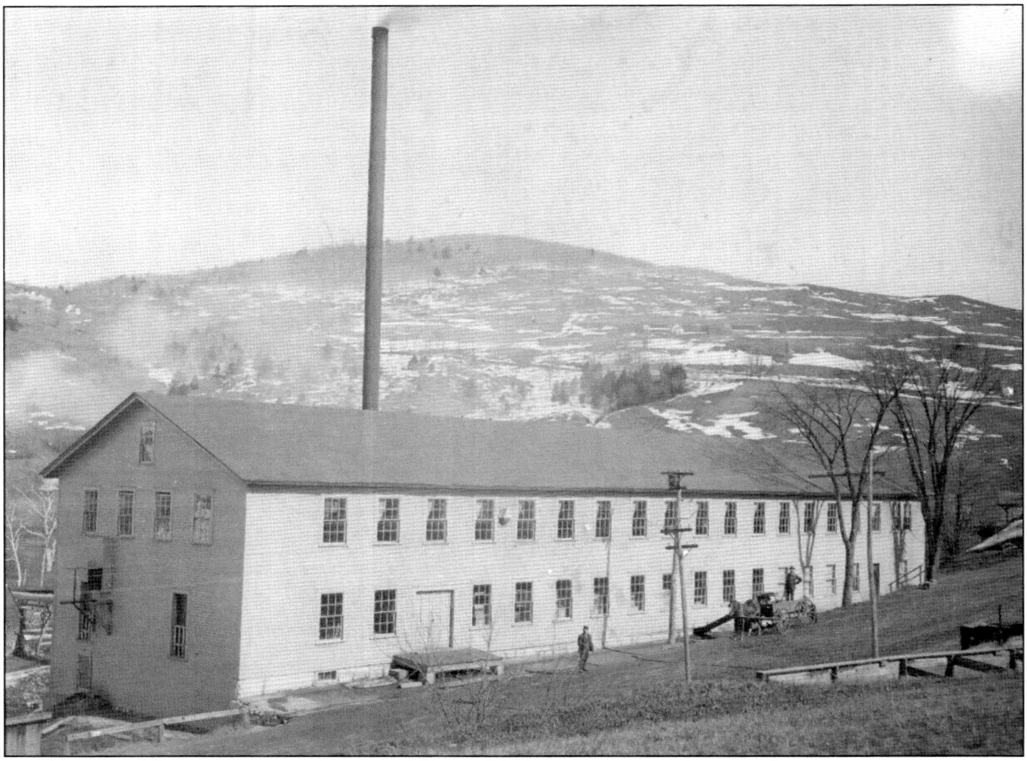

Vermont Hosiery & Machinery Co. began operation in 1907 with 10 workers and 10 knitting machines, producing a stocking called Lasherhose. Just prior to World War I, the mill was producing 175 dozen pairs of stockings a day. A knitter would work 10 hours a day and take home $6 a week. By 1943, the mill was still in operation, with 56 employees.

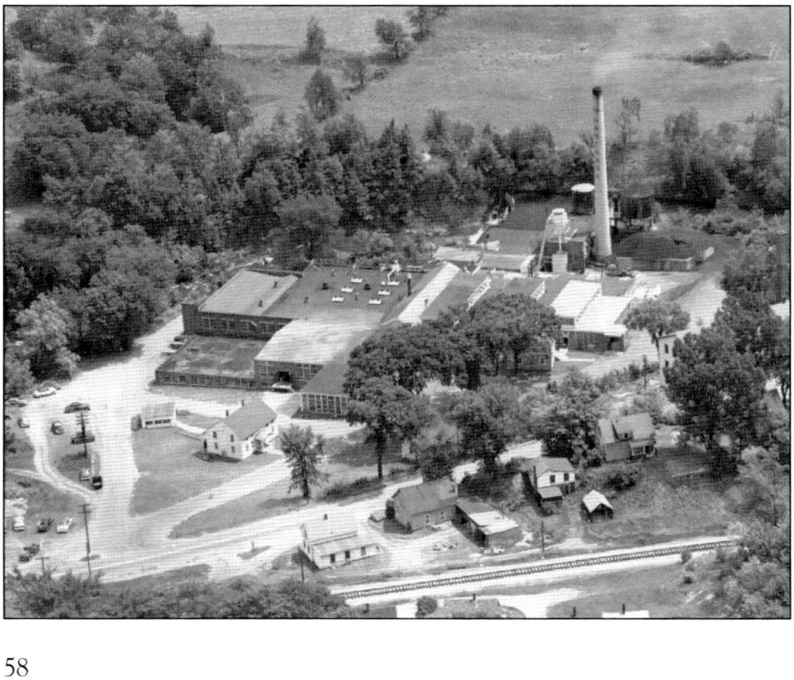

Certainly a landmark in town is the 135-foot-tall Nantana chimney, built in 1925. At the time it was constructed, it was considered a symbol of prosperity for the town. This mill was designed to manufacture men's fine worsteds, but it was severely damaged in the 1927 flood and then changed owners to be become the Northfield Mills.

Four

The Train Comes to Town

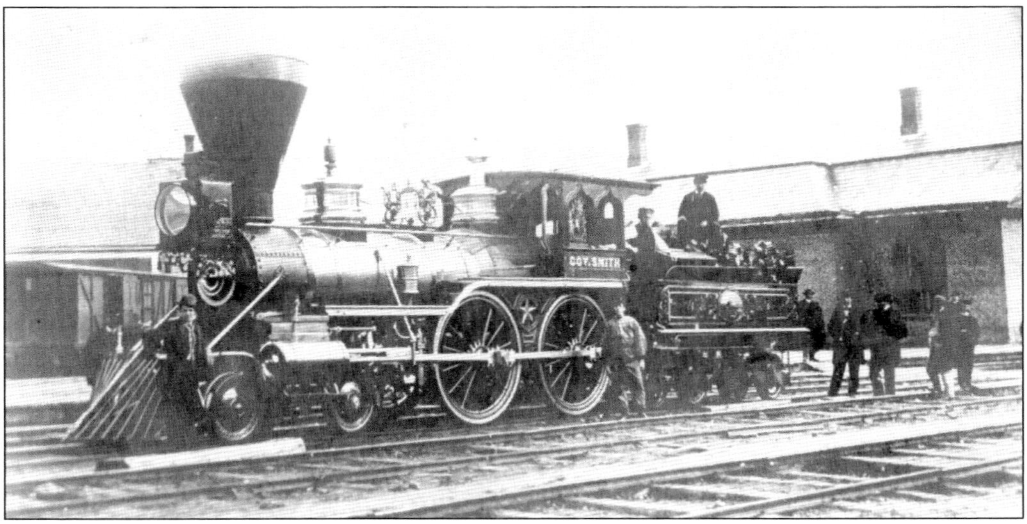

The locomotive pictured here was built in Northfield in 1868. All the wheels were painted vermilion and lined with gold leaf and blue. The tender and frames were painted brown. The inside of the cab included walnut rubbed to an oil finish and stained-glass windows. The cost of this engine was $19,500.

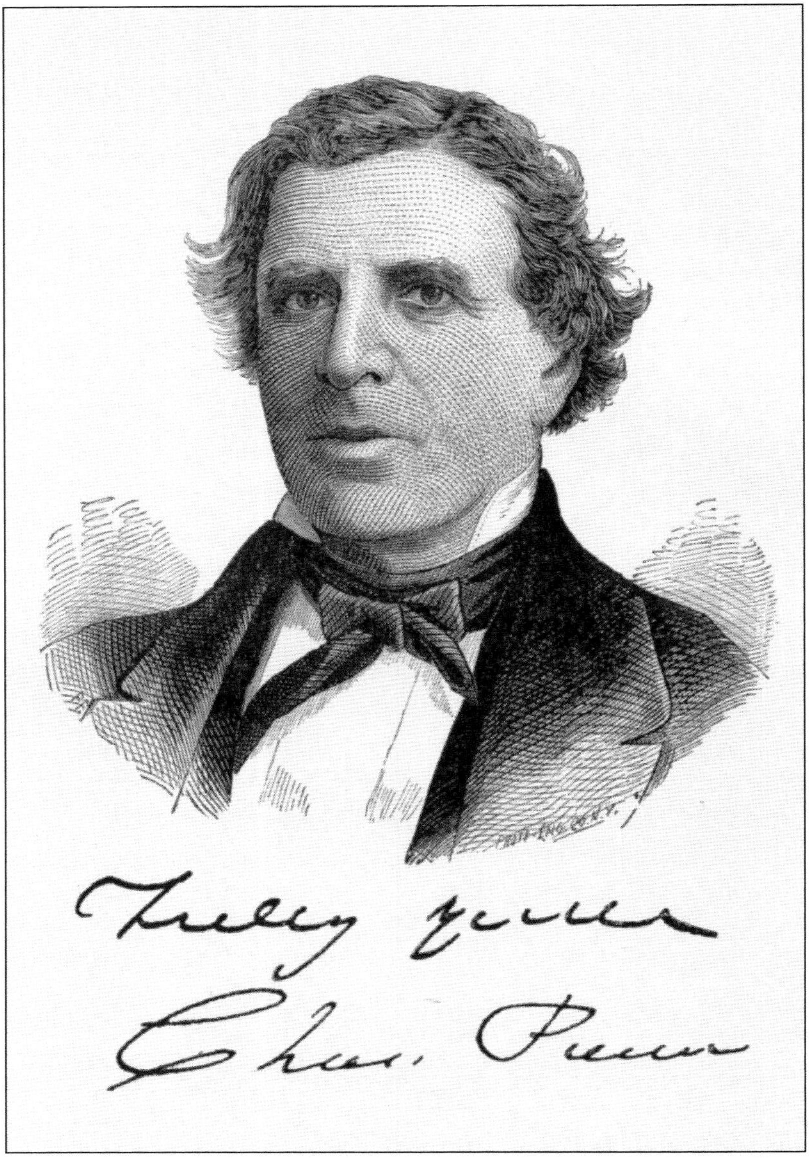

Born in Williamstown in 1799, Charles Paine was considered Northfield's great benefactor and one of Vermont's illustrious sons. After graduating from Harvard in 1823, he was given the woolen mill to manage for his aging father, Elijah Paine. Elijah had started to develop the town, and Charles continued the project. Charles built the Congregational church, the Northfield House, and the Paine Block and was instrumental in planning the layout of the town. He was elected governor of Vermont in 1841 as a Whig party candidate, serving until 1843. With his power and influence, he orchestrated the railroad path through Northfield. After becoming president of the Vermont Central Railroad, he brought the headquarters to Northfield, and the village became a thriving town. His home, the Governor Paine House, is located on Main Street and is currently home to the Northfield Historical Society. He was buried in front of the Congregational church but was later moved to Elmwood Cemetery. His monument was donated to the town and is now the Soldiers Monument, located on the Common.

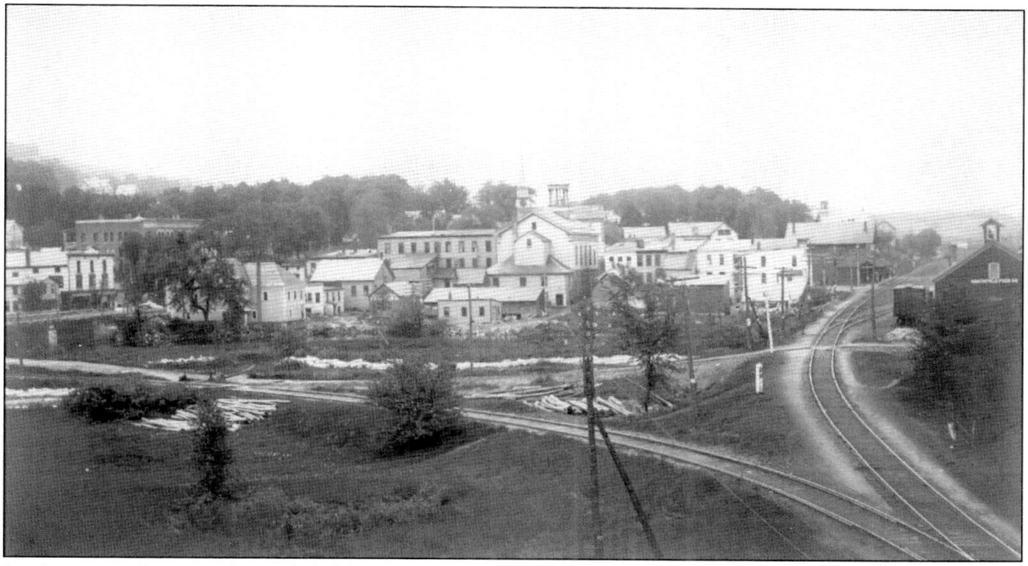

Looking south toward Northfield, one of the railroad spurs is seen. This one led to Cross Brothers Granite Company in the early 1900s. Now, Kenyon's Hardware Store and Water Street are located in this area. Another spur is seen branching off to the right toward the old railroad yard.

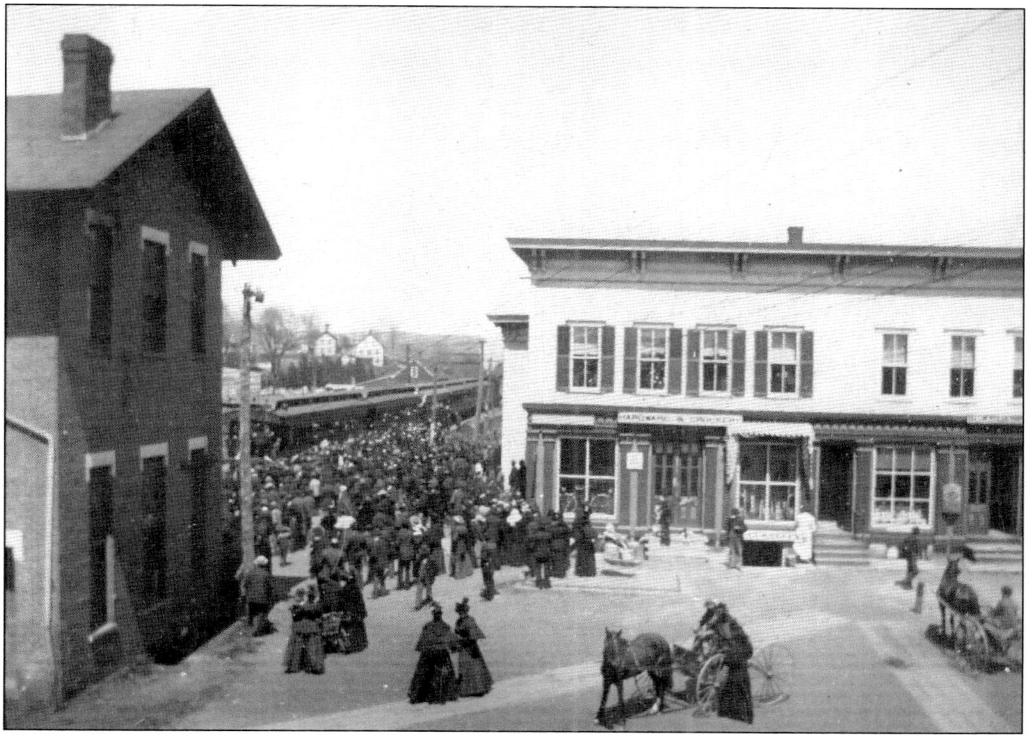

In this 1890s photograph, the Northfield depot is crowded with citizens saying goodbye to the soldiers going off to the Spanish-American War. The train was headed northward to Montpelier. This was a momentous day in Northfield, as the townspeople gathered to watch the troops depart for training and eventual combat.

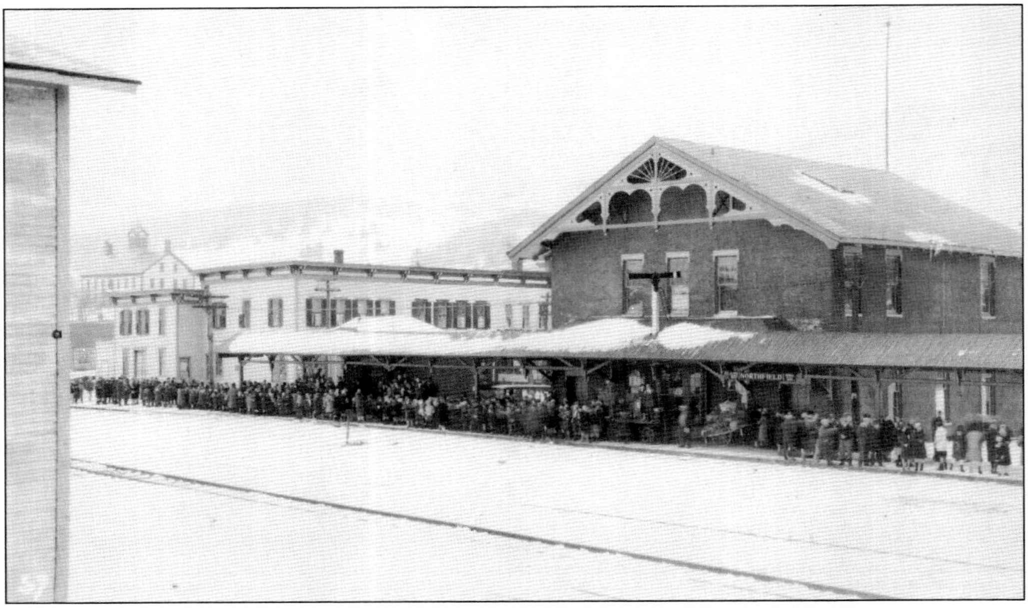

The crowd here shows a bustling depot in the 1920s or 1930s. The original brick wings are gone from the passenger house, and a covered platform exists. This line from White River Junction to Burlington opened travel from Boston and on to New York's Erie Canal and Canada. The Vermont Central Railroad instituted the first regular train service in Vermont.

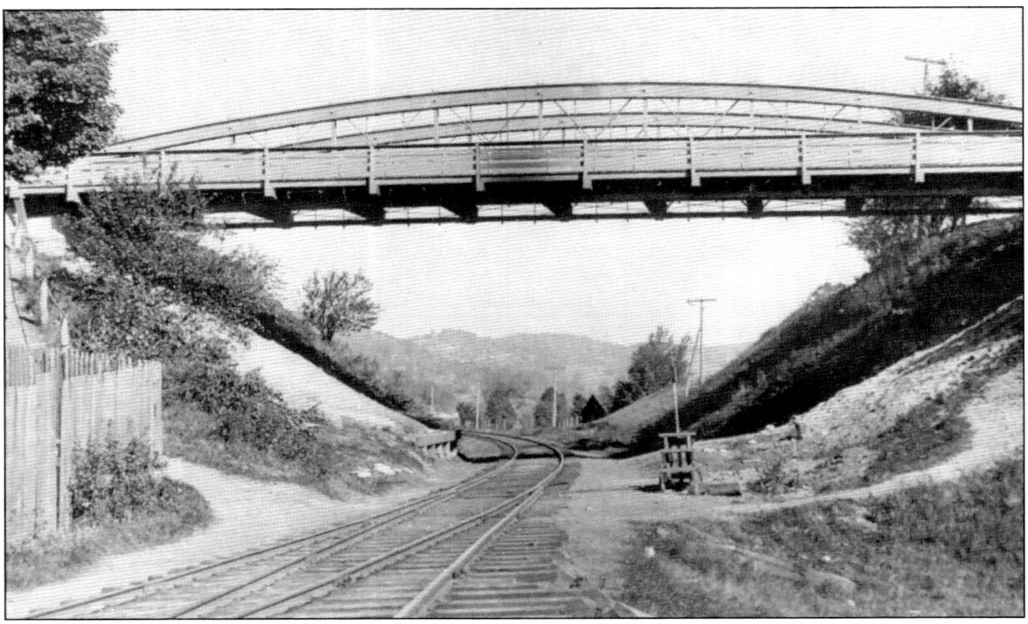

The Dry Bridge on Vine Street is shown here in this undated photograph. The spur in the foreground is going to Cross Brothers Granite Company on South Main Street. Gov. Charles Paine was a passenger on the first train to arrive in Northfield. The engine was named the *Abigail Adams* after Pres. John Adams's wife.

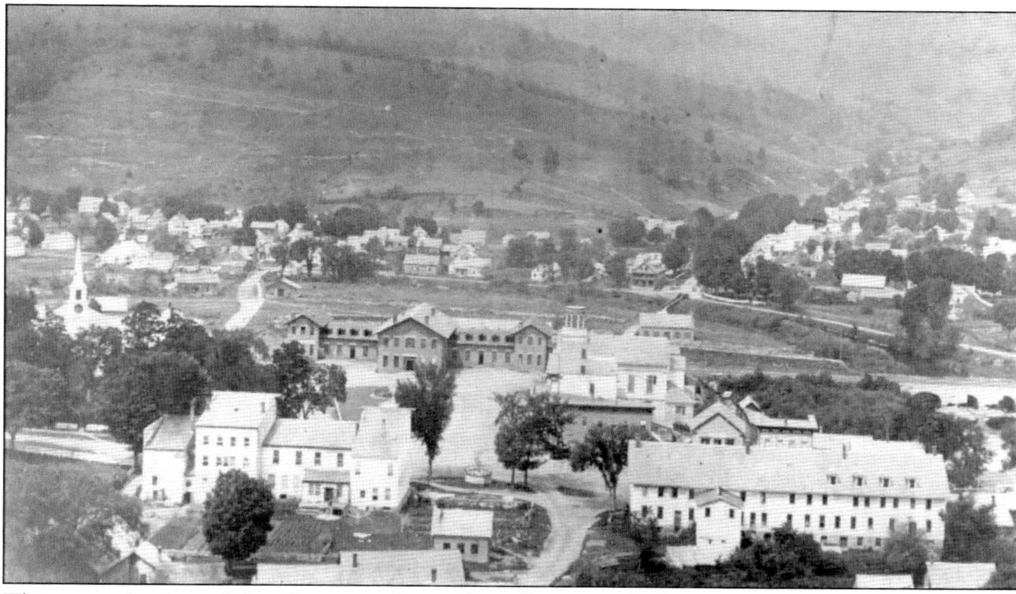

This westerly view of the Common shows the village as it looked in 1887. The railroad depot is seen in the center, with its large brick wings extending north and south. The railroad yard was behind the depot and contained a roundhouse, a paint shop, a car house, and an engine house. Note the extensive woodpiles to the left of the station. The early trains had to stop every 30 miles to "wood up."

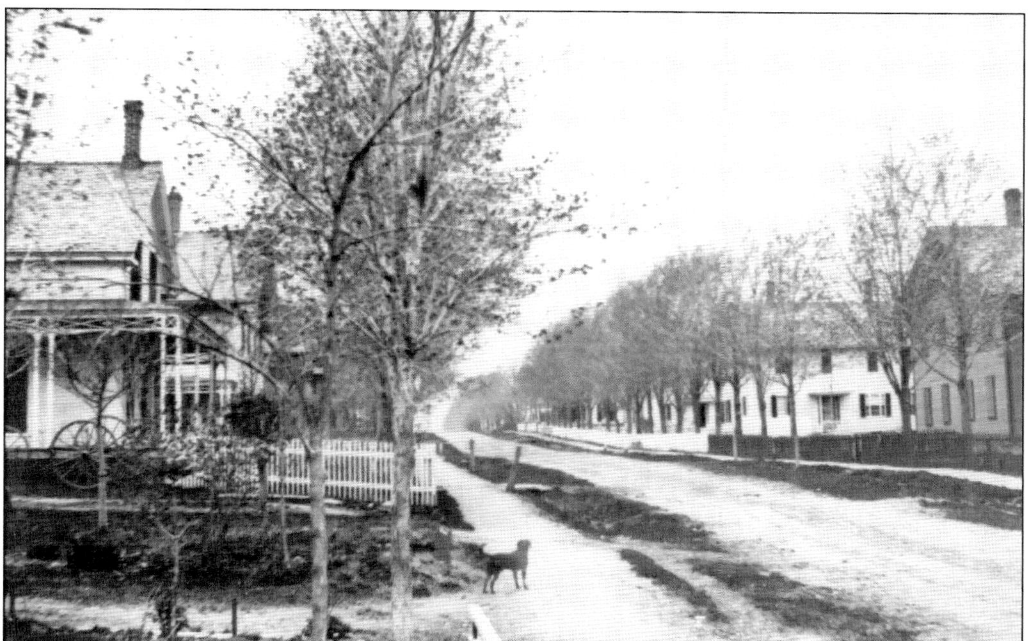

In this 1861 photograph of lower Central Street, the railroad houses are shown. On both sides of the street, there were 10 two-family houses. They were erected in the 1850s by the Central Vermont Railroad to house its officers. The houses were built exactly alike, but, over time, porches and ells were added. The railroad sold the houses in 1872 for $1,500 each.

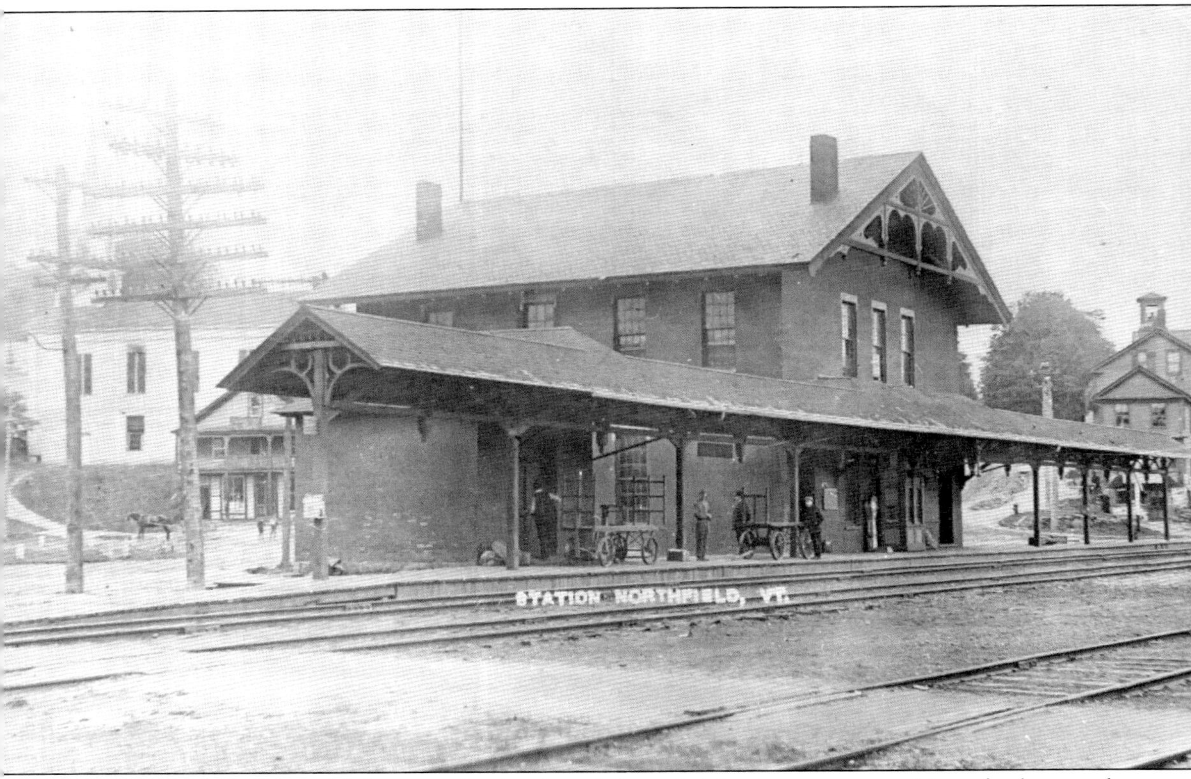

Here, in this undated photograph, the depot's large brick wings are gone. Note the large poles filled with insulators, however, as electricity had been installed at the station. Northfield was an overnight stop, and the train would drop people off at the Northfield House. More than a dozen trains per day stopped at the depot in the 1850s and 1860s. Northfield was a prosperous town with an influx of newcomers, travelers, and workers looking for jobs and housing, and the railroad afforded all of this. Passenger service came to an end in the 1960s.

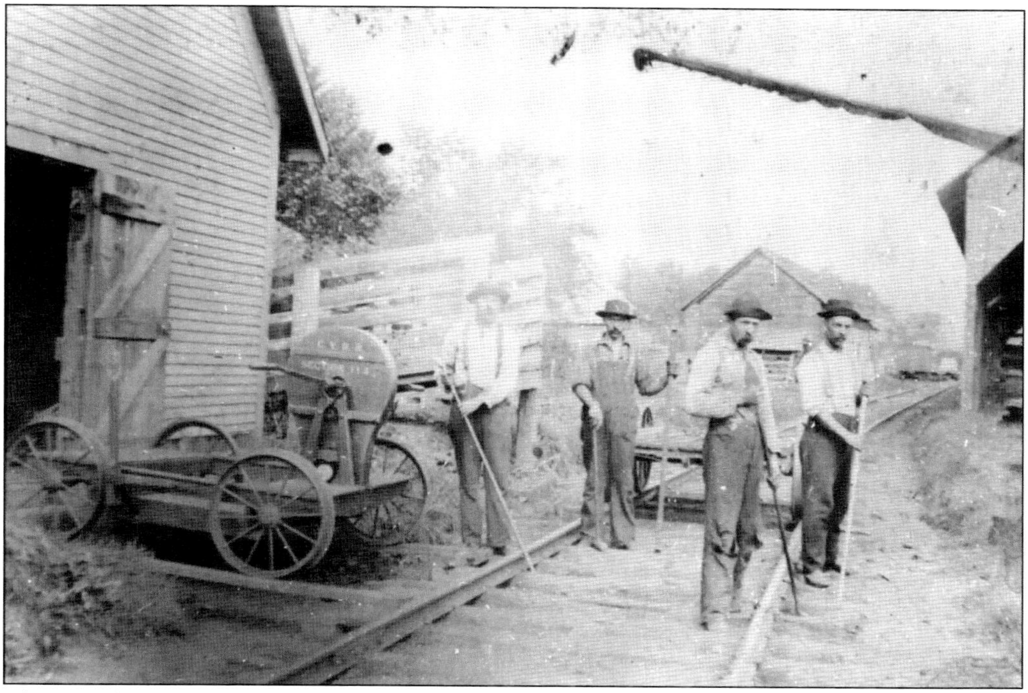

These workers, most likely Irish immigrants, came to Northfield to work for the railroad in the 1850s. They brought vitality and diversity to the town. Many settled on Cox Brook Road and in Turkey Hill. In this photograph, the four men are heading off to work using the railroad handcar. The car on the left has "C.V.R.R." printed on it, meaning that the railroad had changed hands at this time.

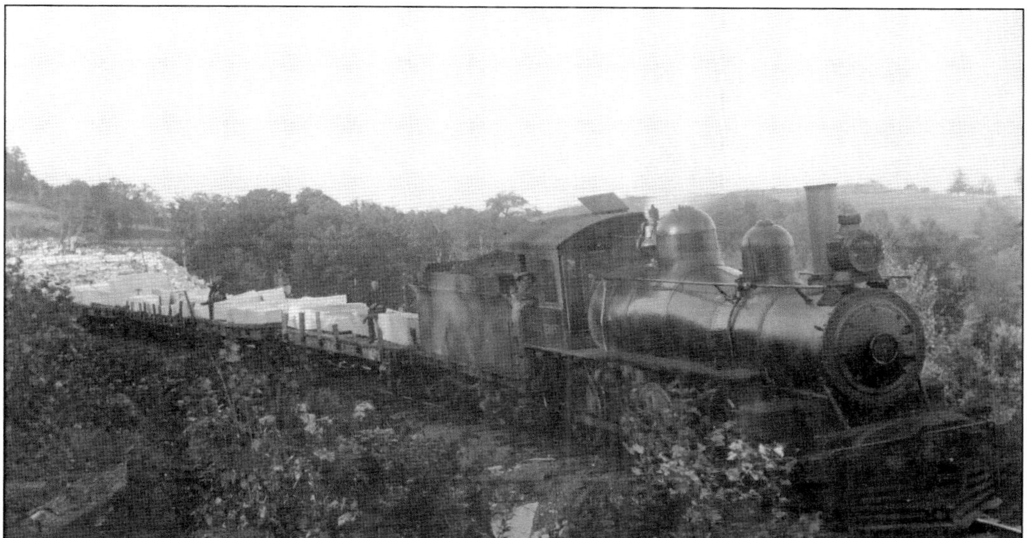

This train hauling granite was owned by the E.B. Ellis Granite Company. This 1906 photograph shows the railroad spur that Ellis built to move granite from his Bethel quarry. The Central Vermont Railroad took the stone to his granite sheds in Northfield. About five carloads a day were needed to fill the contracts and keep Ellis's 300 stone workers busy.

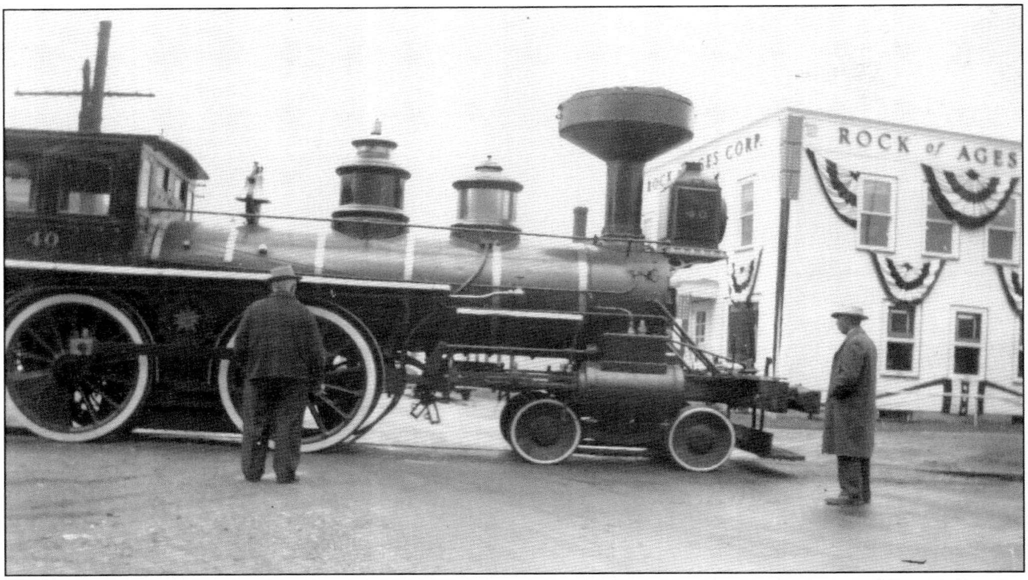

On October 6, 1951, the Central Vermont Railroad lent this Grand Trunk Engine No. 40 for the large celebration to honor the 100th anniversary of Maj. Gen. Grenville Dodge's graduation from Norwich University. He was a Civil War hero and a railroad builder, one of Norwich's famous alumni. There were parades, marching bands, and many prominent people, including Gen. Ernest N. Harmon, attending.

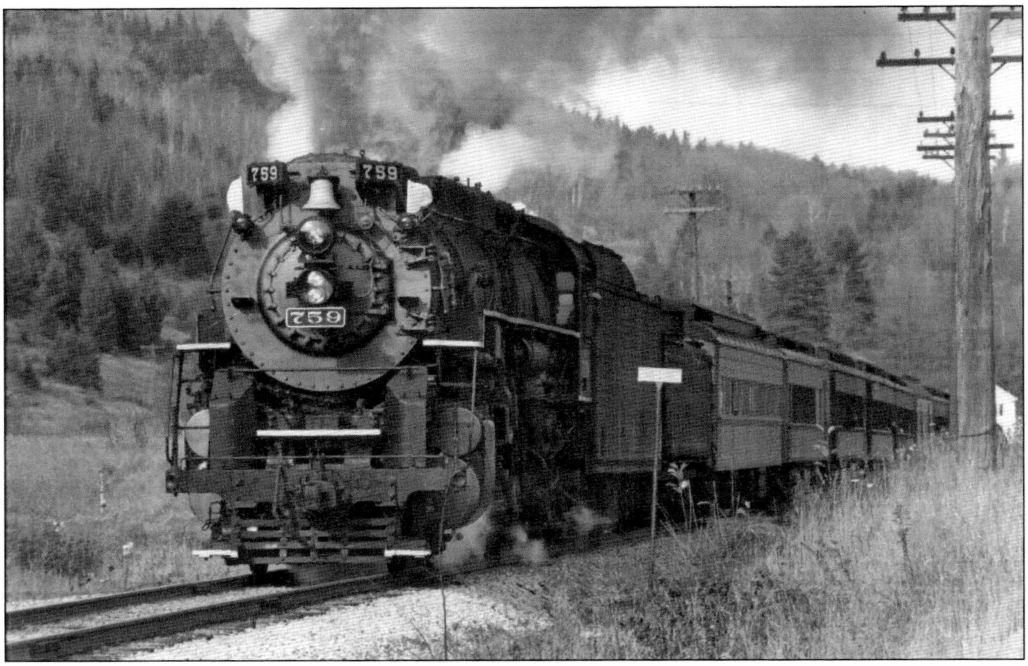

In 1972, Engine No. 759 came through Northfield pulling an excursion train. The train paused briefly, backed up, and came forward slowly so that people could take pictures of one of the last steam engines to come through town. In the heyday of the Vermont Central Railroad, eight steam engines were built in the train sheds in town.

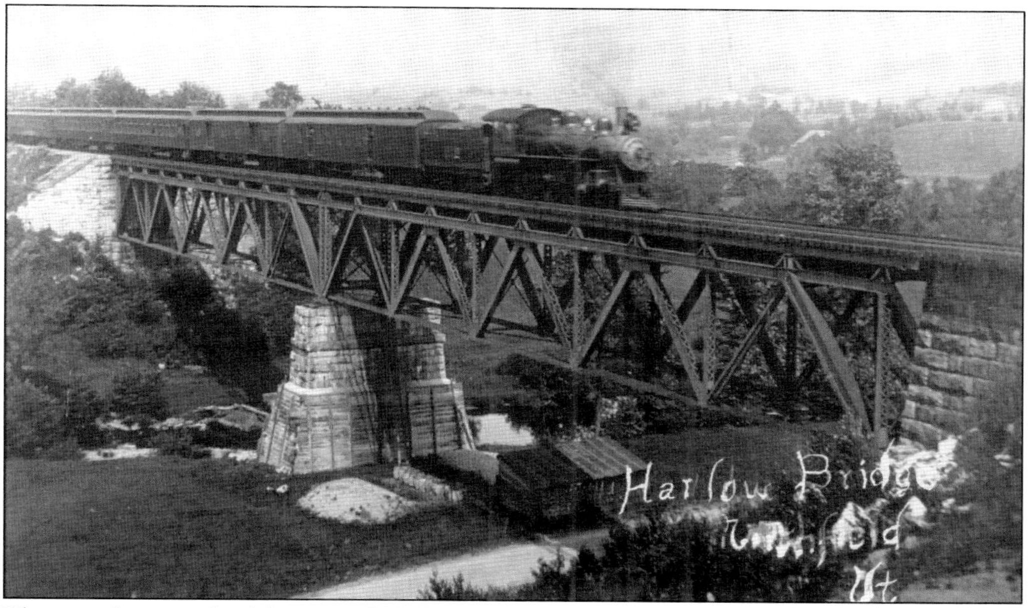

This is a photograph of the second Harlow Bridge, which was completed in 1899. On December 11, 1867, the horrific Harlow Bridge tragedy occurred. An engine, tender, and passenger car were taking 60 workers back to the work site after the noon meal in the Northfield House. The train was going too fast and could not stop in time. A total of 15 men were killed, and 38 people were wounded. Six Northfield men died in the train wreck.

CENTRAL VT. RAILWAY

Corrected to December 31, 1916

TRAINS LEAVE NORTHFIELD, VT. SOUTHBOUND

1:38 a. m. Daily for Boston, and New York. Sleeper to Boston and Springfield.

9:25 a. m. Except Sunday, for Boston and New York.

12:50 p. m. Daily for Boston and New York. For New London, week days only. Parlor cars to Boston and New York.

3;42 p. m. Except Sunday for White River Jct., Bellows Falls and Springfield.

6:52 p. m. Except Sunday for White River Junction.

8:27 p. m. Milk Train and Passenger.

9:10 p. m. Sunday only. Local for White River Junction.

TRAINS LEAVE NORTHFIELD, VT NORTHBOUND

3:11 a. m. Daily. Night Express for Montreal and Chicago.

8:44 a. m. Except Sunday. Local for Burlington, St. Albans and Montreal.

9:07 a. m. Sundays only. Local for Burlington and St. Albans.

11:06 a. m. Milk Train and Passenger.

1;39 p. m. Except Sunday for Burlington.

3:42 p. m. Except Sunday. Mail for Burlington, St. Albans and Montreal.

6:10 p. m. Daily. For St. Albans Montreal and Chicago.

This 1916 Central Vermont Railroad train schedule illustrates the importance of rail transportation to the town. With daily passenger trains heading south to Boston and New York and night express trains to Montreal and Chicago, the Northfield depot was a busy place. Note the daily run of a milk train.

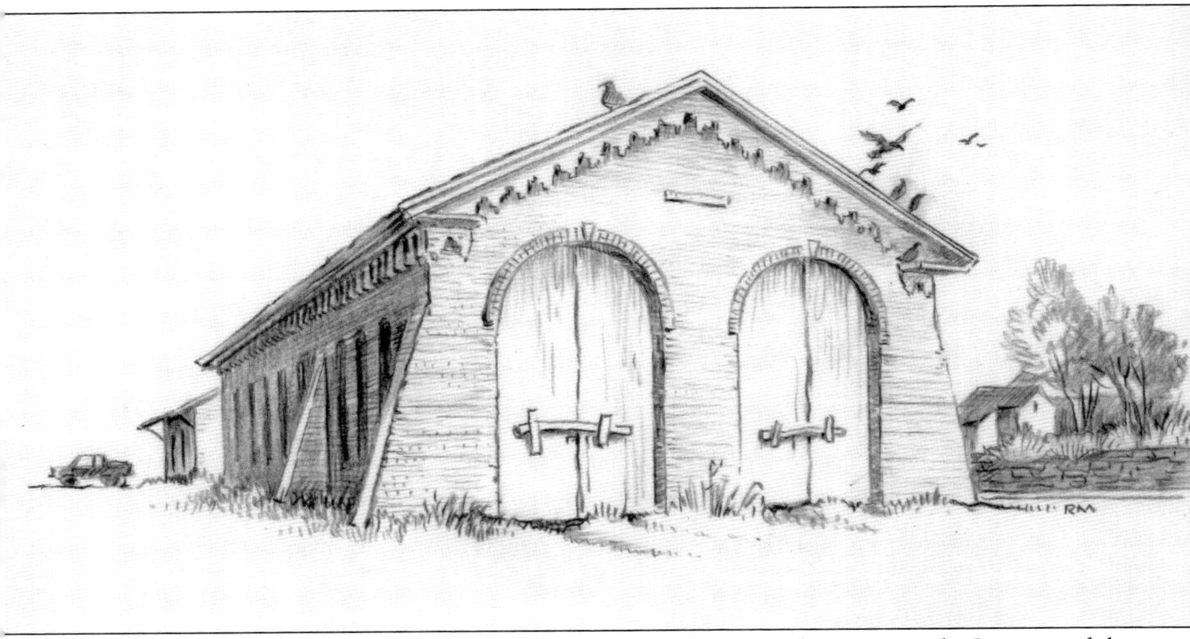

This double-door engine shop, drawn by Becky Merrilees, is Italianate in style. It is one of the oldest railroad structures standing today in the state. The archway details and window cornices are two of the interesting features of this building. Along with the original train station on the Common, it is one of the last buildings representing the strong railroad history of Northfield. Merrilees has also drawn the old freight shop behind the engine shop. The old freight shop has been converted many times, but the outside structure is still recognizable. The arches of Norwich's White Chapel originally supported the train shed, once part of the station. In 1866, a bank opened in the railroad station, and a bank still remains there today. For many years, it was the only bank located in a railroad station in the United States.

Five

Merchants of Main Street

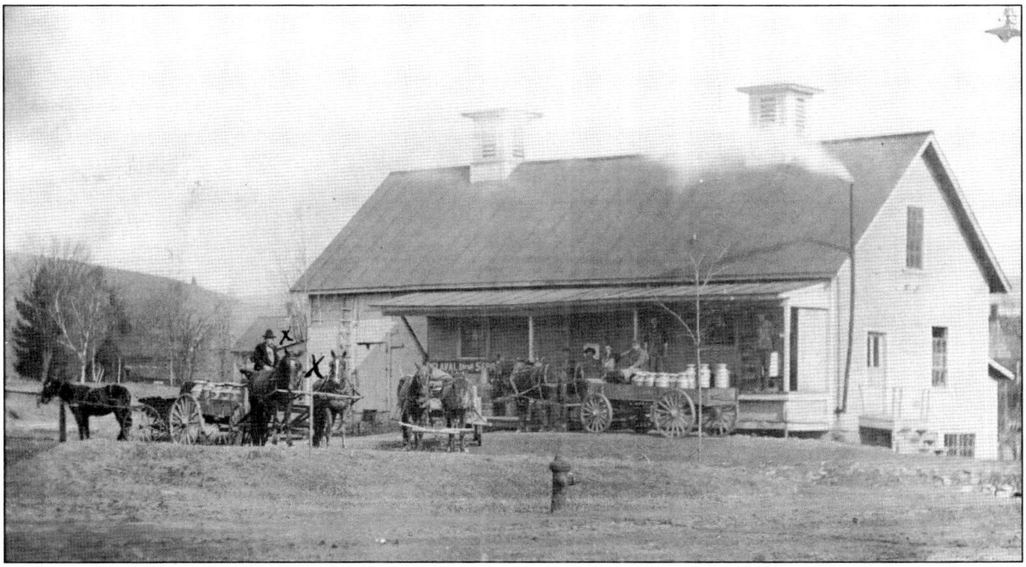

Built in 1894 on the site where Norwich University's Plumley Armory now stands, the old creamery was the place where Northfield farmers brought their milk to be processed. Since the waste from the creamery was dumped in the nearby brook, one can imagine the smell, and the flies, on sultry summer days.

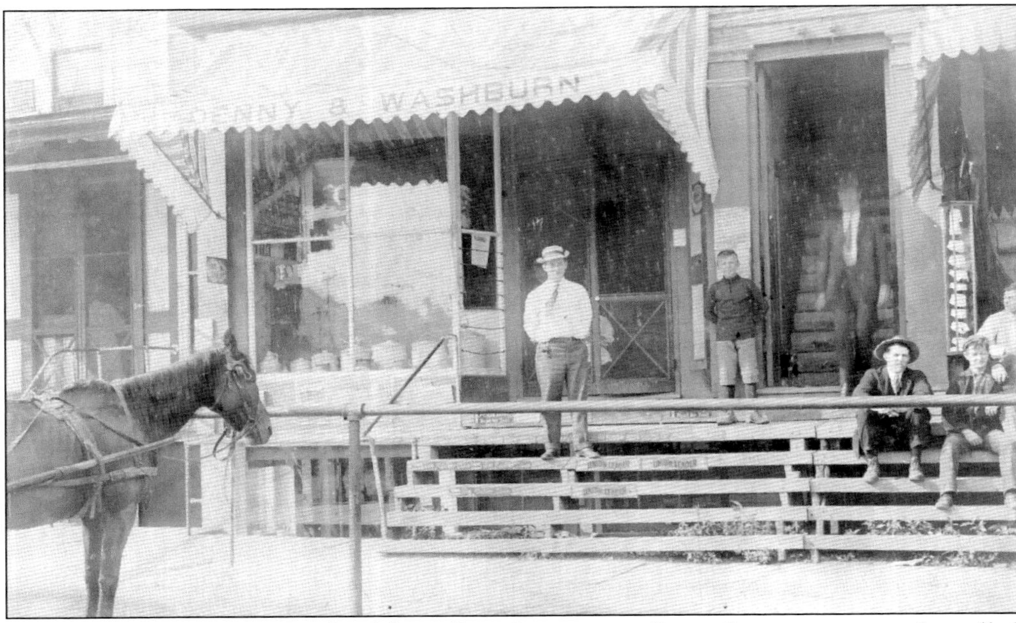

The buildings on the north side of the Village Common, or Depot Square, as it was also called, contained a variety of businesses over the years. In 1906, for example, the Denny & Washburn store sold stoneware crocks of various sizes, which are seen sitting in the front window. Union Leader Tobacco signs are among those nailed to the steps.

NORTHFIELD SAVINGS BANK

Incorporated 1867

NORTHFIELD, VERMONT

The only Mutual Savings Bank in Washington County

Owned by Depositors and Managed in Their Interests

Deposits,	**$1,000,000.00**
Guaranty Fund,	**$100,000.00**

The income from an unusually large guaranty fund being the property of the depositors insures a good rate of interest to them.

FOUR PER CENT interest paid on deposits longer than any bank in this section.

FRANK PLUMLEY, Pres. **JOHN L. MOSELEY, Vice-Pres.**

HEBER C. CADY, Treasurer

By the early 1900s, Northfield Savings Bank had grown from a box safe in a haberdashery to a bank with a vault. This was due to an early robbery. The thieves were not caught in Northfield; however, they were later caught and hanged in Minnesota for other crimes.

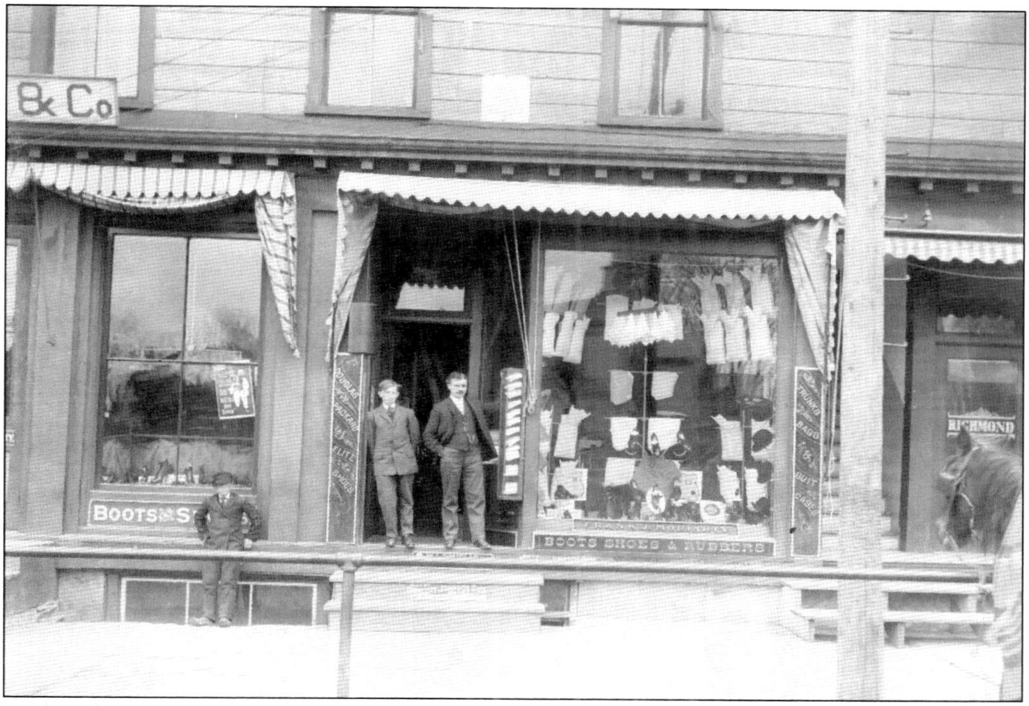

In this photograph, taken around 1913, one sees more of the businesses located in what was called the Central Block. The Frank J. Moriarty Men's Store has a window filled with shirts, stiff collars, shoes, and derby hats. The well-dressed boy on the left is standing in front of a window display of the latest shoes.

The Northfield News

And Its Auxiliary Publications

The Williamstown Herald

... and ...

Mad River Valley News

Covers a field in Central Vermont better than any and all other mediums.

All the Local News, Summary of State and County News, Market Reports, Editorials, Stories and Miscellaneous matter make these publications complete Family Newspapers, read in every home in their territory.

The Business Man

Who is doing business without inviting the patronage of the readers of the News and its Auxiliary publications, through their advertising columns, is losing an opportunity for increased profits.

Rates Are Very Reasonable
Results Are Very Sure

Talk it over with the publishers by letter, 'phone, or call at the publication office of the

Northfield Publishing Company

News Building, Northfield, Vermont

Small Advertisements—For Sale, Wants, etc.—get exceptionally good returns in the above papers.

The *Northfield News*, the local weekly newspaper, was established in 1878. Since its establishment, it has achieved the outstanding accomplishment of having never missed an issue.

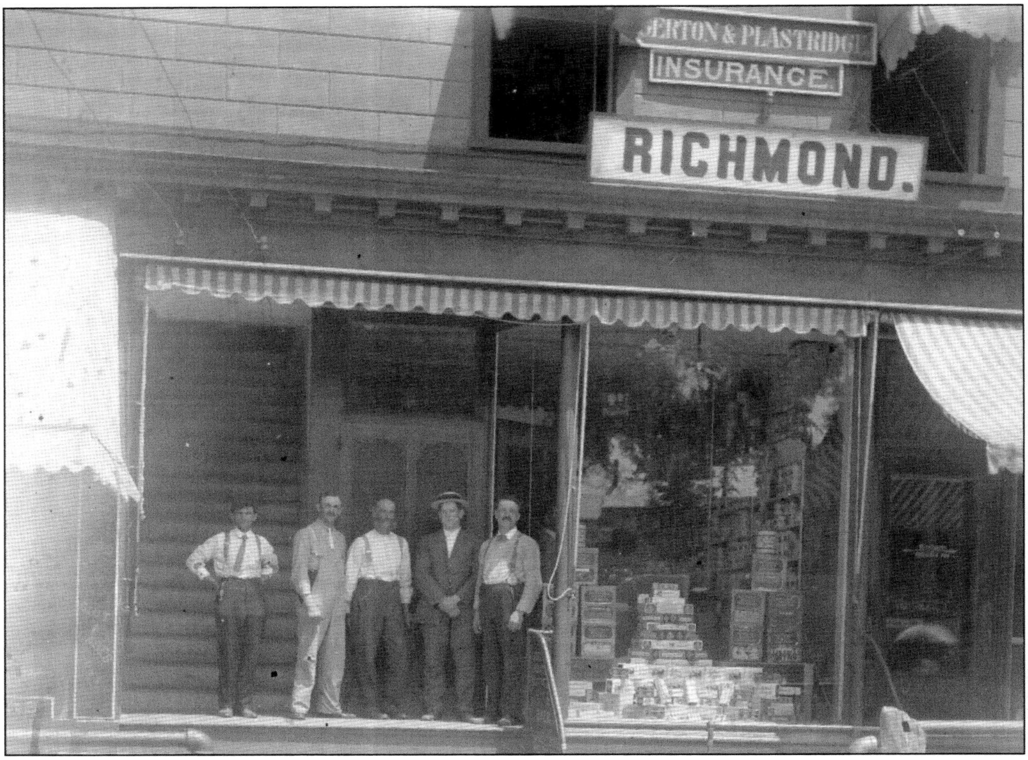

Many businesses were located on the north side of the Common in the early 1900s. Among them was Charles Richmond's grocery, shown above with boxes of the National Biscuit Company's cookies and crackers on display. The shelves on the right are filled with a wide variety of foods. It was common practice for local farmers to bring in their produce, such as eggs, potatoes, and other vegetables, to trade with Richmond for needed staples. The offices of the Egerton & Plastridge Insurance Company were located on the second floor, above the store.

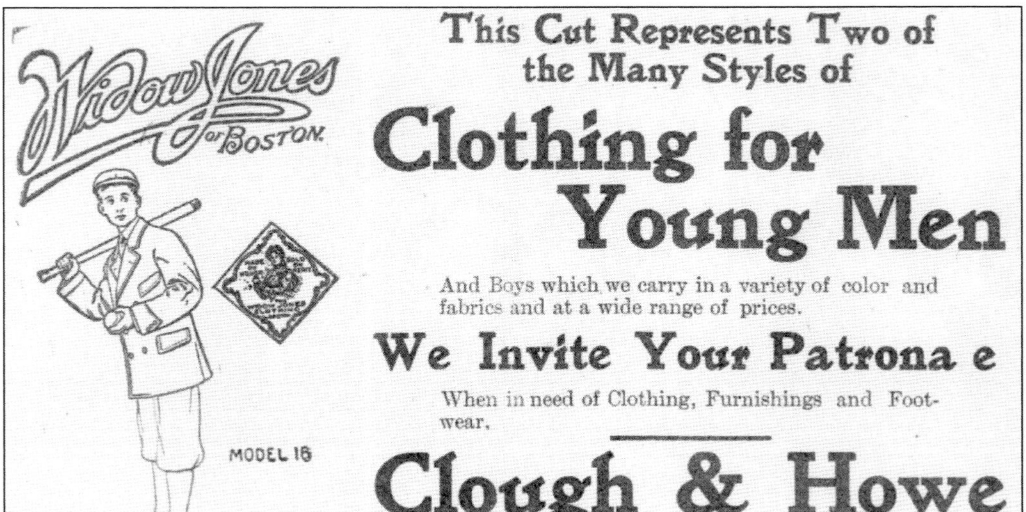

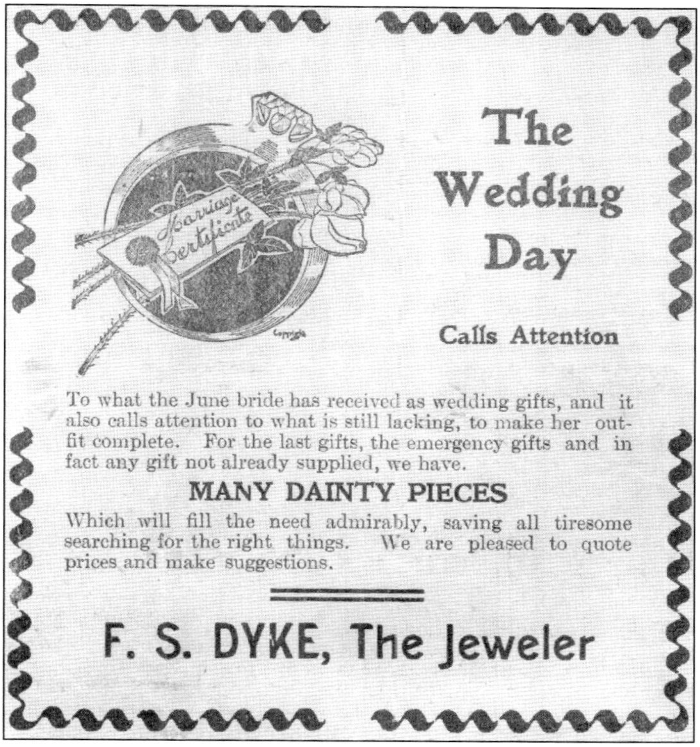

F.S. Dyke was an optician and jeweler, who, along with clocks, watches, and silver tea urns, also sold Edison and Victor phonographs and records. Below, in the lower left, on the steps below Dyke's shop and the Richmond grocery, Mr. Kovalsky, the tailor, stands proudly with his tape measure over his shoulder. Minnie Smith's millinery shop is the last business located on the first floor of this block. Some of her most exquisite creations are on display in her shop window. W.S. Woodbury's barbershop, beneath the millinery shop, was the place to get a shave and a haircut and have one's shoes shined.

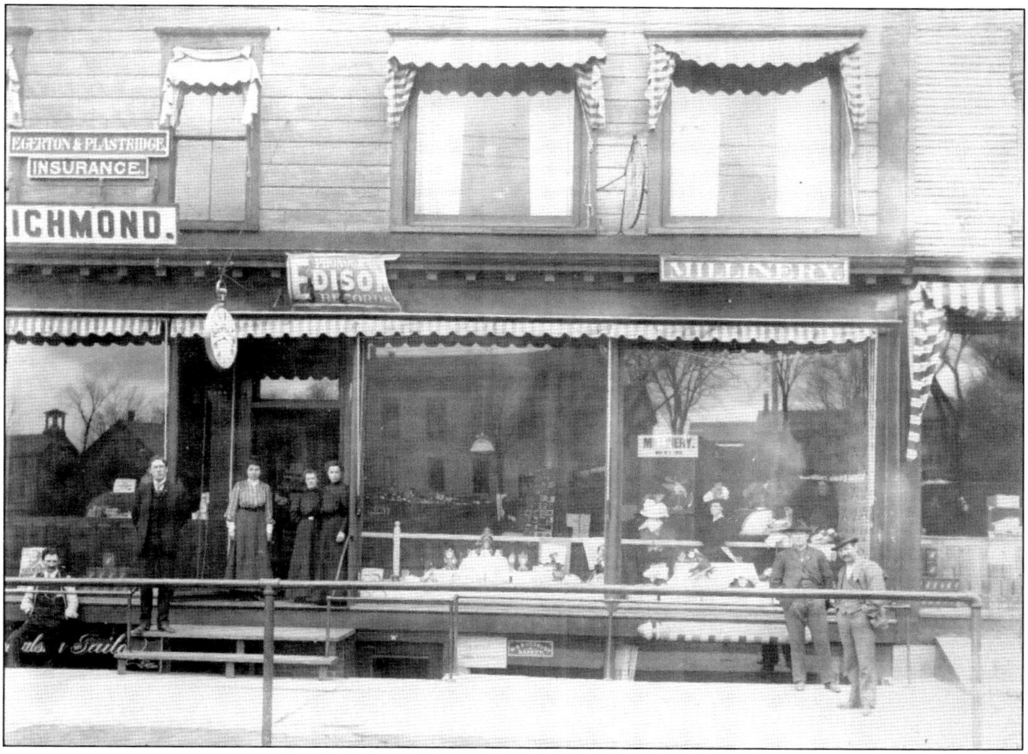

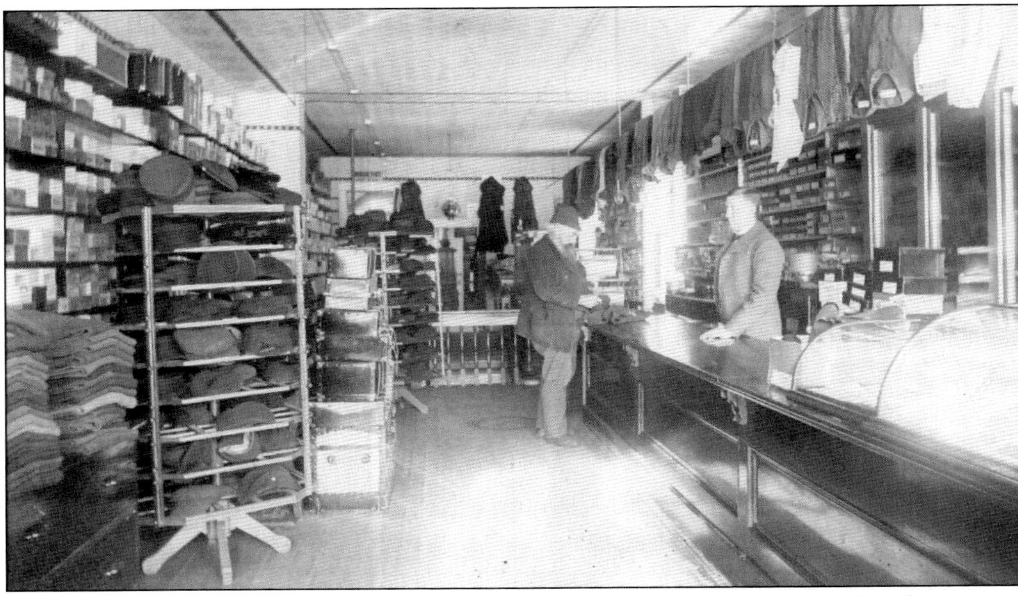

In the early 1900s, the eastern side of Depot Square was dominated by a variety of clothing stores. Clough & Howe Men's Clothing Store (above) had a large supply of woolen trousers, as well as two revolving racks of winter hats and caps. The long ceiling rod held shirts of every size and color. The store was stocked from floor to ceiling with every type of clothing a well-dressed boy or man would need. Trunks and suitcases were also sold in the store. It was located to the right of where Trombly's Florist shop is today. The advertisement below for the Northfield Telephone Company promotes that its service was important to businesses.

THE NORTHFIELD TELEPHONE CO.

Telephone Connections Anytime

day or night with thousands of phones throughout New England

Indespensible in Business

and social affairs about town

Call "Central" or write for information

It must have been a cold day when the photograph below was taken in an unnamed store, perhaps a competitor of C. Denny & Co. (right). The lady in the background is wearing an elegant floor-length fur coat and a fur hat, while the gentleman beside her is also suitably dressed for a wintry day on the streets of Northfield in the early 1900s. The two well-dressed clerks are busily assisting customers with their purchases, perhaps robes or blankets. The store boasted up-to-date electric lights that illuminated the vast array of goods for sale. Note the variety of men's hats that are for sale to the right of the photograph.

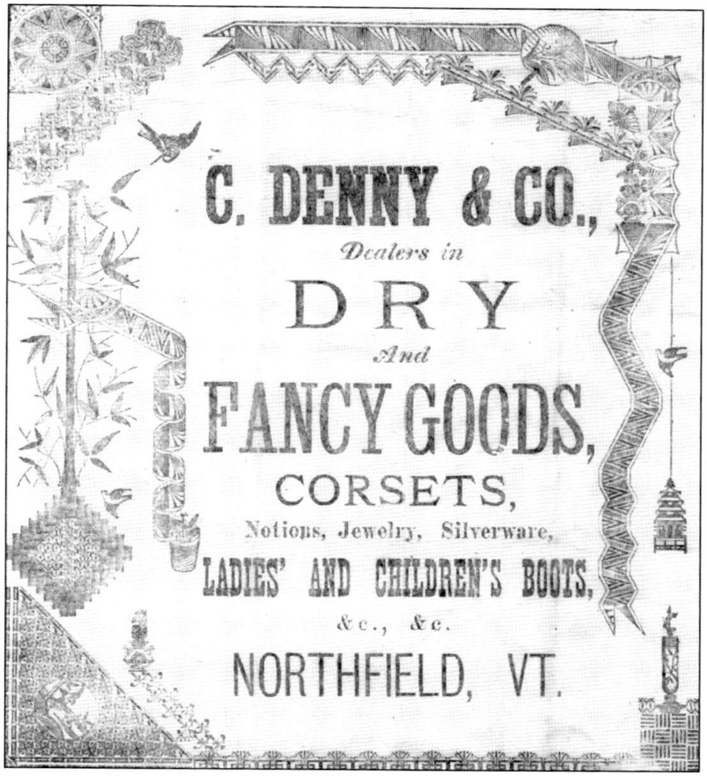

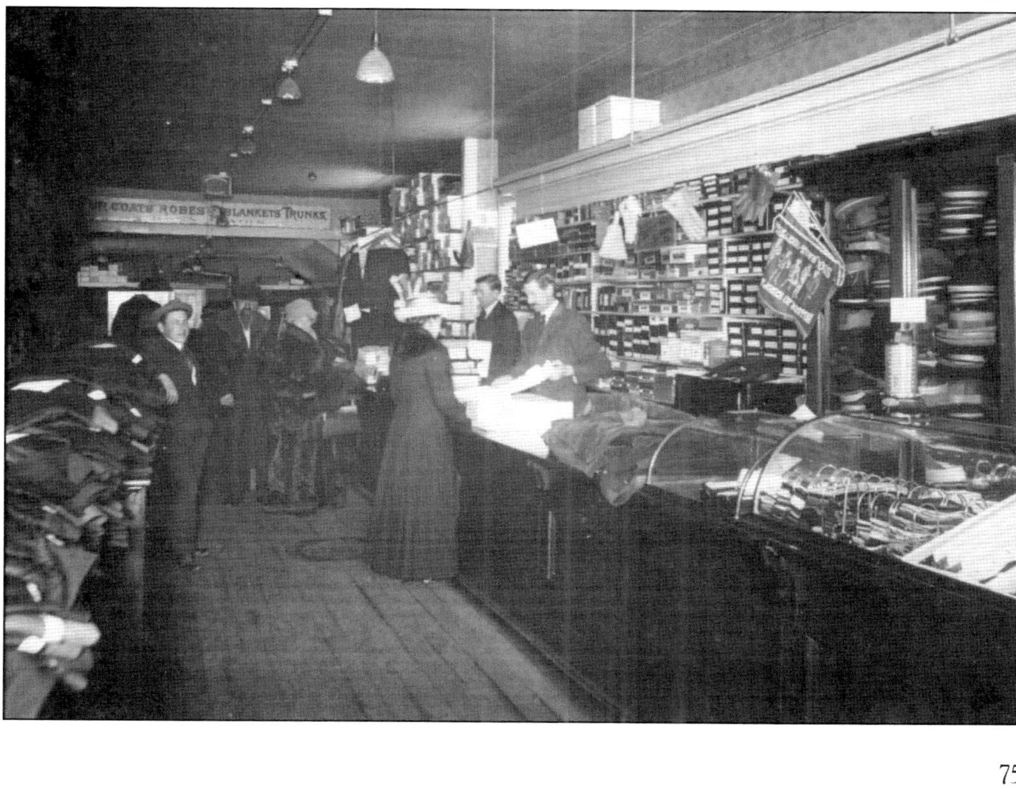

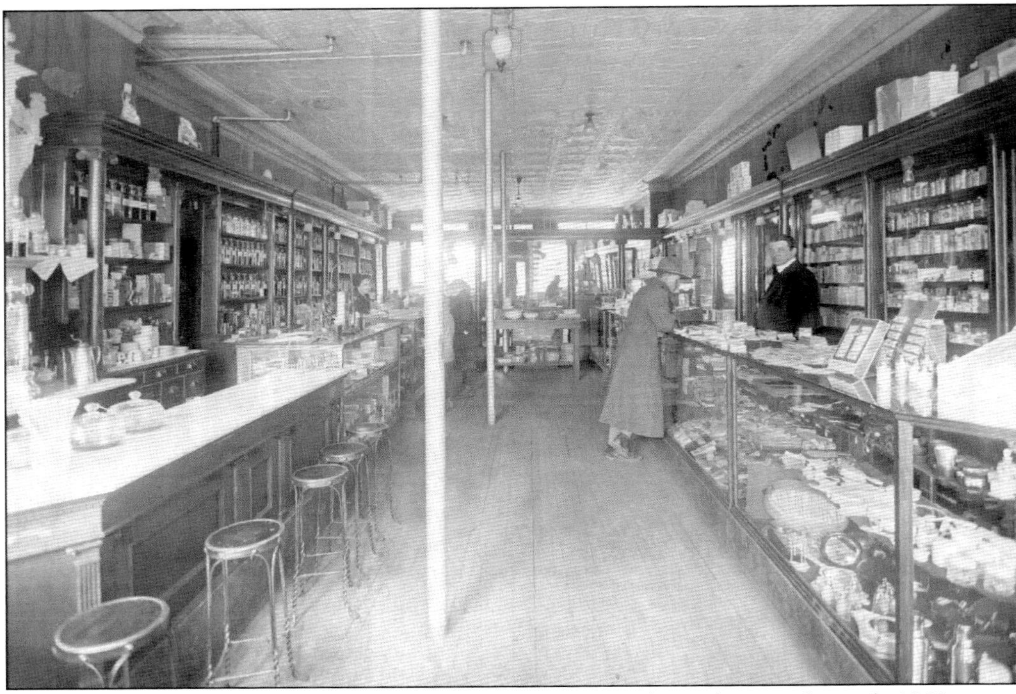

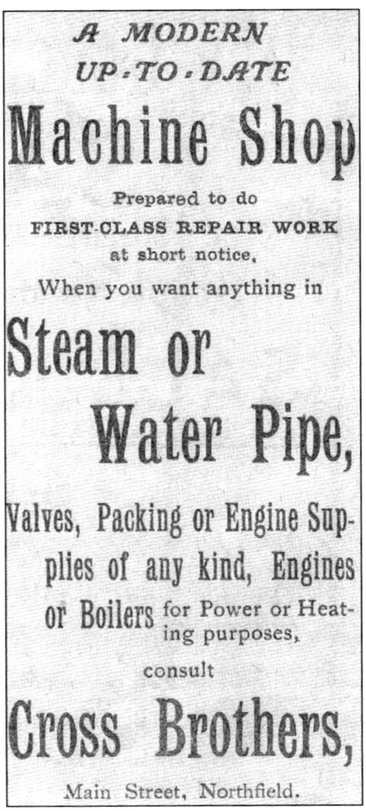

Ned Ray's Drug Store, shown here in the early 1900s, was an interesting place of business, from its marble-topped soda fountain counter to the display cases filled with shaving mugs, hair brushes, mirrors, and other items. Note the young man in a military coat and hat, perhaps a cadet down from the hill, perusing picture postcards, while two youngsters are pondering the sweets at the penny candy counter. Behind the clerk at the candy counter is shelf upon shelf of apothecary jars—their mysterious contents now long forgotten. Ned Ray's was located where the Northfield Savings Bank is today. At left is an advertisement for the Cross Brothers machine shop.

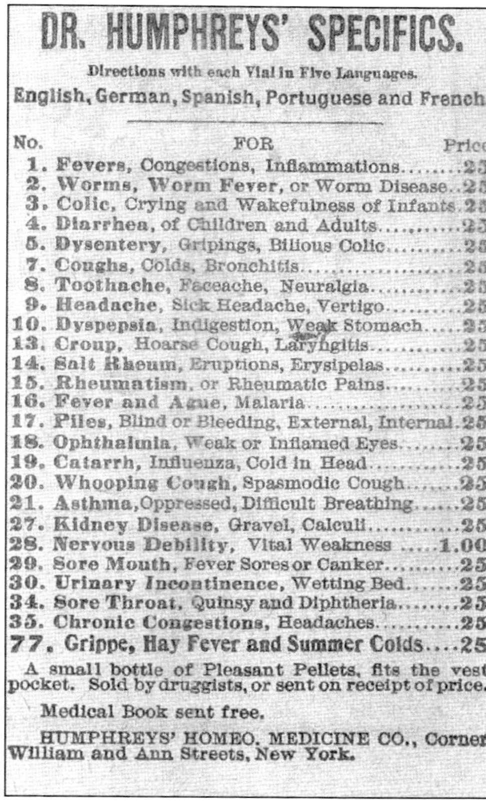

DR. HUMPHREYS' SPECIFICS.

Directions with each Vial in Five Languages.

English, German, Spanish, Portuguese and French.

No.	FOR	Price
1.	**Fevers**, Congestions, Inflammations	.25
2.	**Worms**, **Worm Fever**, or Worm Disease	.25
3.	**Colic**, Crying and Wakefulness of Infants	.25
4.	**Diarrhea**, of Children and Adults	.25
5.	**Dysentery**, Gripings, Bilious Colic	.25
7.	**Coughs**, Colds, Bronchitis	.25
8.	**Toothache**, Faceache, Neuralgia	.25
9.	**Headache**, Sick Headache, Vertigo	.25
10.	**Dyspepsia**, Indigestion, Weak Stomach	.25
13.	**Croup**, Hoarse Cough, Laryngitis	.25
14.	**Salt Rheum**, Eruptions, Erysipelas	.25
15.	**Rheumatism**, or Rheumatic Pains	.25
16.	**Fever and Ague**, Malaria	.25
17.	**Piles**, Blind or Bleeding, External, Internal	.25
18.	**Ophthalmia**, Weak or Inflamed Eyes	.25
19.	**Catarrh**, Influenza, Cold in Head	.25
20.	**Whooping Cough**, Spasmodic Cough	.25
21.	**Asthma**, Oppressed, Difficult Breathing	.25
27.	**Kidney Disease**, Gravel, Calculi	.25
28.	**Nervous Debility**, Vital Weakness	1.00
29.	**Sore Mouth**, Fever Sores or Canker	.25
30.	**Urinary Incontinence**, Wetting Bed	.25
34.	**Sore Throat**, Quinsy and Diphtheria	.25
35.	**Chronic Congestions**, Headaches	.25
77.	**Grippe, Hay Fever and Summer Colds**	.25

A small bottle of Pleasant Pellets, fits the vest pocket. Sold by druggists, or sent on receipt of price.

Medical Book sent free.

HUMPHREYS' HOMEO. MEDICINE CO., Corner William and Ann Streets, New York.

Dr. Winifred S. Humphrey was an optometrist with an office on the second floor of the Mayo Building. She is shown below in the 1920s, awaiting a patient in her well-equipped examination room. She was in business until the early 1950s. Note the sight-testing chart over the doctor's chair, which would be displayed in the mirror hanging over the counter on the right side. As a patient entered her office, which also happened to be part of her apartment, they could look right into her living room.

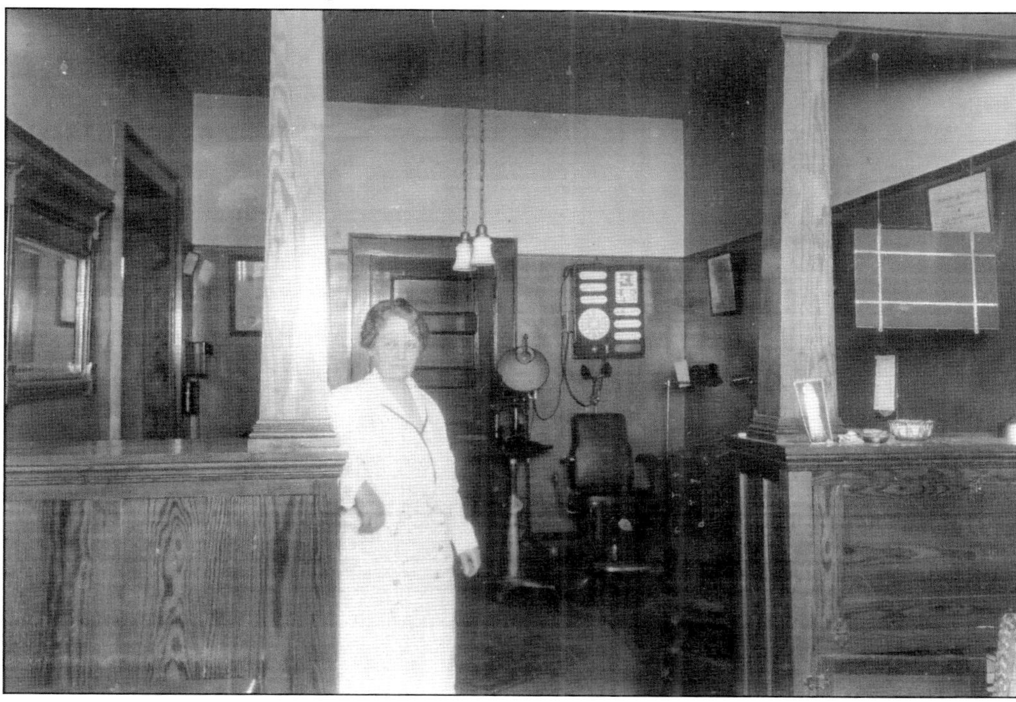

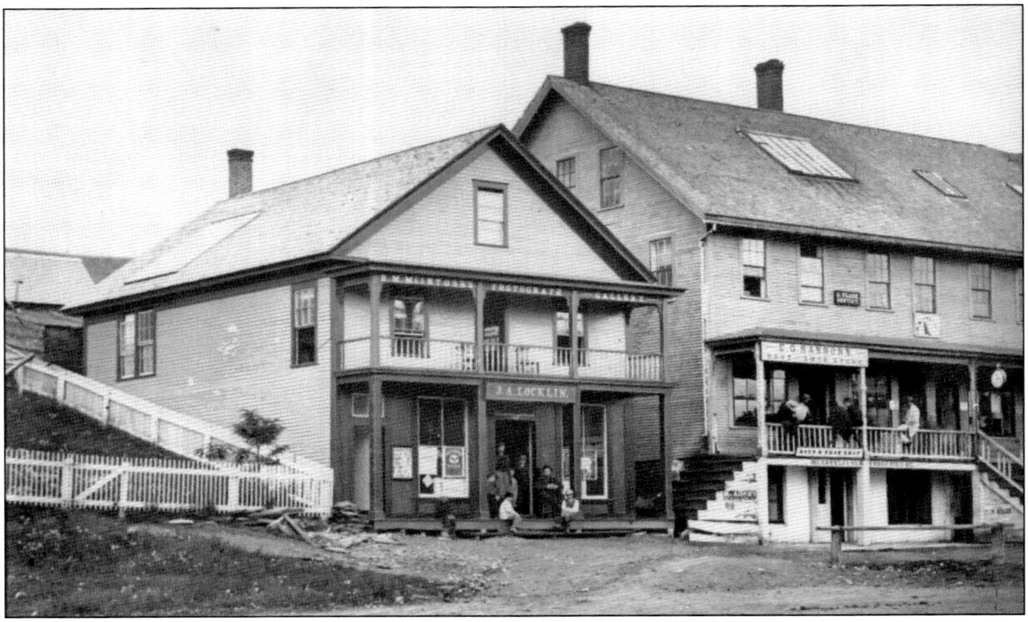

A portion of the south side of the Common is shown in this 1880s photograph. The photographic gallery of Northfield photographer Reuben McIntosh was located on the second floor of the building on the left. The large skylight on the left side of the roof provided the natural light essential for the early photographic studio.

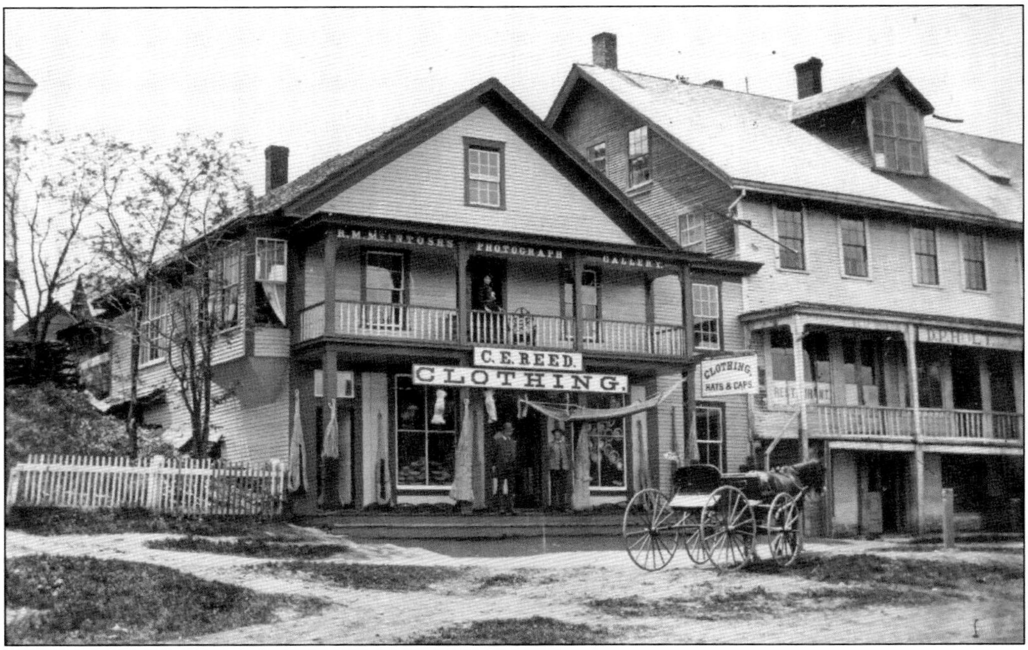

Some changes have taken place in the businesses as one compares this picture with the one above. C.E. Reed Clothing, with hammocks hung everywhere, has replaced J.A. Locklin's grocery store, and, in the Union Block, a restaurant is located in the former boot and shoe store. Also, an addition now connects the two buildings.

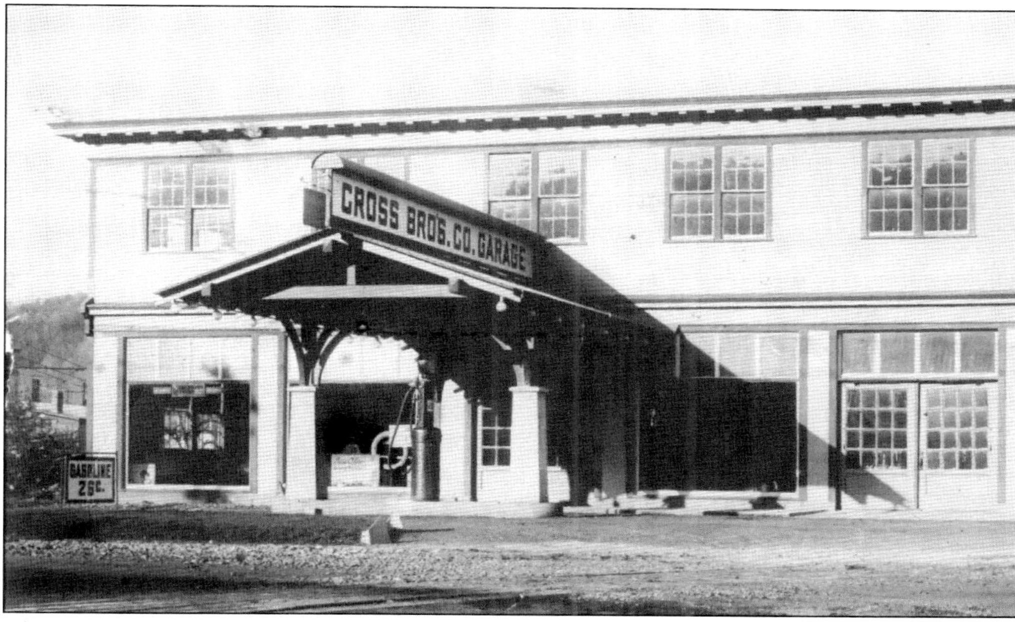

The Cross brothers built their spacious garage around 1918 on North Main Street, opposite their granite sheds. Here, they sold Ford cars and trucks and Fordson tractors. A gallon of gasoline cost 26¢ at this time.

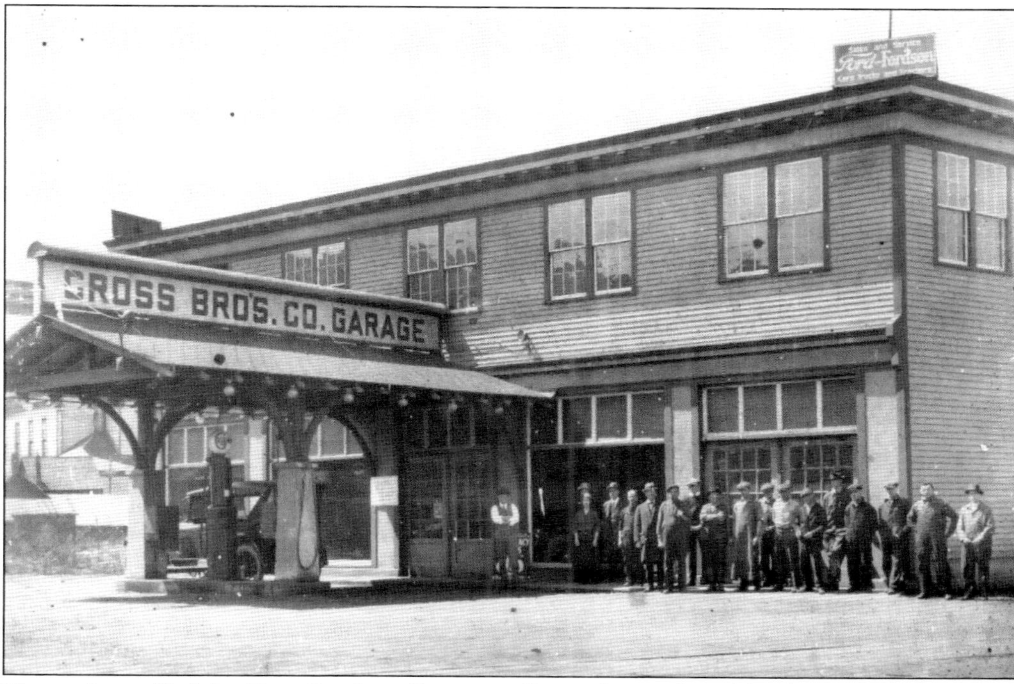

The entire staff of the Cross Brothers Company Garage has gathered for this group photograph, with a new Ford Model T touring car parked in the portico. For a time, Gene Nadon ran his knitting company from the second floor of the garage, where he knit high-quality socks from circular knitting machines.

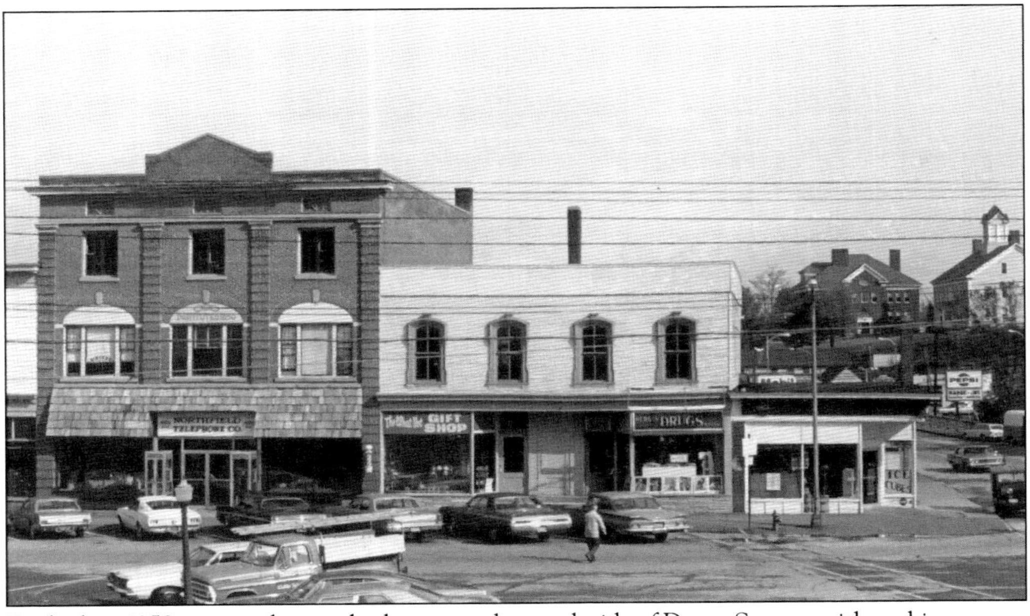

By the late 1950s, many changes had come to the north side of Depot Square, with parking spaces for automobiles replacing the old hitching rails. The brick Odd Fellows Building, erected in 1930, had replaced the old Central Block. Only the location of the barbershop remained the same.

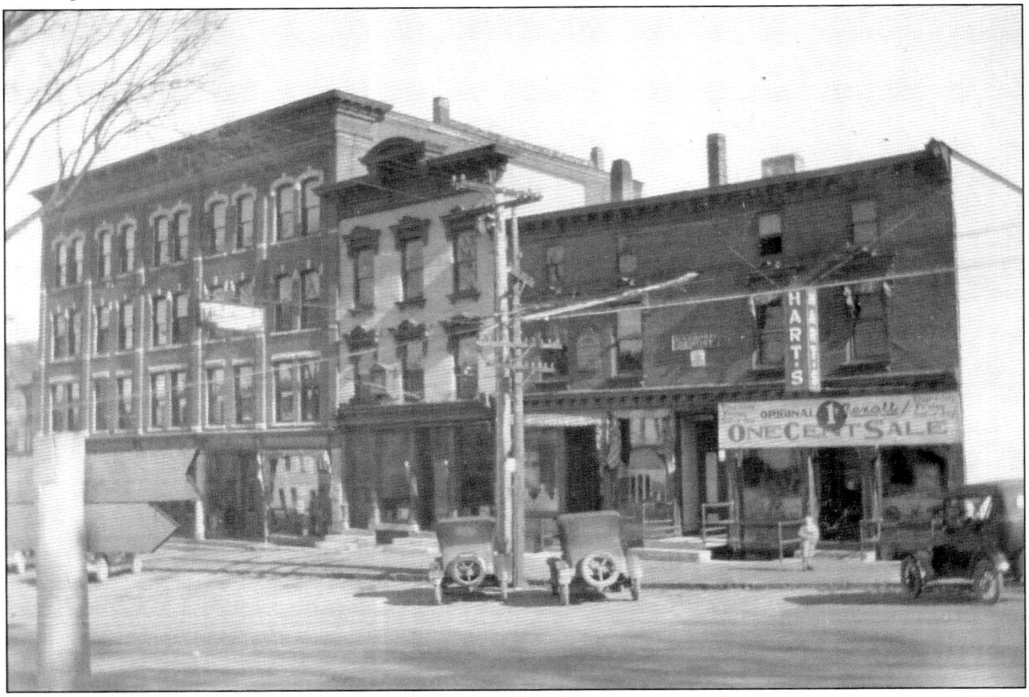

Here, in the early 1920s, the horse-and-buggy mode of transportation has given way to automobiles. The stately Mayo Building dominates the eastern side of Depot Square, as it still does today. Dr. W.G. Huntley's dental office is located above Hart's Rexall Store. On the sidewalk, a boy in knickers gazes at the photographer.

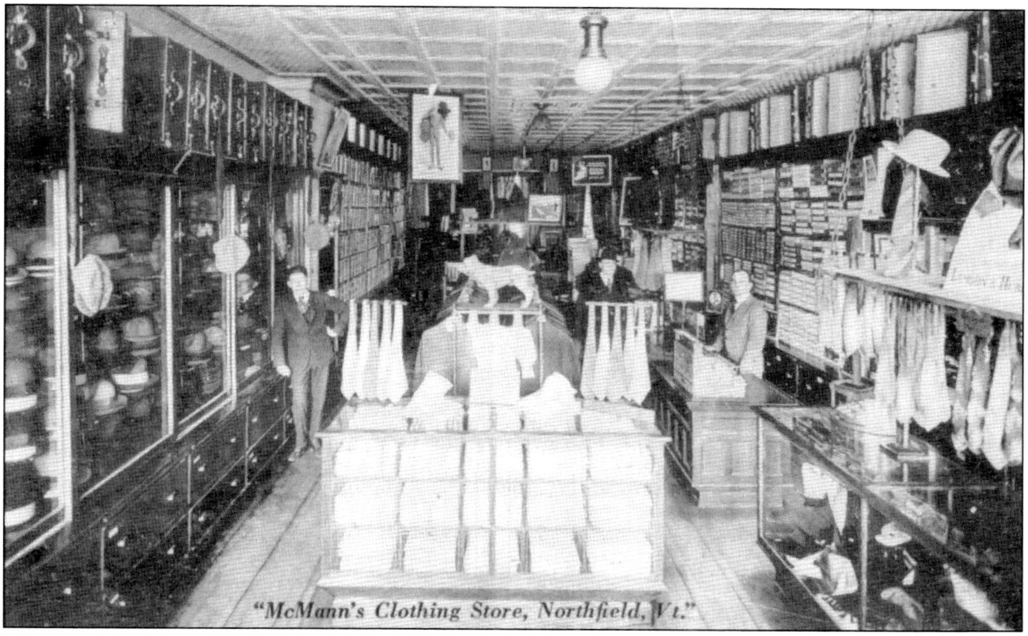

McMann's Clothing Store was well stocked, as shown in this advertising card. Neckties seem to be everywhere!

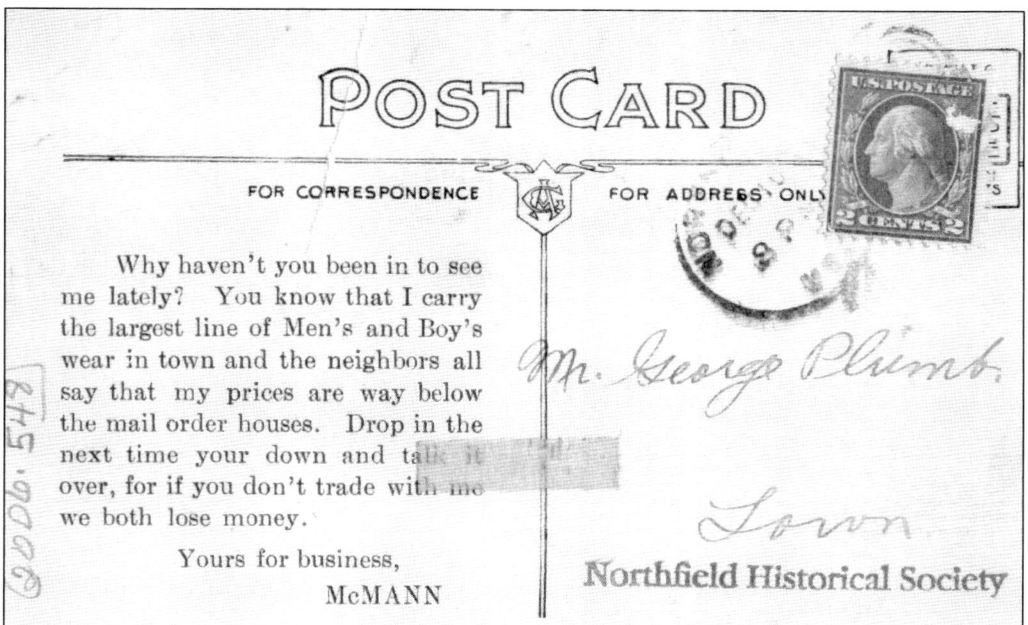
POST CARD

FOR CORRESPONDENCE FOR ADDRESS ONLY

Why haven't you been in to see me lately? You know that I carry the largest line of Men's and Boy's wear in town and the neighbors all say that my prices are way below the mail order houses. Drop in the next time your down and talk it over, for if you don't trade with me we both lose money.

Yours for business,

McMANN

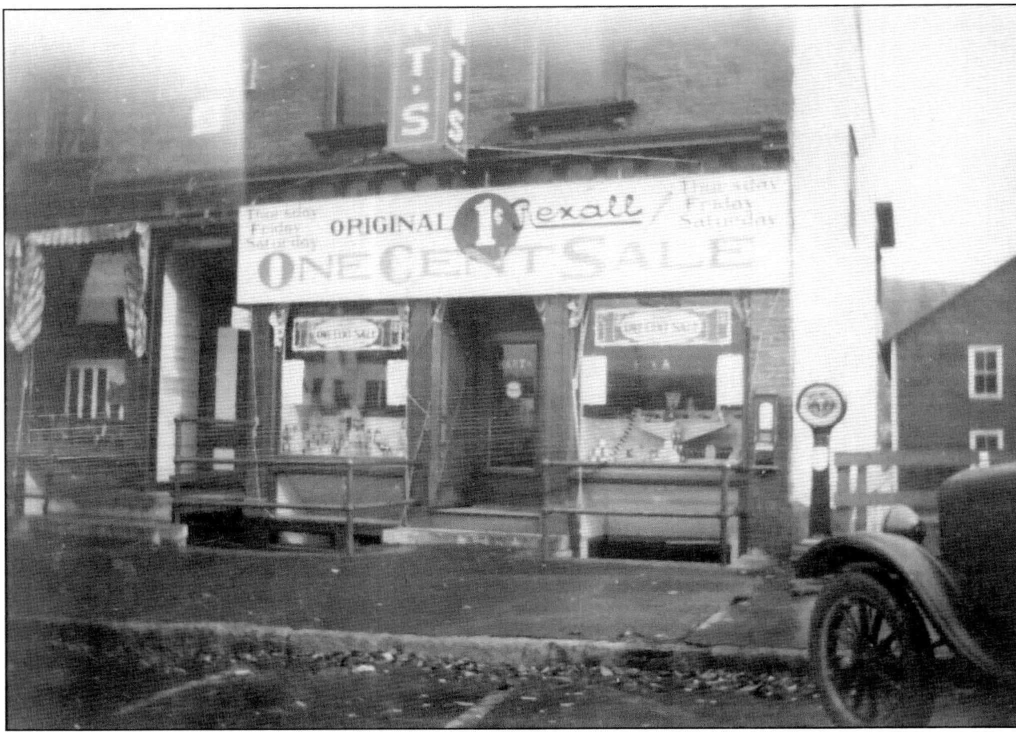

The Northfield Savings Bank now stands on the former site of Hart's Rexall store. Popular for many years, Hart's was located there until the 1950s. Schoolchildren would stop by to visit with Mrs. Carla Despart and have an ice cream soda. Thrifty housewives most likely took advantage of the 1¢ sale to replenish their home medicine cabinets.

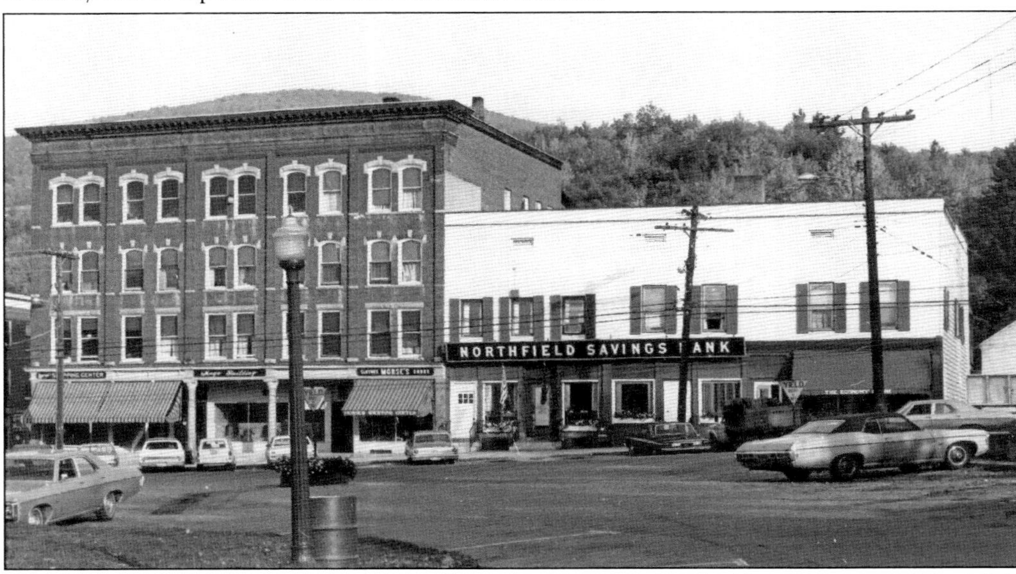

In the late 1950s, the Mayo Building was still standing, but a modern building housing the Northfield Savings Bank had taken the place of the old buildings that once stood there. Fortunately, the new architecture of the renovated building restores the character of old Northfield.

Six

DARK CLOUDS OVER NORTHFIELD

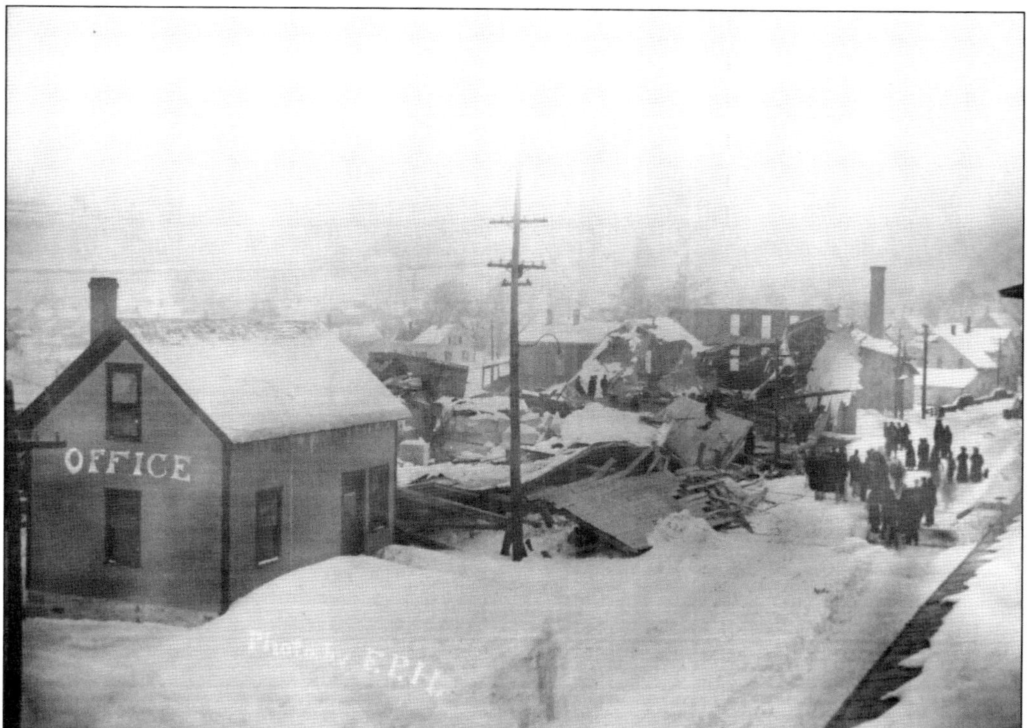

In the winter of 1910, after a heavy snowfall, the Burns granite shed, on the north side of Water Street, collapsed under the weight of the snow.

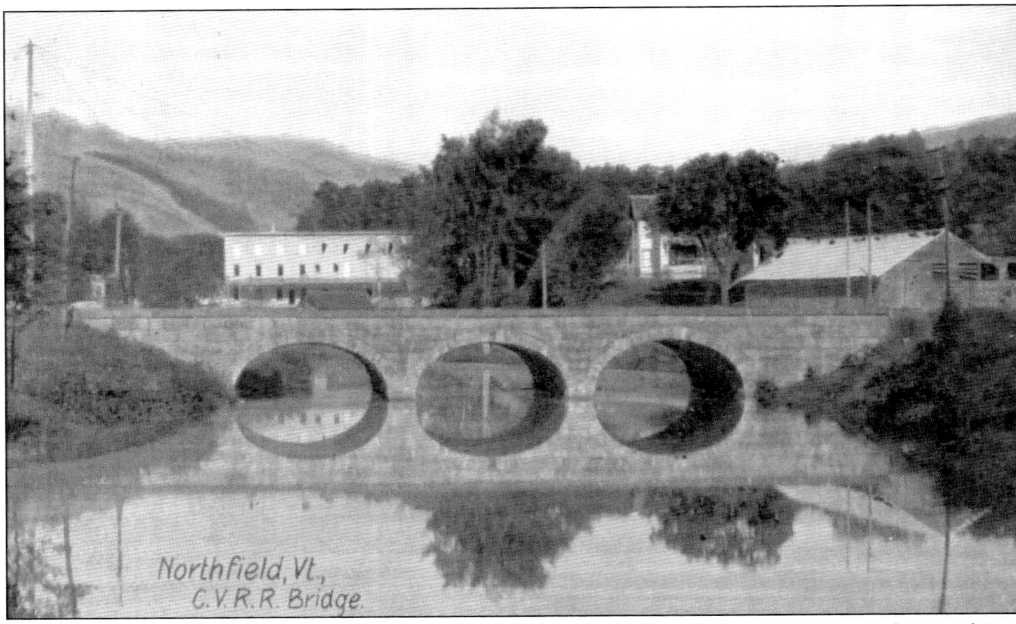

The beautiful Arch Bridge was constructed in 1852. Henry Campbell, an engineer who was hired by the Vermont Central Railroad, designed it. It was located west of the Main Street Bridge, where the steel railroad bridge is today. The Arch Bridge stood for 75 years until the 1927 flood destroyed it.

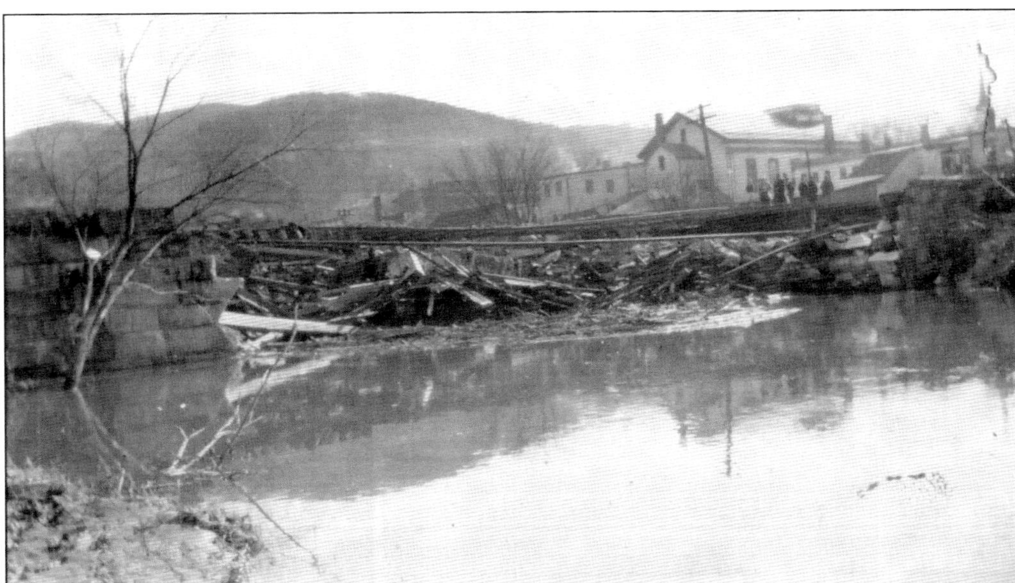
This photograph shows the Arch Bridge after the flood, with just the ends intact. The rest of the stones lay in the Dog River below the railroad tracks. No Northfield lives were lost in the 1927 flood, but the Arch Bridge was not the only bridge lost. The Lovers Lane covered bridge went out with the floodwaters, as did another one over Bull Run Brook at Harlow Bridge.

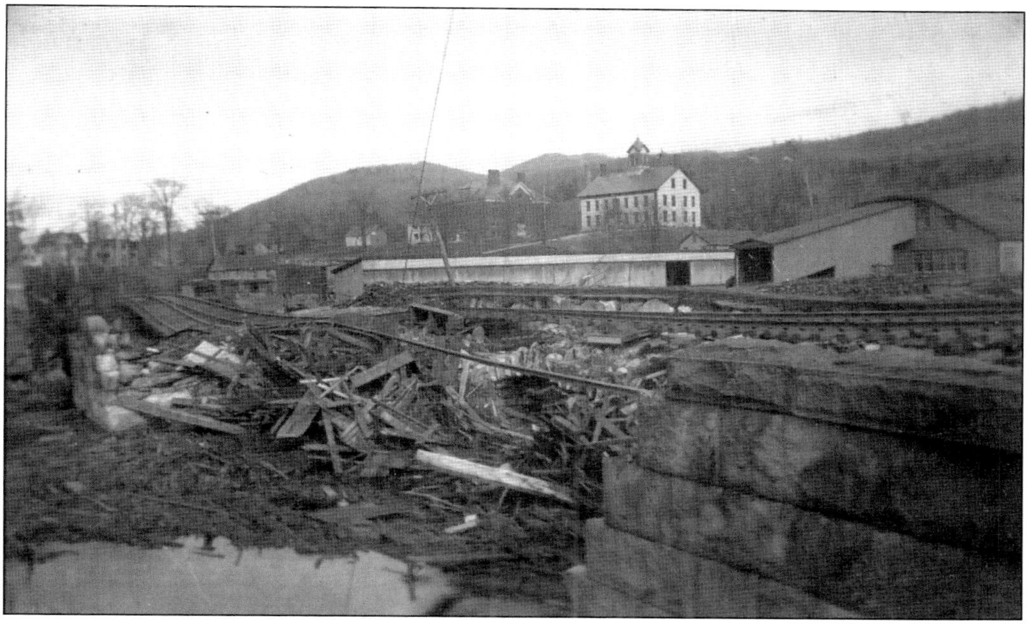

Here are close-up views of the remains of the Arch Bridge and the railroad tracks that ran over it. Inside the pile of debris, one of the arches can be seen. Today, remains of the bridge still lie in Dog River. In 1928, the Central Vermont Railroad replaced the former, beautiful Arch Bridge with a practical and sturdy steel one.

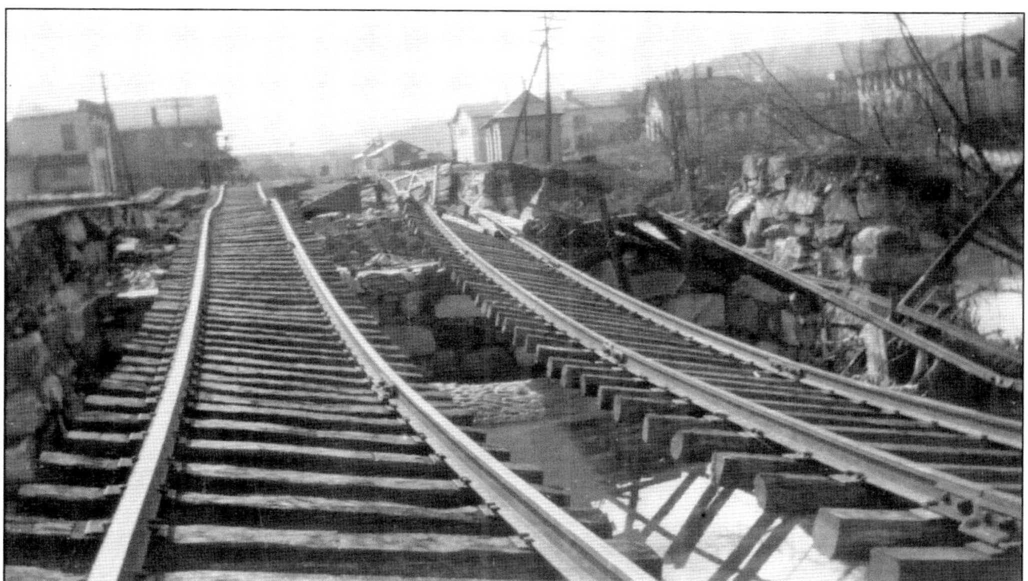

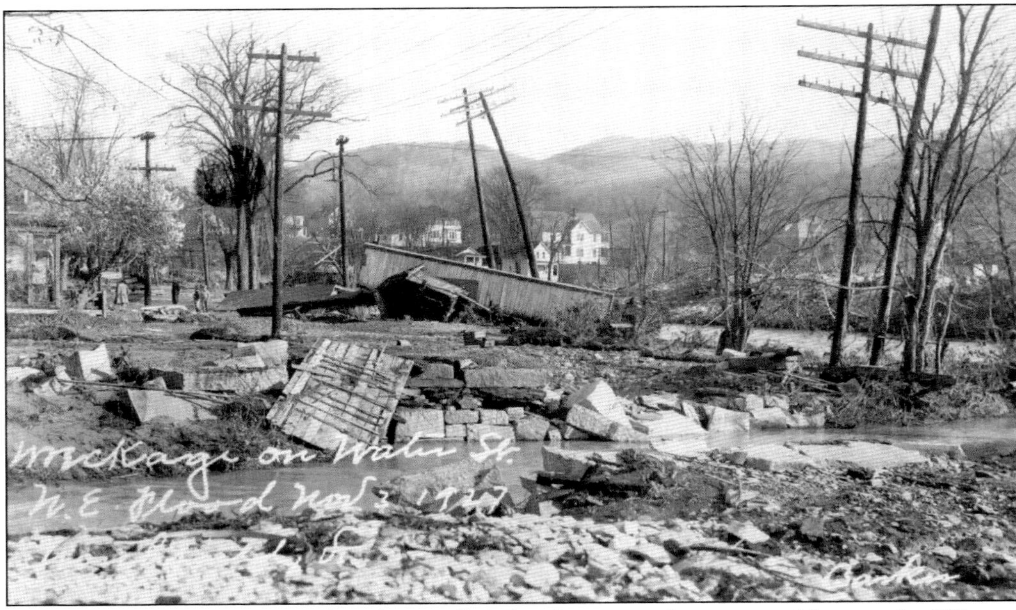

On November 3, 1927, a Canadian front collided with a tropical storm over Vermont for 39 hours. Northfield received 8.61 inches of rain. The town was totally isolated, and martial law was put into effect. This photograph shows Water Street where Union Brook and the Dog River meet. The Union Brook Bridge foundation is all that was left of the bridge.

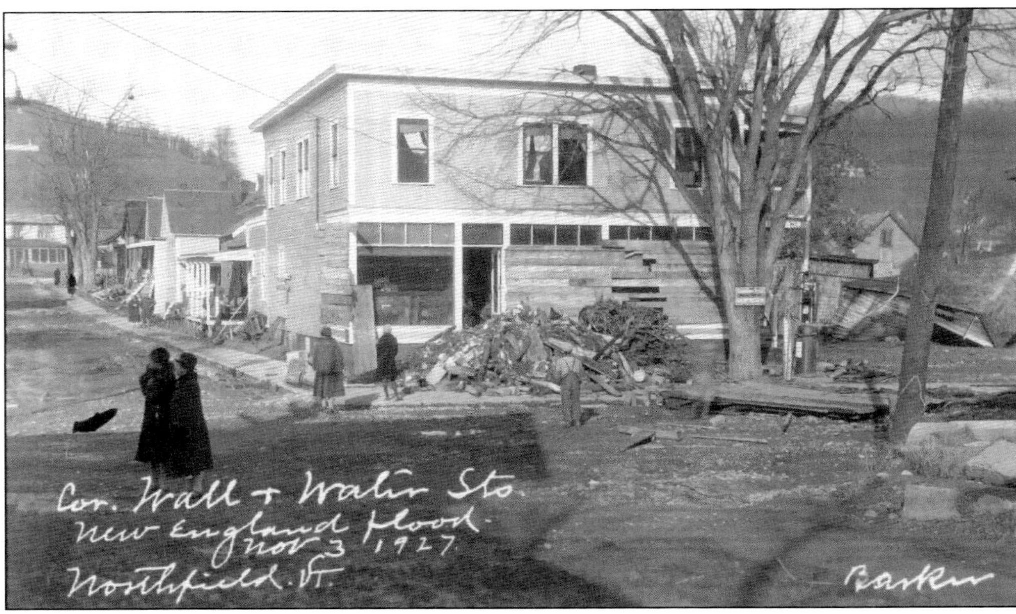

This photograph shows the corner of Water and Wall Streets following the 1927 flood. The extent of the destruction can be seen here, as Diego's store is boarded up with debris boards. A collapsed building on the right is visible. A total of 75 people were killed in the 1927 flood, none of them from Northfield.

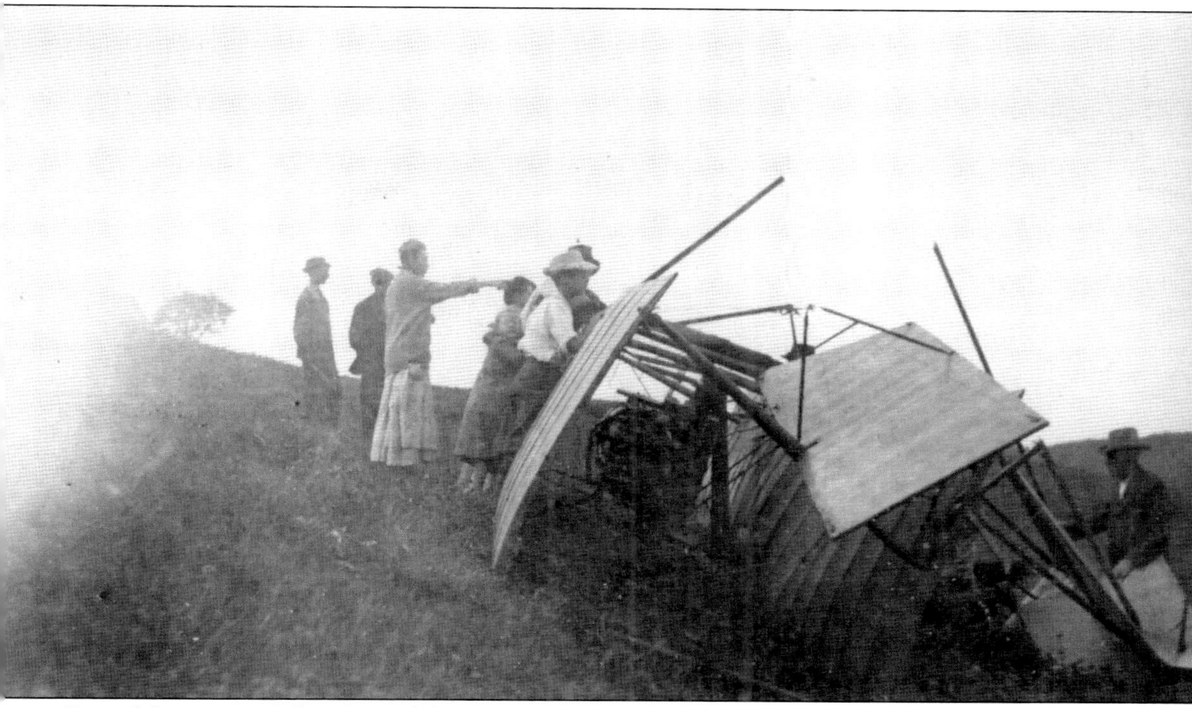

One of the most popular songs of the era was "Come Josephine in My Flying Machine," so there must have been a good deal of excitement among the people of Northfield and the surrounding area in 1913 when it was announced that one of the latest and improved biplanes would be appearing on September 3–4 at the Dog River Valley Fair. On the days when the weather was fine, Charles Baysdorfer, the pilot, planned to make two or more flights over the fairground and the valley. It was during one of these flights over the Bannister farm, at the end of Winch Hill Road, that his "Josephine lost her flying machine." The plane took a nosedive into the field below. Luckily, the pilot was not seriously injured, but the plane lay in a splintered heap where it fell, as a curious crowd of onlookers gathered to inspect it. One can almost hear an old farmer in the crowd making the observation, "If God had meant men and women to fly, He would have given them wings."

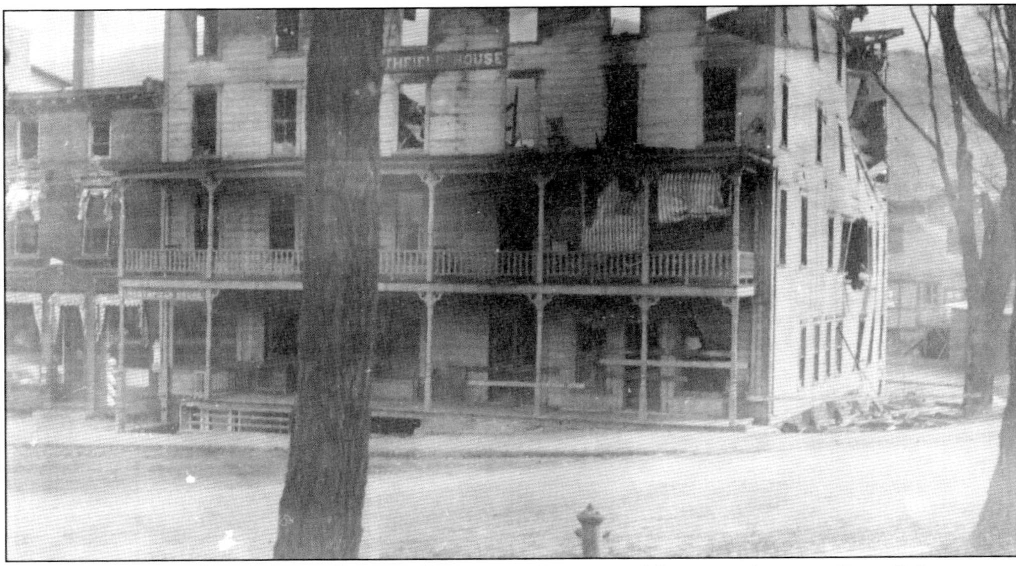

Northfield has suffered through many fires over the years. Here are the remains of the second Northfield House, which burned down in 1916. It was built in 1880 by George Fisk and was four stories high. It was located where the Northfield Savings Bank is now. The first Northfield House was built in 1837, and it burned down in 1879. They both offered affluent lodging.

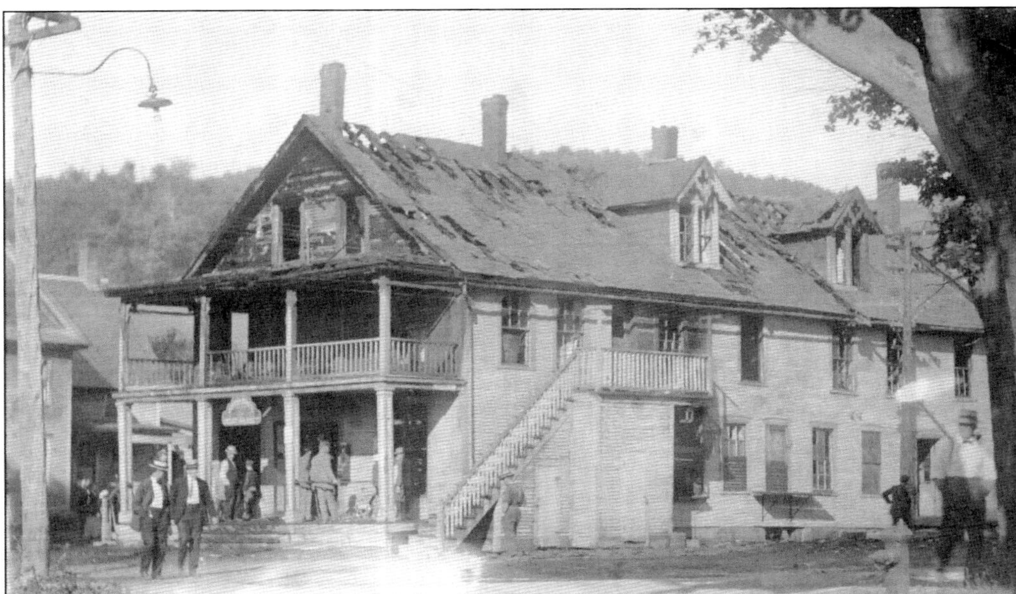

Shown here following a 1911 fire is the Kerr Brothers Meat Market, at the corner of Water and Union Streets. Thankfully, this fire did not take the entire building, and it later became Fernandez's Market. Northfield residents were about to experience some frightening years to come in town, with major fires destroying many buildings.

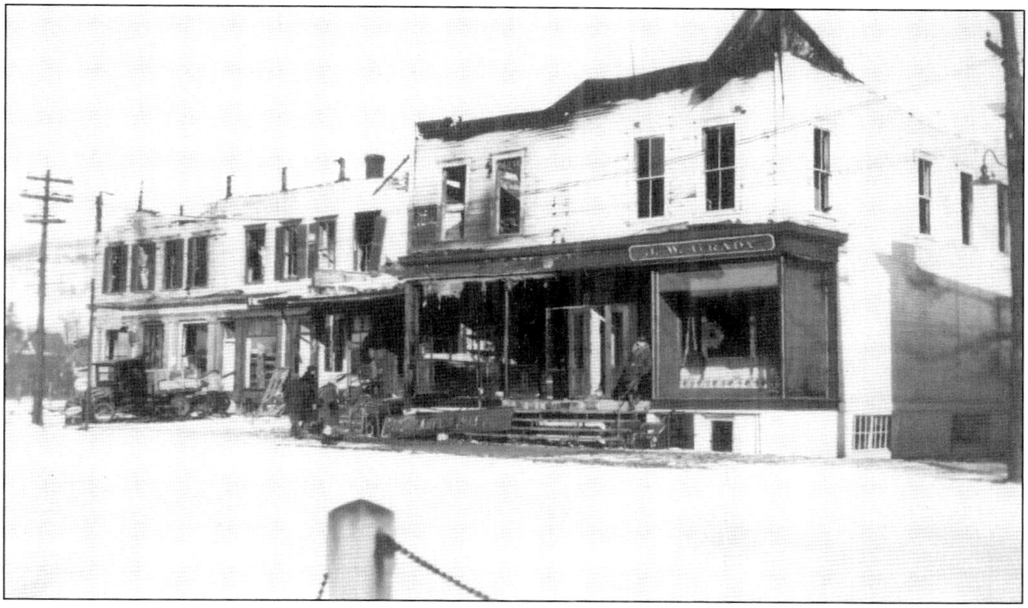

The burned remains of the north side of the Common are shown here in 1928. The Provost Restaurant and the J.W. Grady store burned down in separate fires about a month apart. A total of 11 major fires occurred between 1925 and 1928. Other huge losses were the Central Block and the Universalist church. Arson was suspected but never proven.

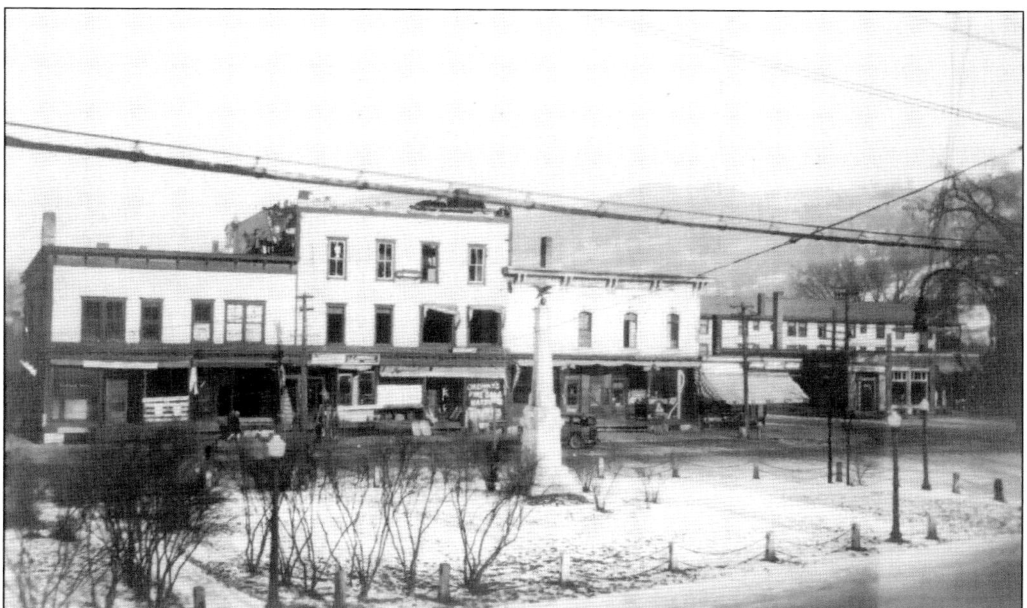

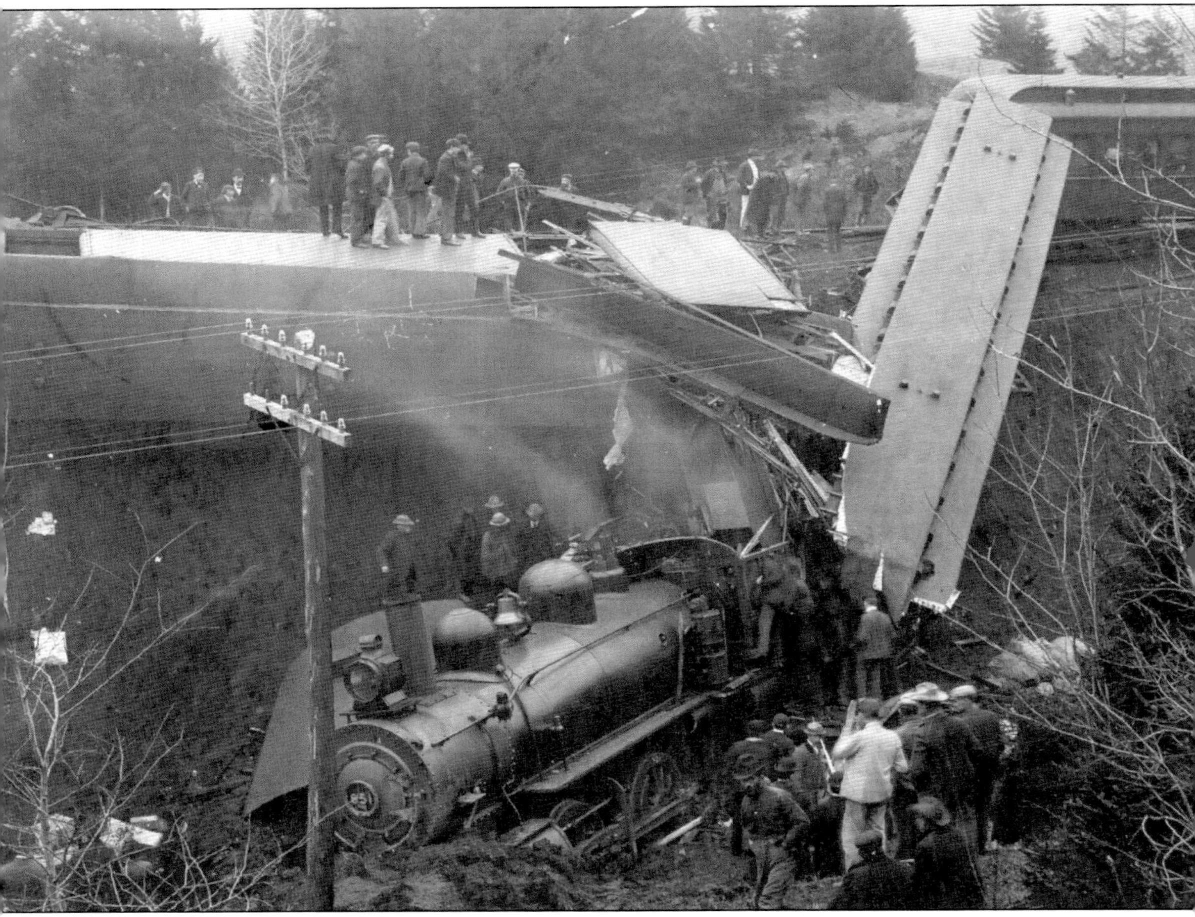

This train wreck occurred 1.5 miles south of the Northfield depot, at Elbow Bridge, in April 1903. Engine No. 851 was returning from Boston when engineer James Lynch noticed a rock slide on the tracks in front of him. Lynch could not stop in time and ran into the slide at 30 miles per hour, plunging the engine 25 feet down the embankment to the left of the track. Lynch escaped the crash without the slightest injury. The baggage and express mail cars rested on the side of the embankment and were badly damaged.

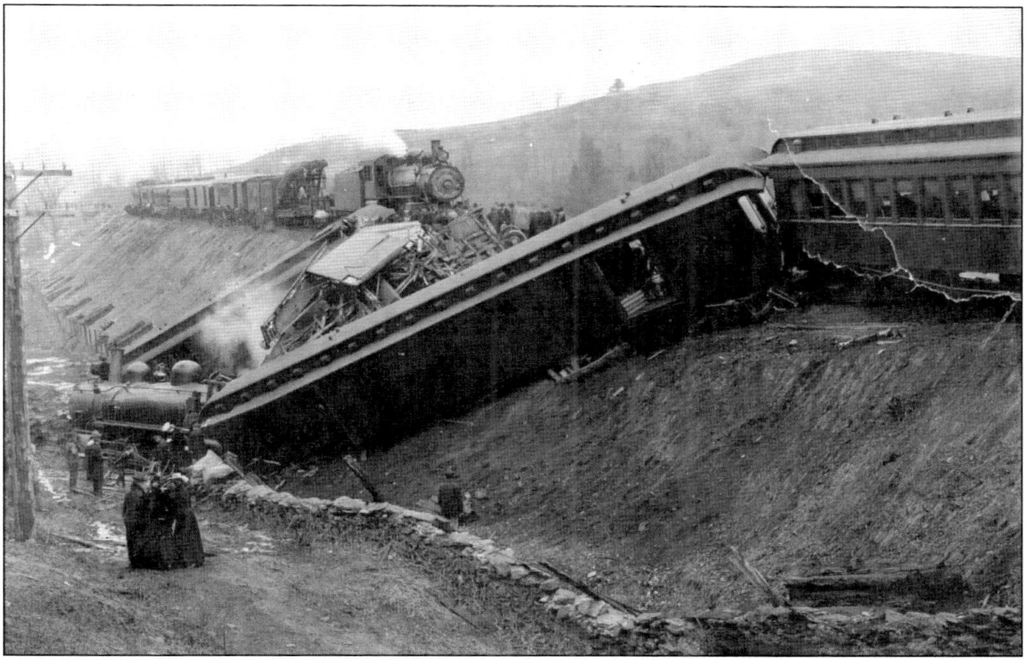

Here is another photograph of the 1903 train accident. Another train has stopped, and people line the tracks. The engineer was thrown from the cab but was unhurt. The train's fireman, Timothy O'Neil, was killed instantly, as he was caught between the boiler and the tender and was crushed to death.

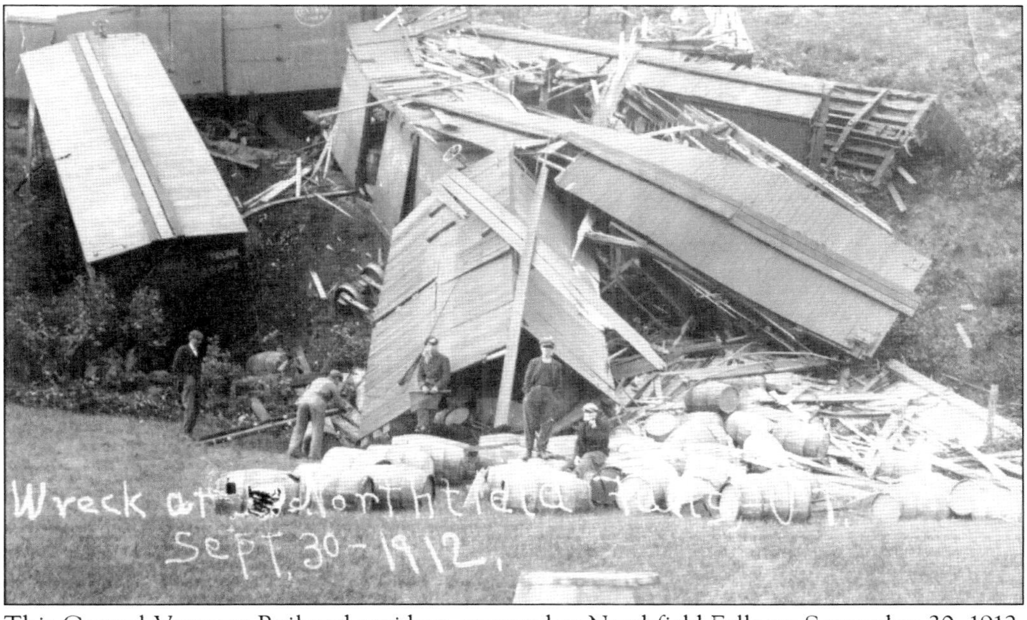

This Central Vermont Railroad accident occurred at Northfield Falls on September 30, 1912. Five railroad cars fell from the tracks, and four of them were destroyed beyond repair. The cargo contained in the numerous wooden barrels can be seen scattered below the train wreck and out into the field.

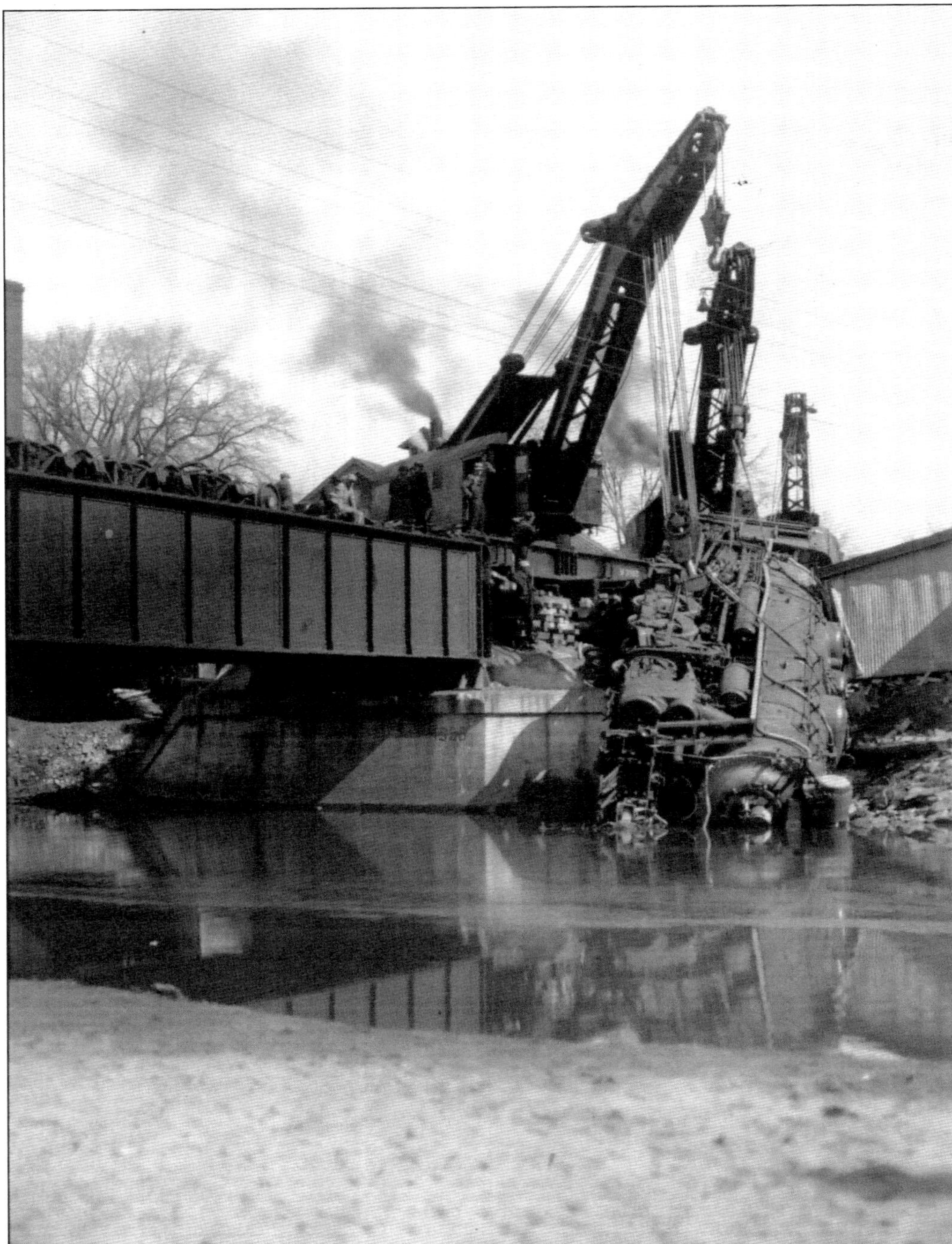

The *Northfield News* headline about this train wreck read, "Spectacular Wreck Here, Huge Engine Leaves Rail, Crashes into Bridge and Topples into the Dog River." The article went on to describe the crash, which took place on May 7, 1936, writing, "This was indeed a spectacular wreck that killed a brakeman. There were 62 cars bound for New London, Connecticut, and as it passed under the Vine Street Bridge, it jumped the tracks."

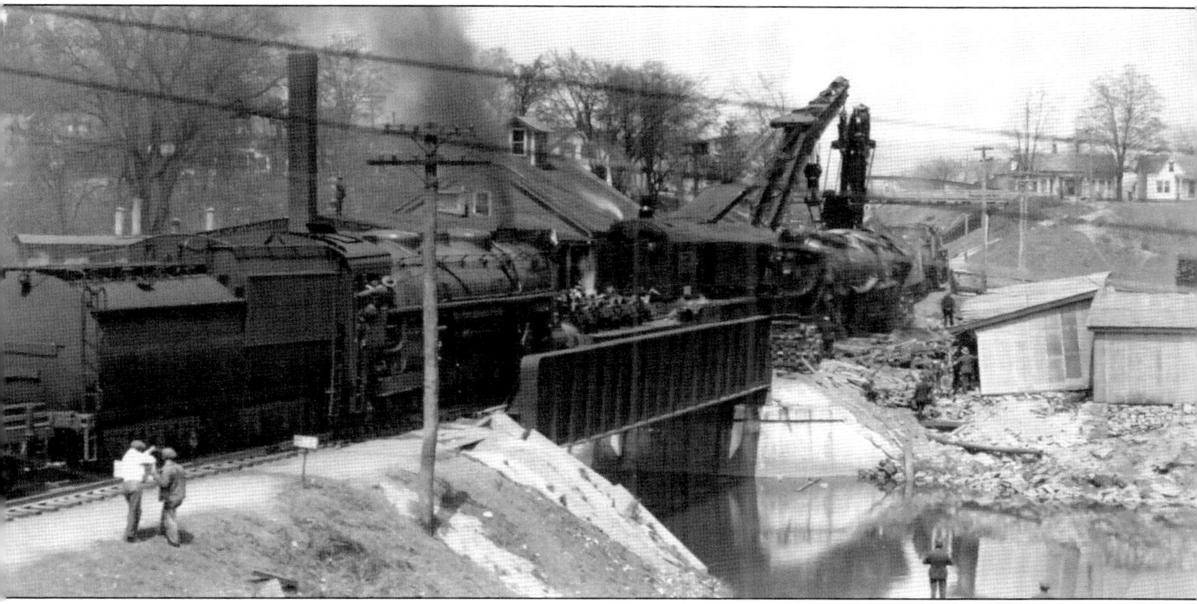

The first two freight cars behind this engine that crashed into the Dog River were carrying 200 head of cattle. The injured cattle were taken to Jesse Cook's farm, but many had to be killed, as the injuries were too severe. Heavy cranes needed to be brought to town to first lift the bridge back onto the abutments and then lift the locomotive back on the tracks.

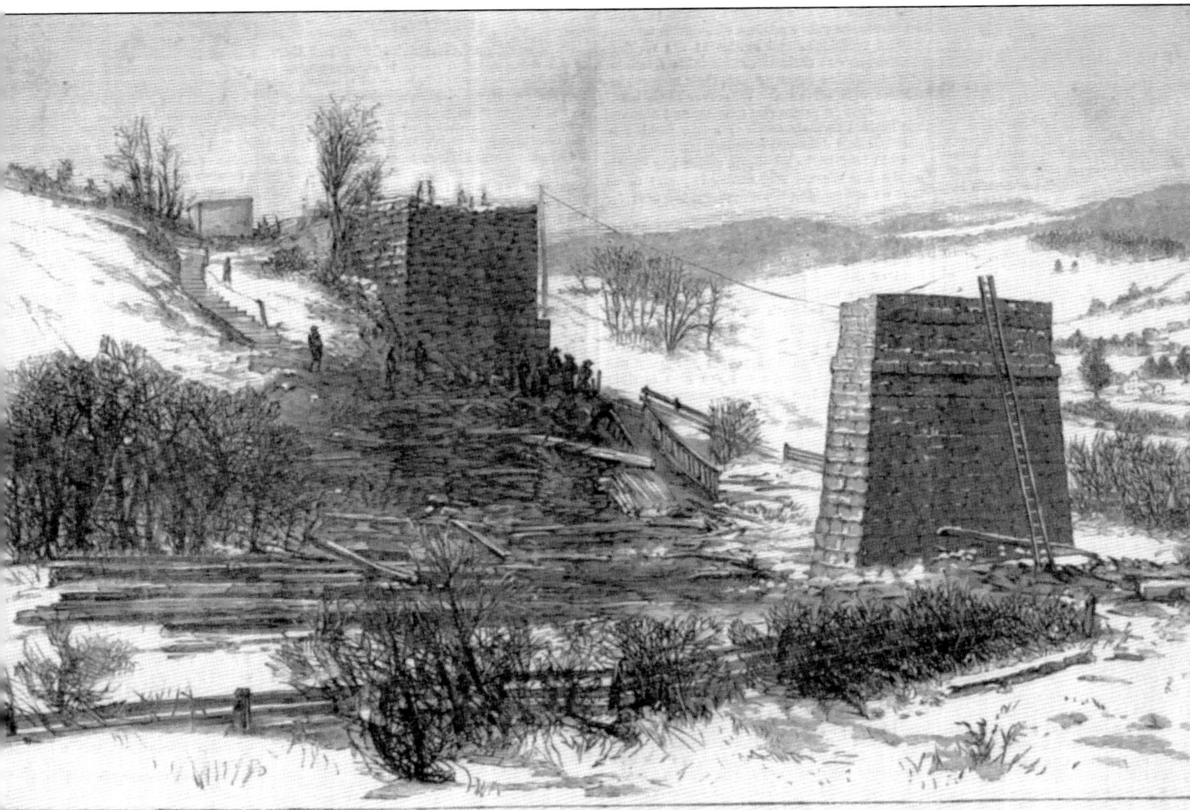

RAILROAD DISASTER NEAR NORTHFIELD, VERMONT.—[PHOTOGRAPHED BY R. M. M'INTOSH.]

This newspaper clipping from a newspaper in New York on December 11, 1867, shows a photograph by Reuben M. McIntosh, a well-known photographer and resident of Northfield. This was one of the first railroad disasters to strike Northfield. Carrying Harlow Bridge workers back to work from lunch, the engineer was asked to hurry up so that he could go back and pick up more workers. He followed orders, and, as a result, the passenger car plunged 25 feet and broke in two, with one part going 60 feet farther down before reaching the ground. In all, 15 men were killed, and 38 were injured.

Seven

People and Places

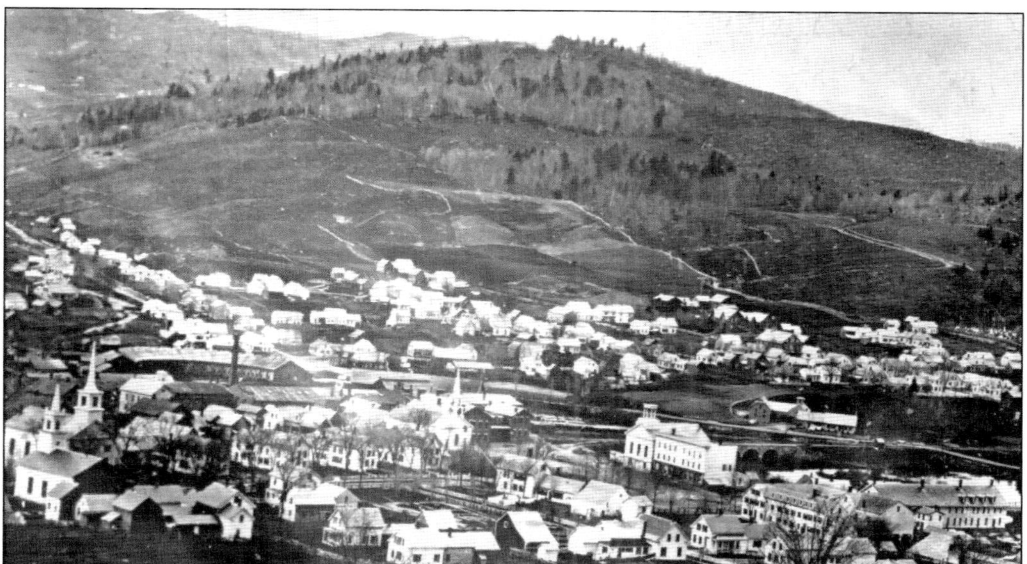

This charming view shows the village in the 1860s. Churches and white houses behind picket fences line the early streets. At the lower right is the Paine Block, and to its left is the first Northfield House. The only buildings on the north side of the Common are the Central Block and the Unitarian church, with its distinctive columned belfry. The Common's western side is dominated by the depot building, the roundhouse, and the train sheds.

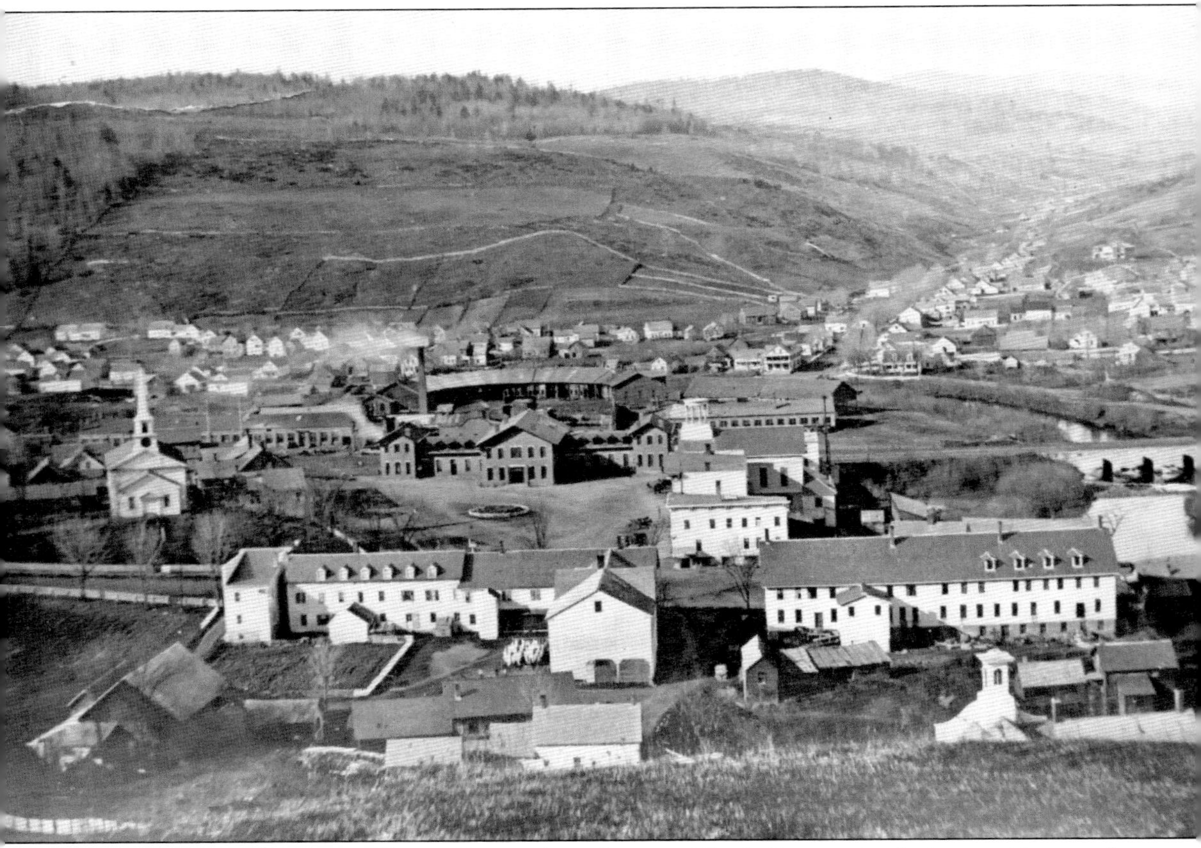

It is 1875 in this view of Depot Square from the east. The bell tower in the lower right was the chapel adjoining the first Catholic rectory on East Street. Immediately in front of the chapel is the Paine Block, with the Northfield House on the left. Note the load of wash hung out to dry. More buildings have been erected on both sides of the Unitarian church. The numerous railroad buildings still command the western end of the square. The roundhouse, where the engines were stored, had a turntable in front of the building where engines were turned as needed.

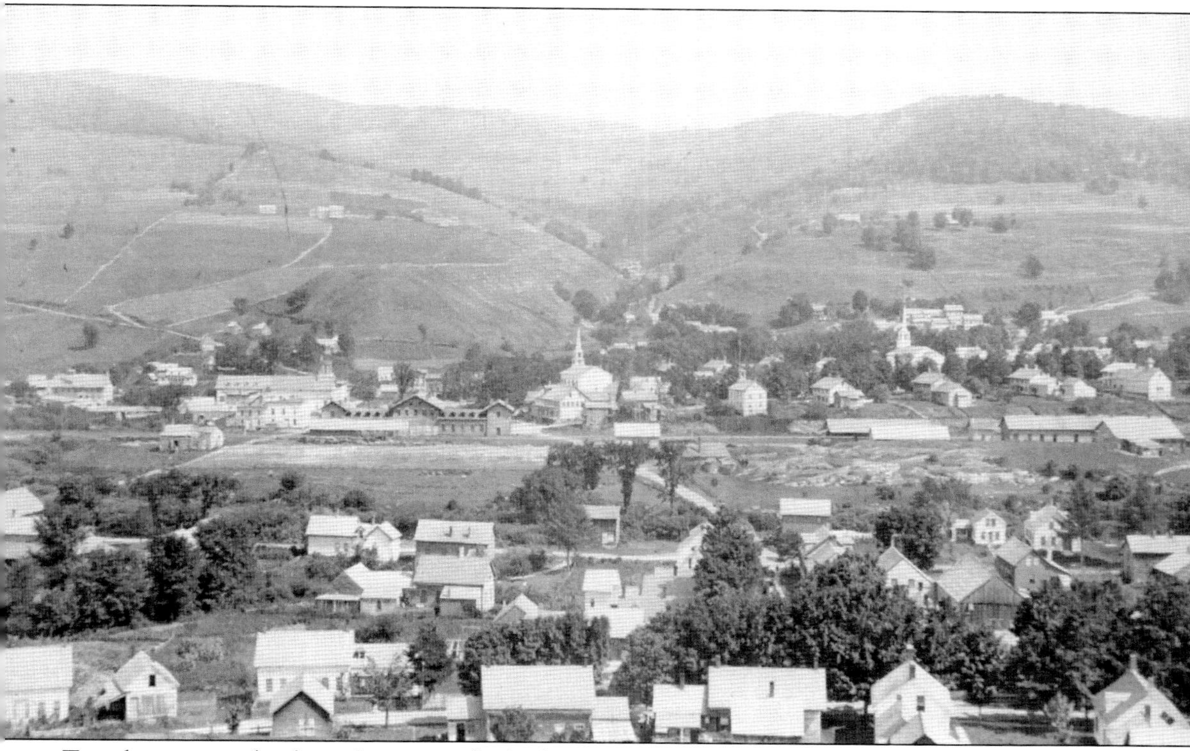

Two changes are clearly evident as one looks down on Northfield from the west in the 1880s. The engine roundhouse and all of the train sheds near it are now gone. Only the depot building and some sheds to the south remain of the once-thriving Vermont Central Railroad. Note the treeless hills above the town; in the days of the wood-burning engines, trees were cut for fuel.

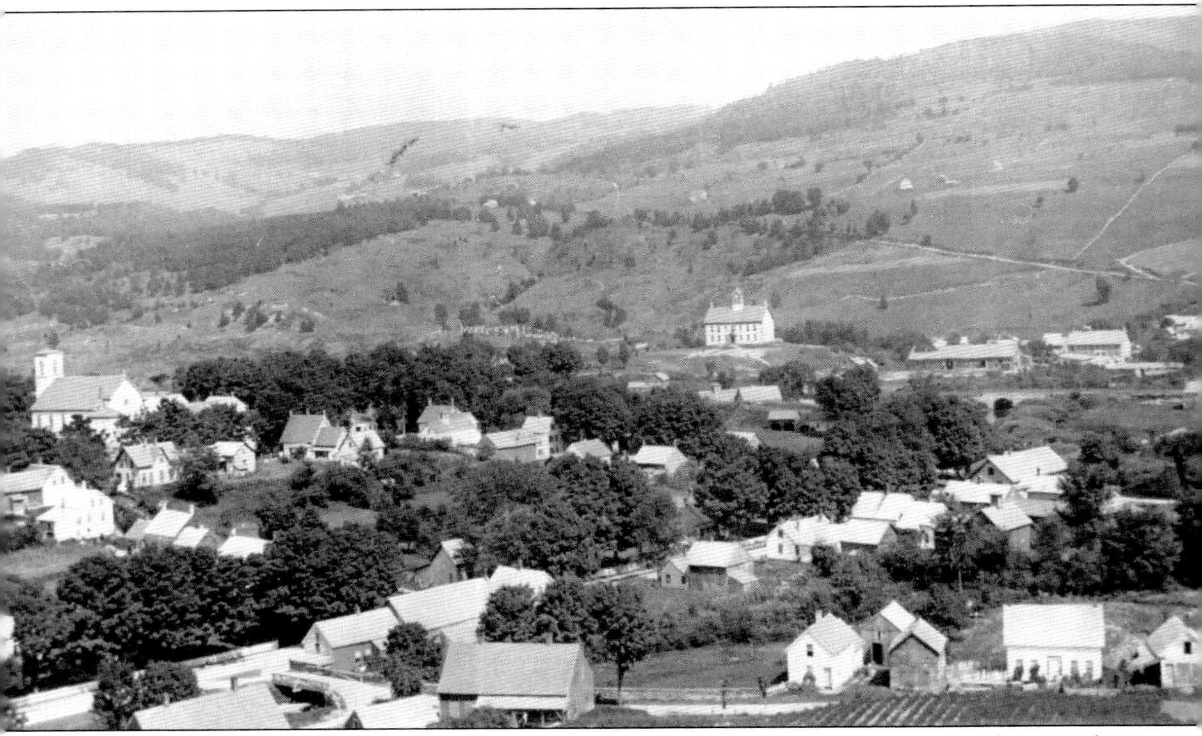

Here is Northfield in the 1880s. Running diagonally across the bottom of the photograph is Union Street. The original Catholic cemetery on King Street can be seen in the distance, and the new Catholic church, dedicated in 1877, can be seen on the left. The Northfield Academy building stands majestically on the hill above the village. One of the arches from the graceful Arch Bridge can be seen.

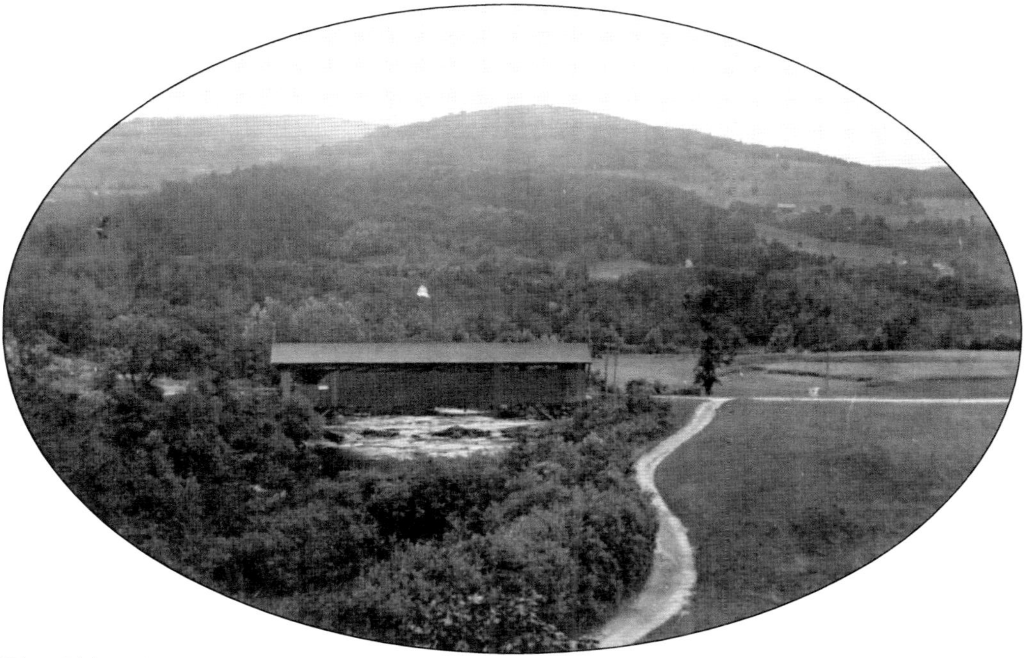

The Old Red Bridge, as it was called, crossed the Dog River on the road to the Falls. This photograph was taken above where Aubuchon Hardware and Tops Market are today.

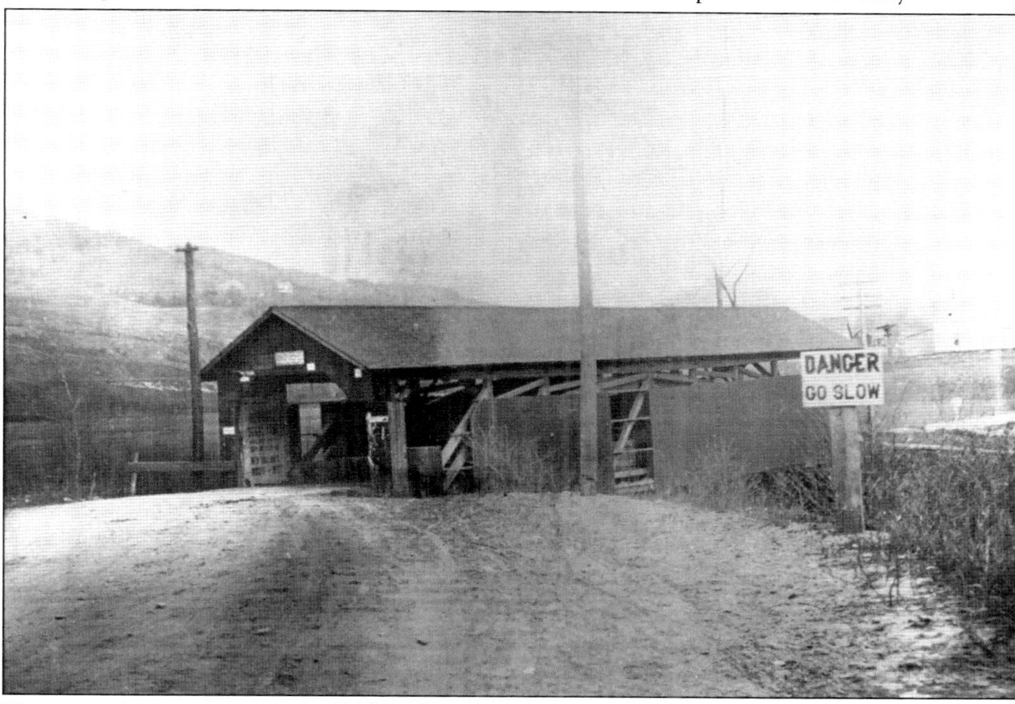

Here is a close-up view of the Old Red Bridge in 1914. It sports a Vermont State Fair sign on the inside left. The bridge was soon replaced by a new cement structure, as the sharp right turn proved to be especially difficult for automobiles.

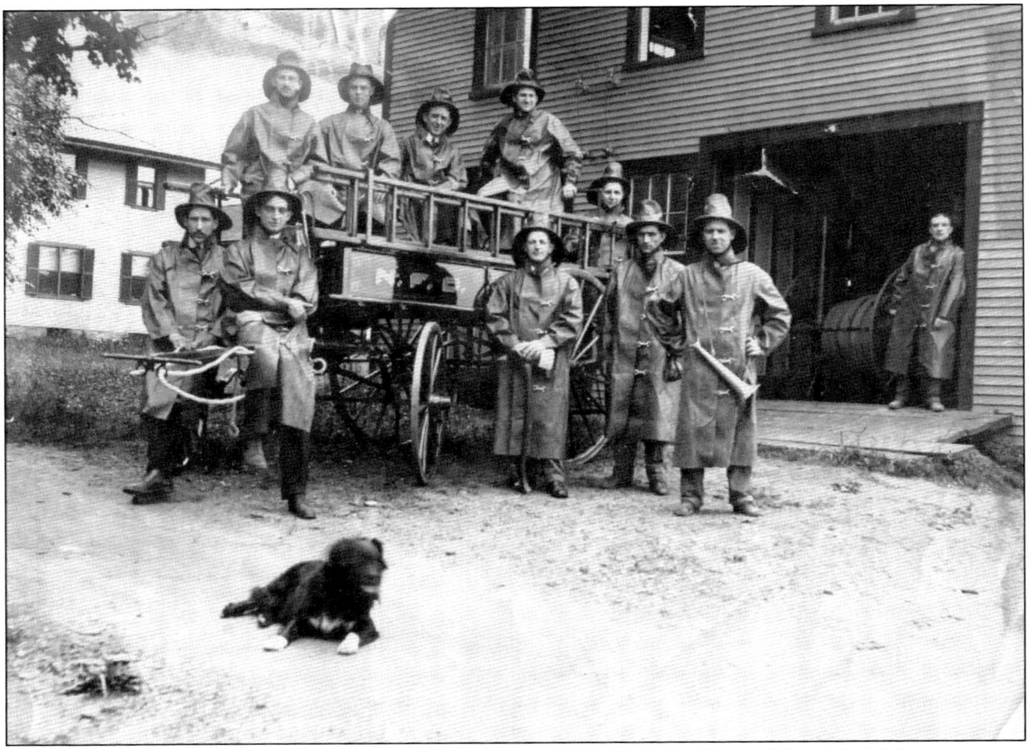

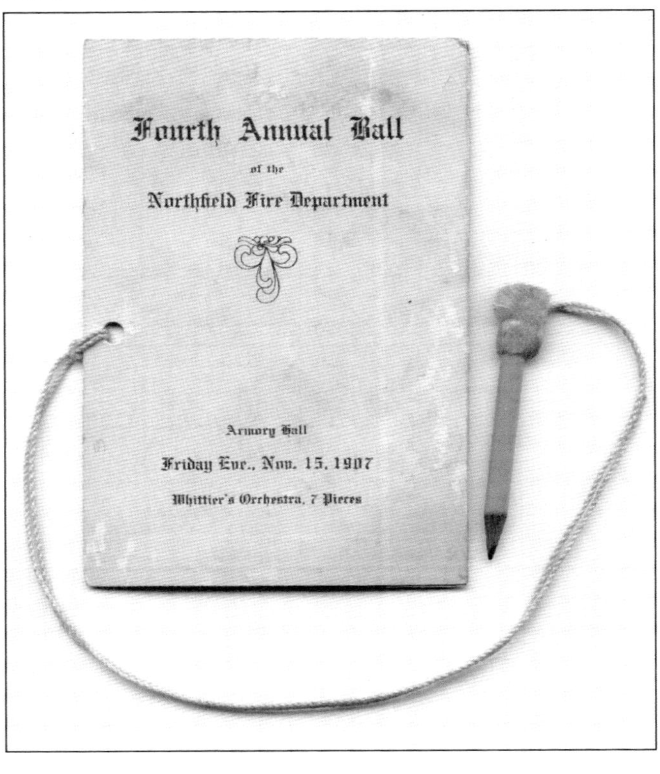

Above, Northfield firemen pose together in the 1890s with their hand-drawn wagon and their dog Jip in front of the Central Street firehouse. Alex Eddie, the fire chief, stands in the doorway. At this time, there were two fire stations in town, one on Vine Street and one on Central Street.

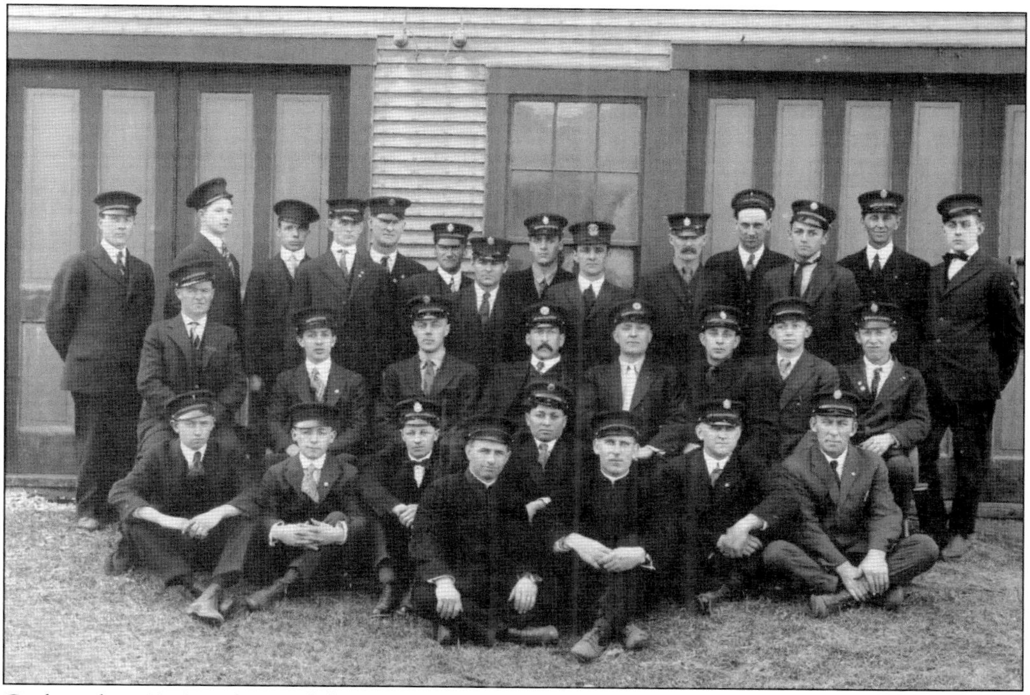

Gathered in 1910 in front of the village hall are volunteer firemen. The fire equipment at this time was stored in the village hall. Seated on the ground, fourth from the left in the second row, is Charles Goodrich, captain of the volunteer fire department.

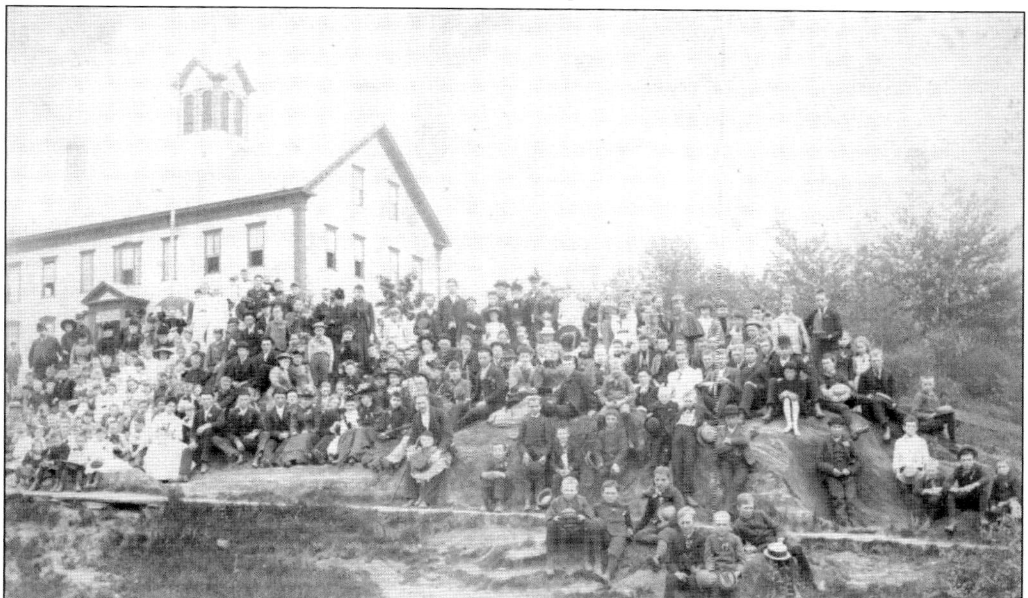

No information is given about this picture, but it must have been a very special occasion, because everyone is dressed in their best. They have gathered just below the school building, probably around 1890. At that time, and for most of its years, the building was painted cream with a dark red trim.

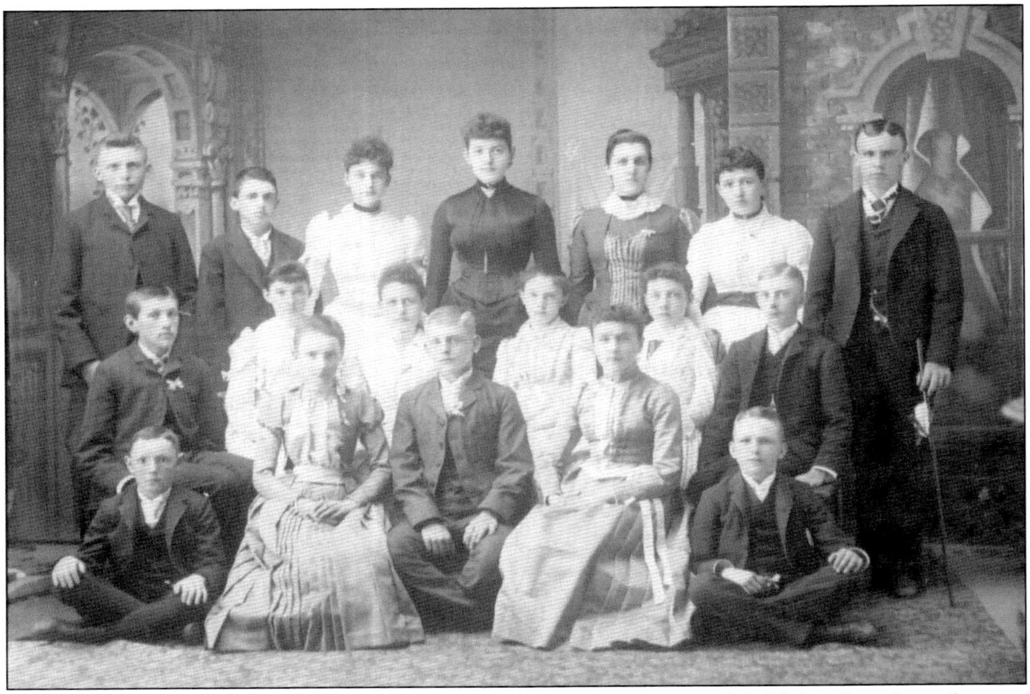

Here, dressed in "best bib and tucker," their Sunday best, is the Northfield Academy's graduating class of 1890, with teacher Mamie Hassett Juckett, who appears to be almost as youthful as her students.

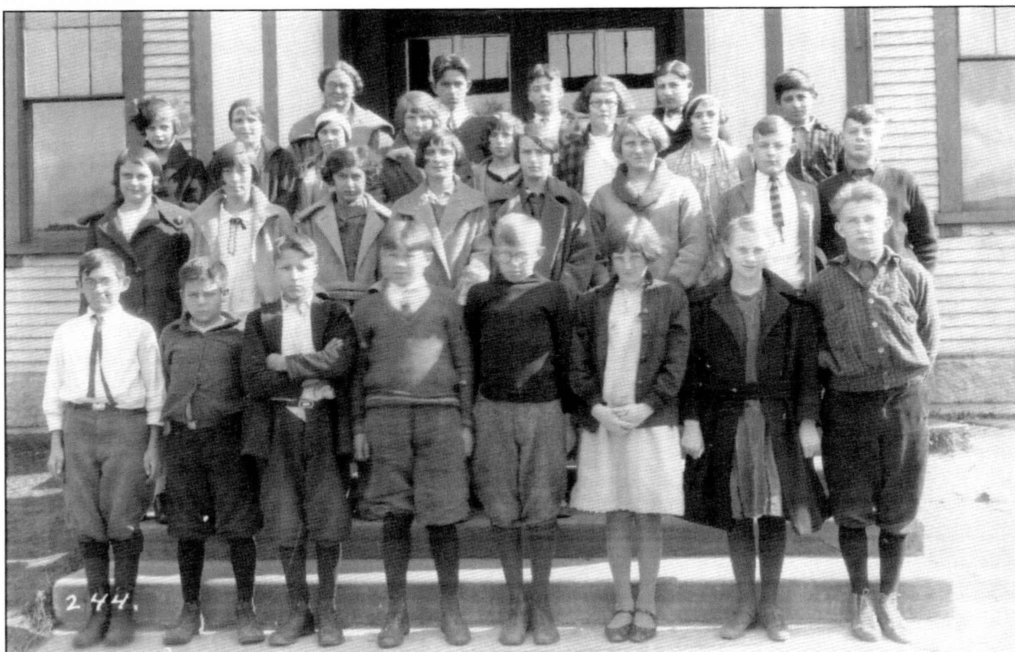

Standing before the front door of the school is the eighth-grade class of 1926, with teacher Inez Perkins. It seems evident that Perkins did not tolerate much nonsense.

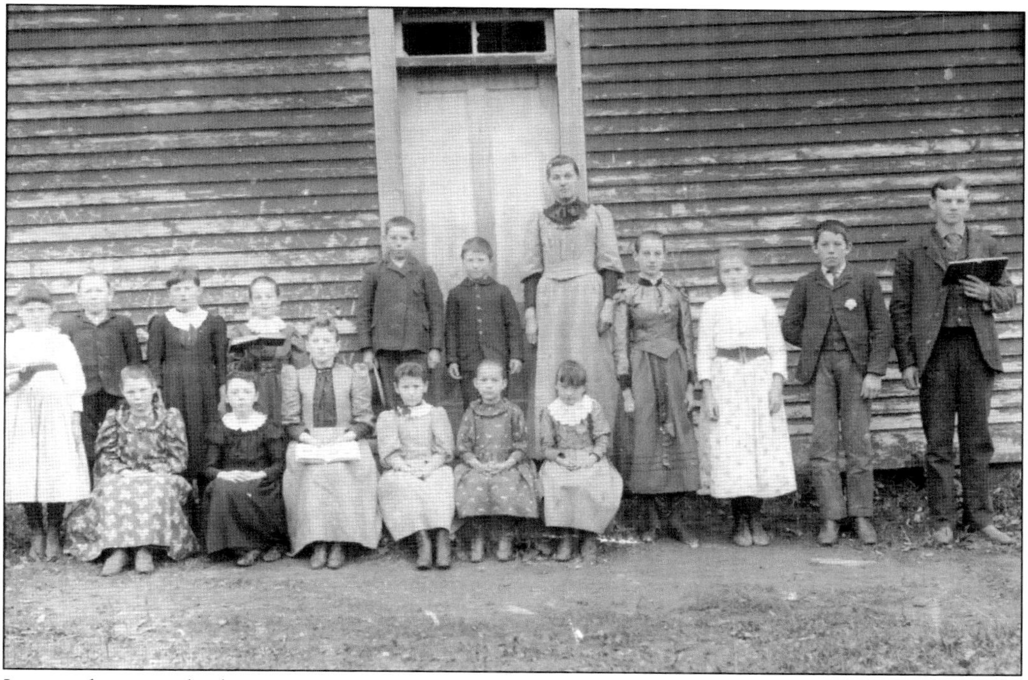

It is not known which one-room school in Northfield these students attended, but they represent any one of the 19 rural schools that existed in the town in 1890. Dressed in their best, they stand with their teacher. Four students are holding textbooks. For the majority of these girls and boys of long ago, their entire education would take place in this little rural school.

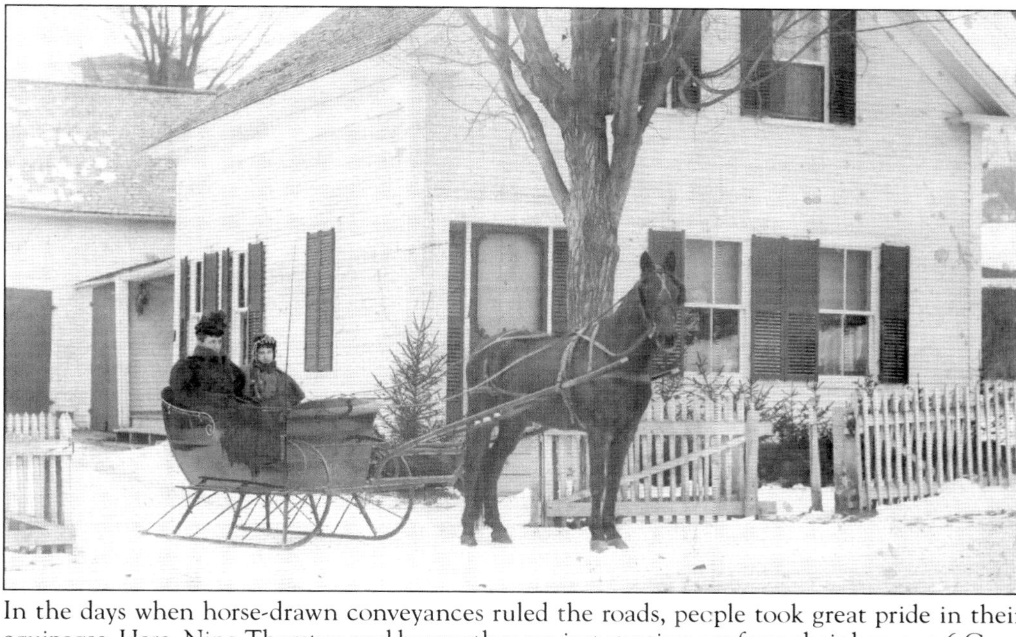

In the days when horse-drawn conveyances ruled the roads, people took great pride in their equipages. Here, Nina Thurston and her mother are just starting out from their home at 6 Cross Street. The ladies are fashionably dressed, the sleigh shines, and the horse is well groomed. Even the three brass bells on the sleigh shaft glisten.

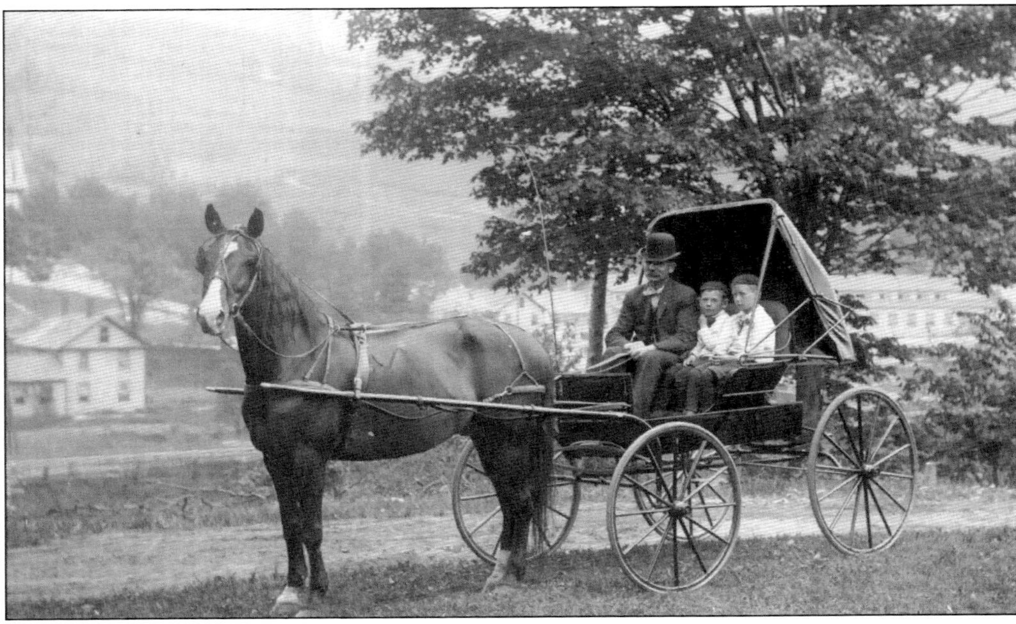

It was in the early 1900s when this father and his sons stopped on Carpenter Street. Pride is written all over this photograph. Dressed in their best, they pose in a gleaming buggy, with a horse that has been brushed and carded until its sides are shining and its mane hangs in waves.

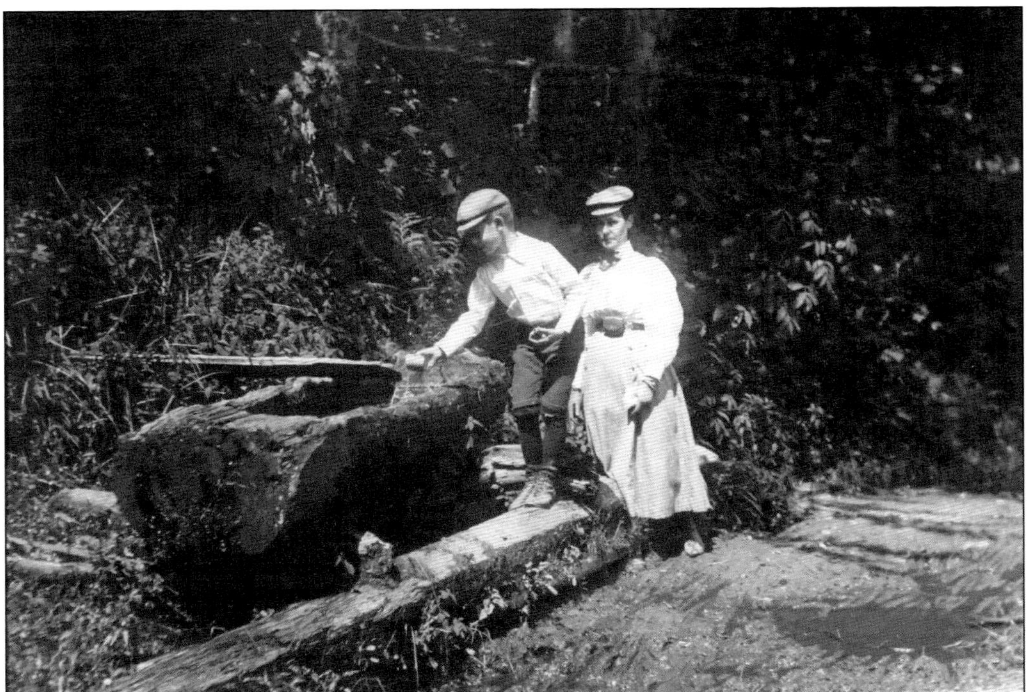

On a summer day in 1898, Jessie Howe and her son Homer have stopped at the watering trough on Stony Brook Road. Homer, it appears, is trying to fill his tin cup with cold water from the wooden spout.

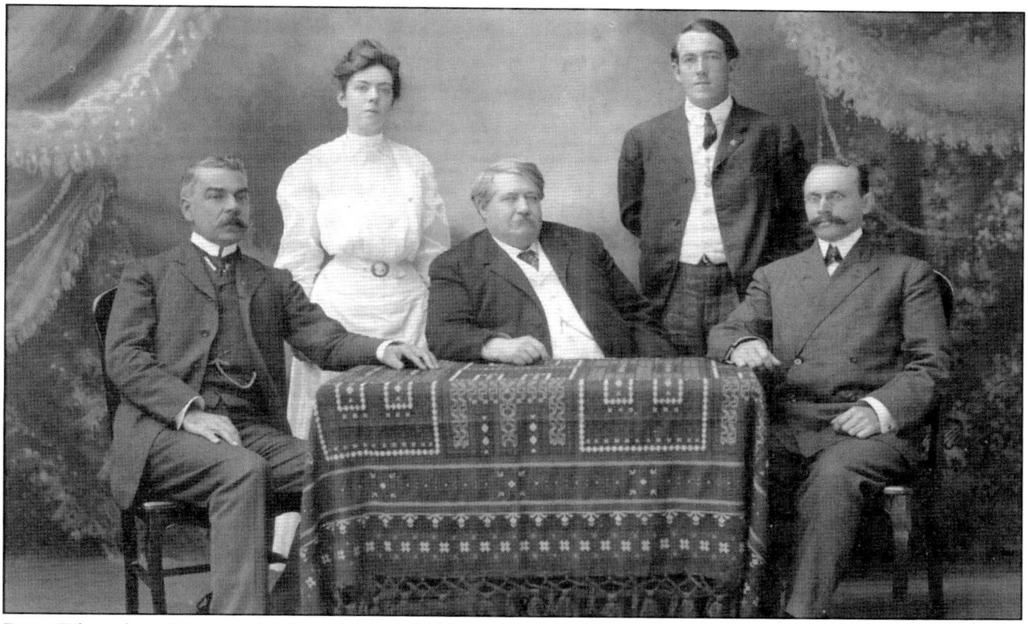

Pres. Theodore Roosevelt chose Northfield lawyer Frank Plumley to serve as umpire of the Mixed Claims Commission in Caracas, Venezuela, in 1903. He was so successful that President Roosevelt asked him to act in the same capacity in 1905. The commission met in Northfield from February to August of that year. In this memorable photograph are, from left to right, (seated) Count de Paretti de la Roca of France; Plumley; and De Jose de J. Paul of Venezuela; (standing) Louise Newell, Plumley's assistant secretary; and Plumley's son Charles. H.R. Roberts, a professor from Norwich, acted as translator.

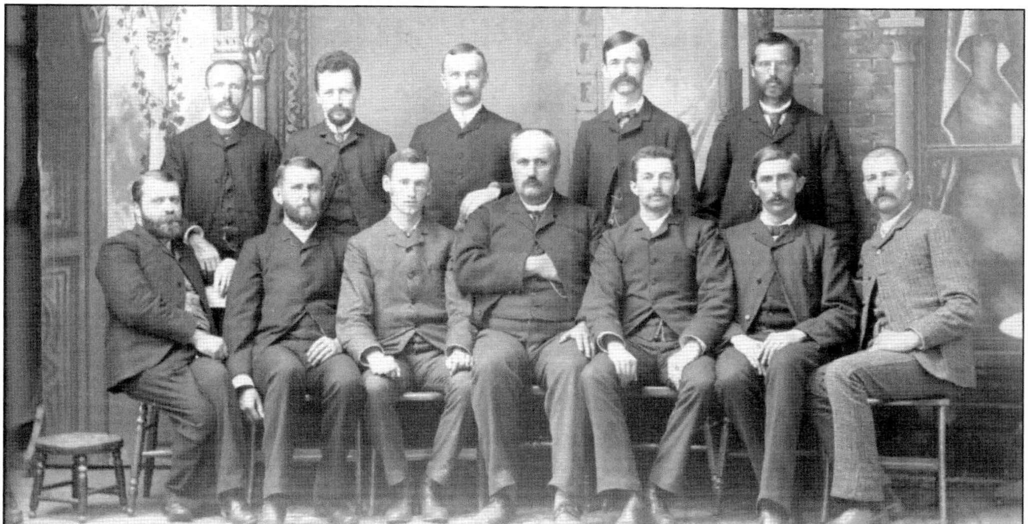

One of Northfield's most beloved and respected benefactors was Dr. William B. Mayo. In this early photograph, taken by Reuben McIntosh, Dr. Mayo is in the middle of the second row, third from the left. The Mayo Building and the East Street Block are two buildings he erected for the people of Northfield. Today, the Mayo Rehabilitation & Continuing Care facility and the Mayo Residential Care facility continue to honor this remarkable man.

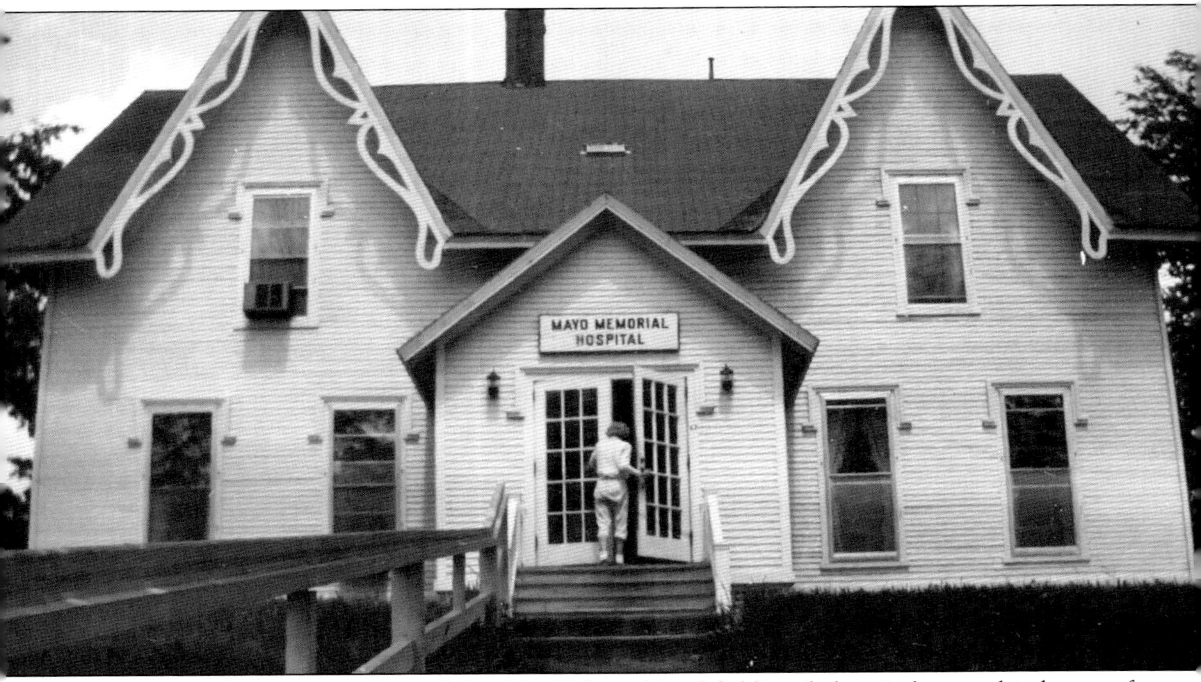

Through the untiring efforts of Cordelia DeLary, Northfield's only hospital, named in honor of Dr. Mayo, opened in 1936 on Vine Street. At the beginning, for hospital equipment, "Cordy," as all who knew her affectionately called her, had just two hospital beds, two bedpans, an emesis basin, and an old operating table.

An outstanding native son of Northfield was William D. Hassett, who served as corresponding secretary to US presidents Franklin D. Roosevelt and Harry S. Truman. Here, President Truman is presenting Hassett with the National Press Club Award for outstanding service to the press over a long period of years. The date is April 26, 1950.

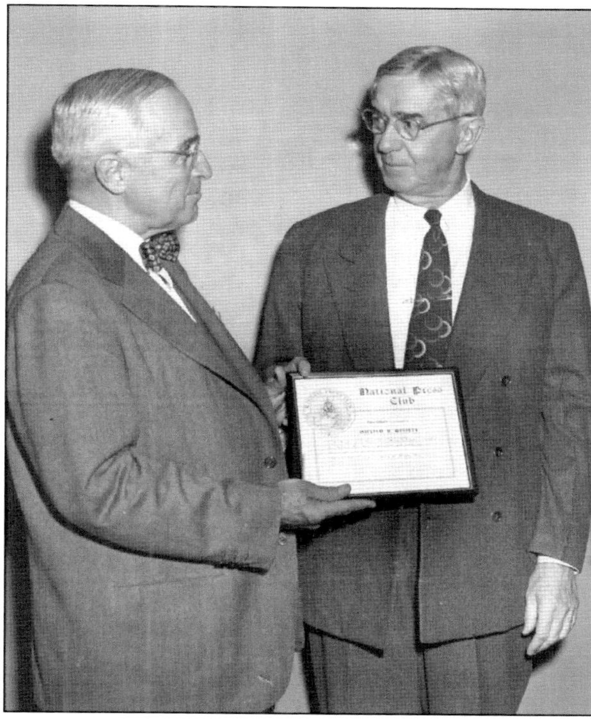

Local resident Christopher Dole built this house on Central Street in the 1850s. He is believed to have built over 20 houses in town. With little schooling and an eye for construction and design, he began making his own tools at the age of 13.

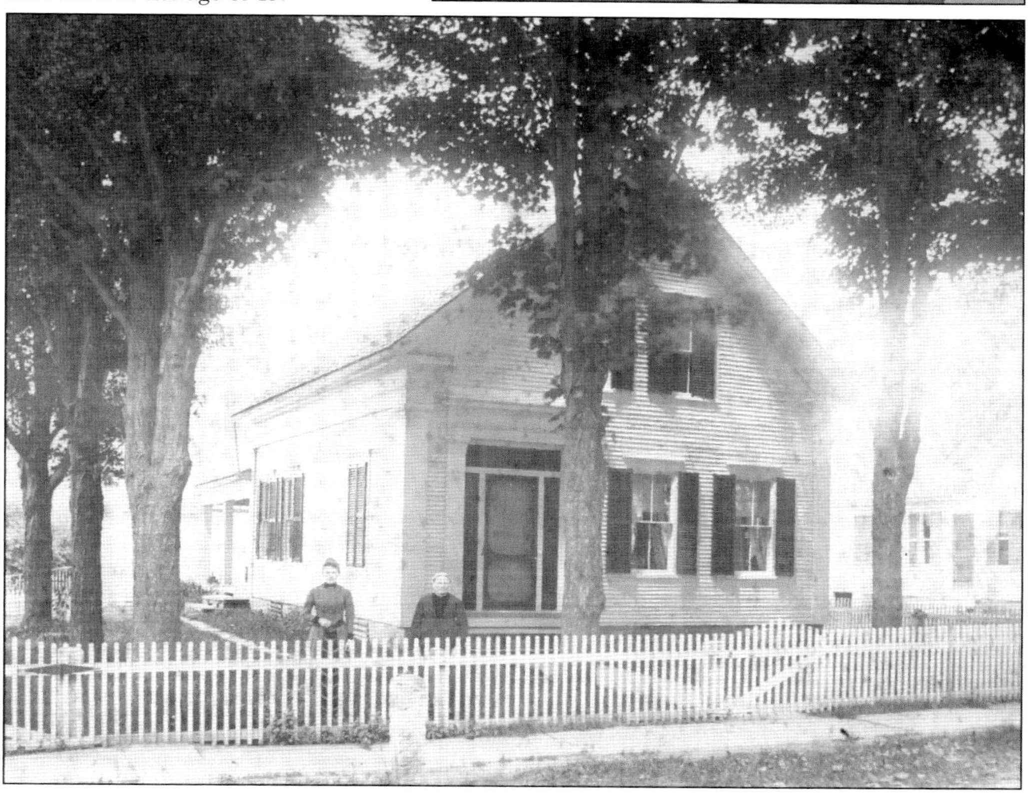

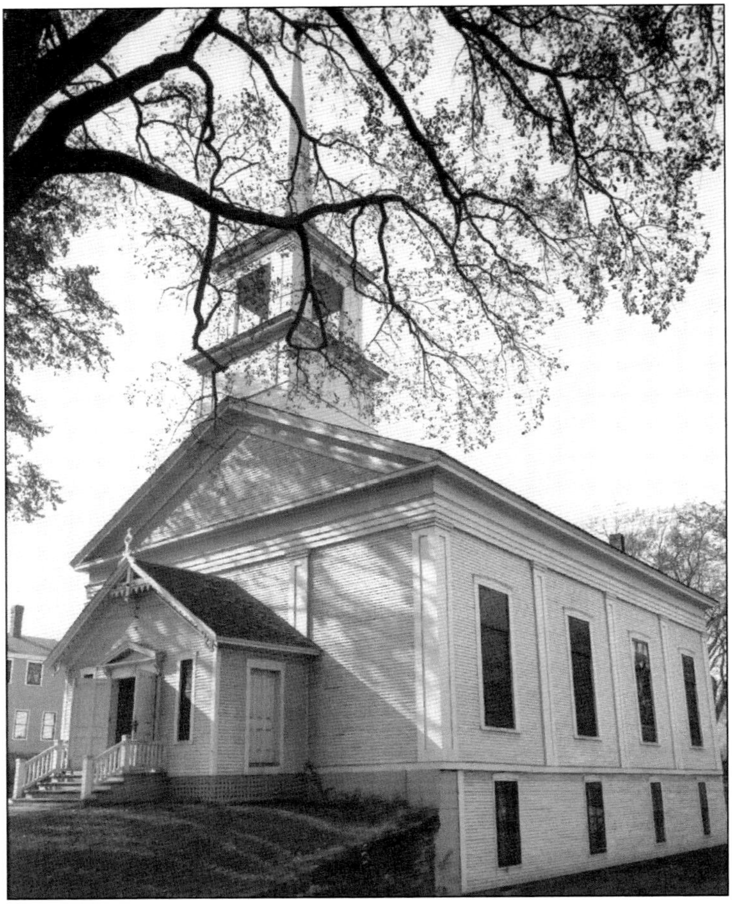

The foundation was laid for the Methodist church on South Main Street in May 1854, as the Methodists needed a place for worship. In 1868, the building (left) was enlarged, and an organ was installed. William B.D. Simmons, who was one of the most highly respected organ builders of the 19th century, made the organ. This mechanical organ is still one of the oldest organs in the state. This church is one of three Greek Revival churches in town. The house pictured below was the Methodist parsonage, located on Prospect Street.

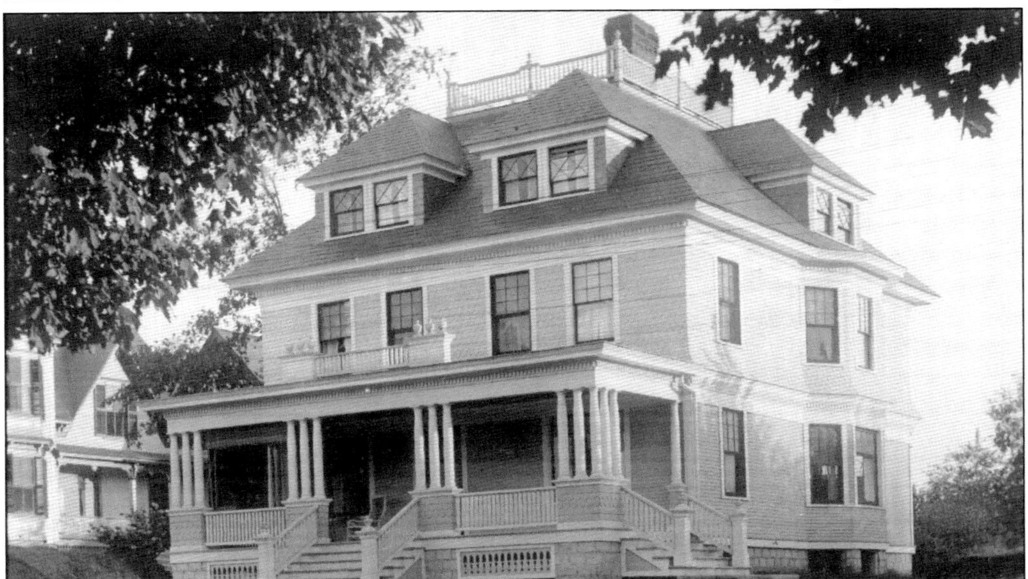

Eight

Celebrations and Fun

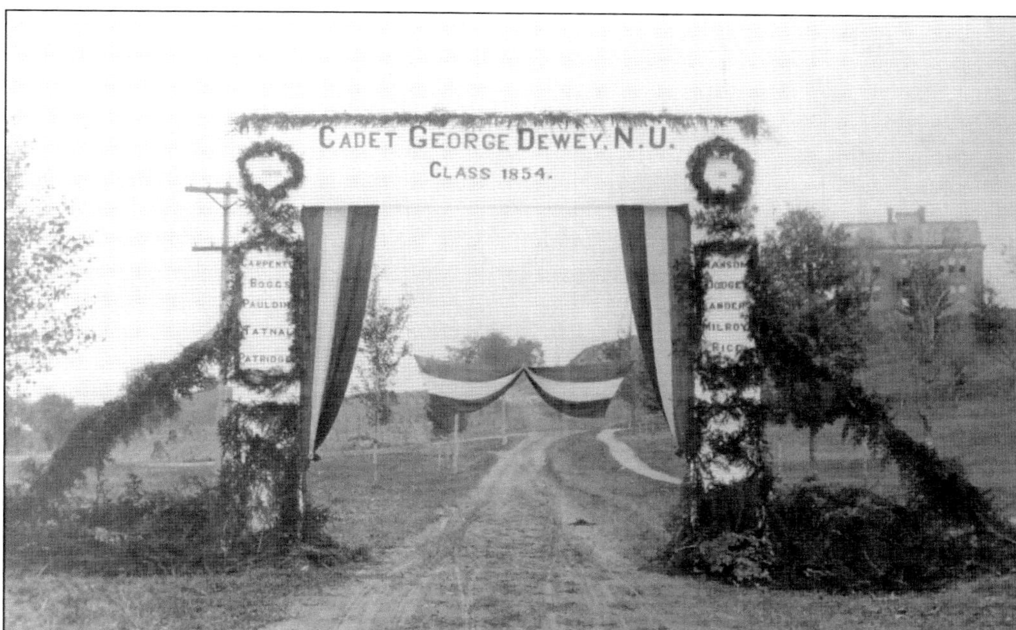

Northfield has had its share of celebrations over the years, from the dedication of the Civil War Monument to George Dewey Day to the Labor Day festivities held every year since 1975. This photograph shows the Dewey celebration banner, standing where Norwich University's north gate is today. The view is from Central Street looking south toward the campus.

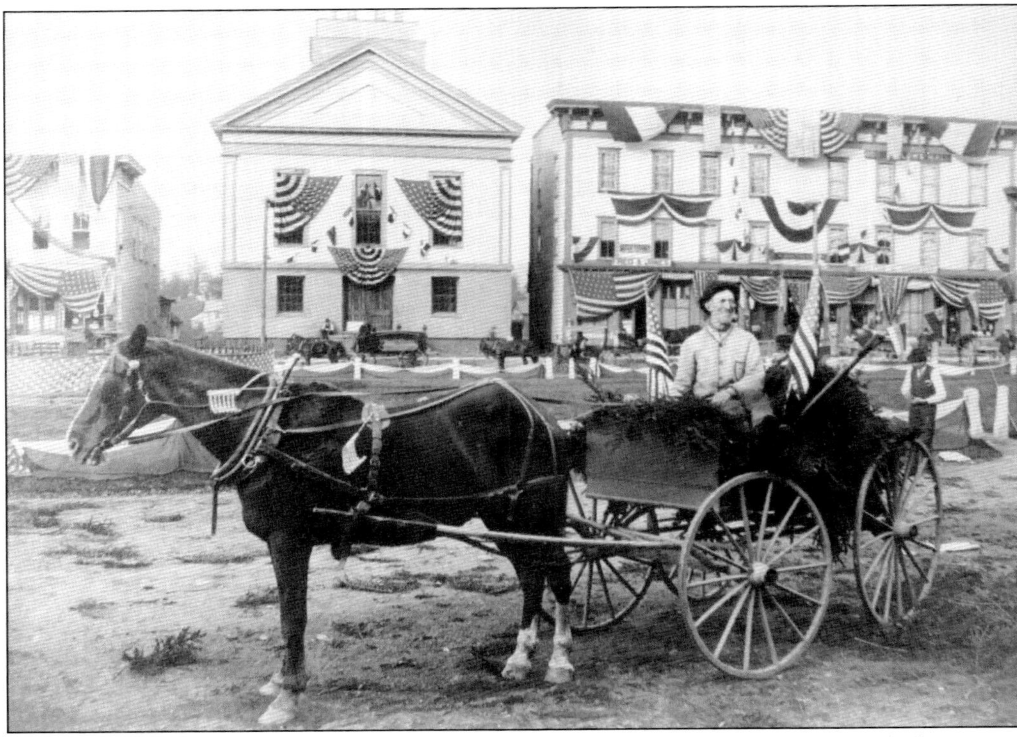

Admiral of the Navy George Dewey, born in Montpelier, Vermont, is best known for his part in the Battle of Manila Bay during the Spanish-American War. He is the only person ever to achieve the rank of Admiral of the Navy. The town of Northfield was privileged to have Dewey Day in October 1899. It was the biggest celebration in the town's history. Six different trains brought people and dignitaries to the town for the celebration. Admiral Dewey attended Norwich University for two years before transferring to the Naval Academy and graduating from there in 1858. The photograph above shows Ed Shaw in the Common, ready for the celebration. The train depot is seen below, with the north side of the Common decorated for the celebration.

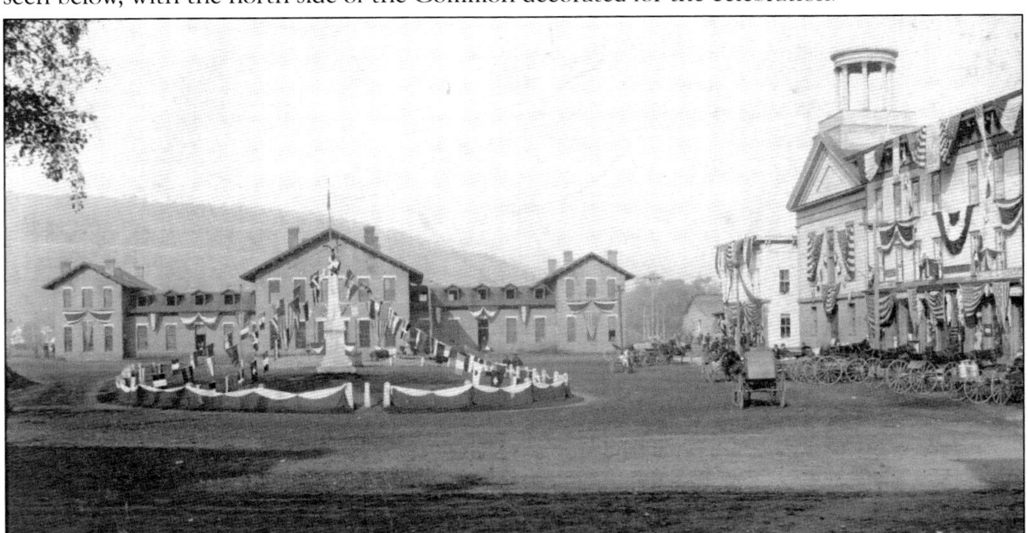

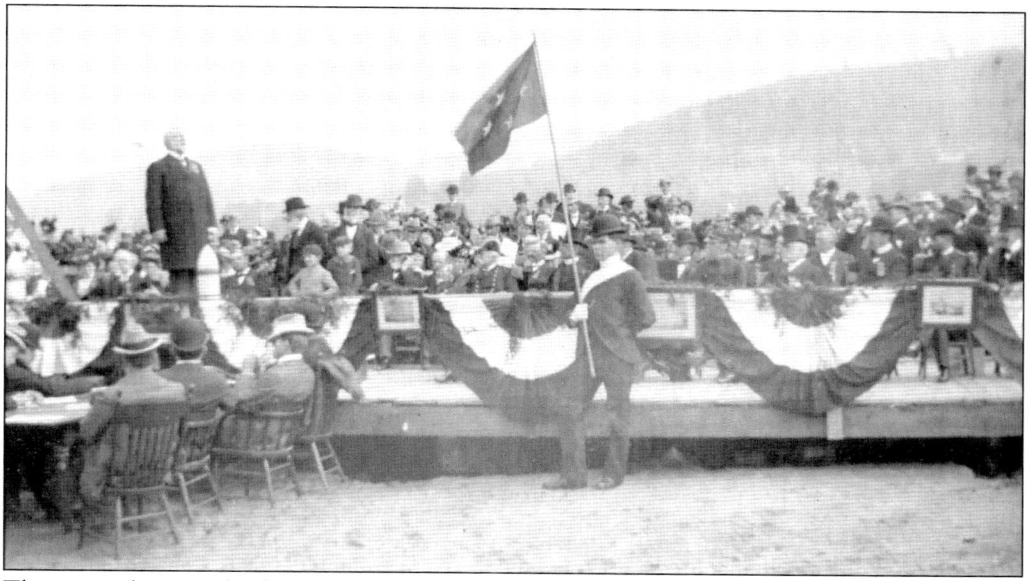

These two photographs show the dedication ceremony for Dewey Hall, on the Norwich University campus, held during the Dewey Day celebration. Before the celebration, about 1,000 people marched around the Common and up Central Street to view the ceremony. Norwich University president Allen Danvers Brown gave the welcoming address, calling Admiral Dewey "the greatest living Vermonter." Note above that Adm. George Dewey is standing on the left side, with Ira Holden displaying the Four Star flag for him. The photograph below shows the laying of the cornerstone for Dewey Hall.

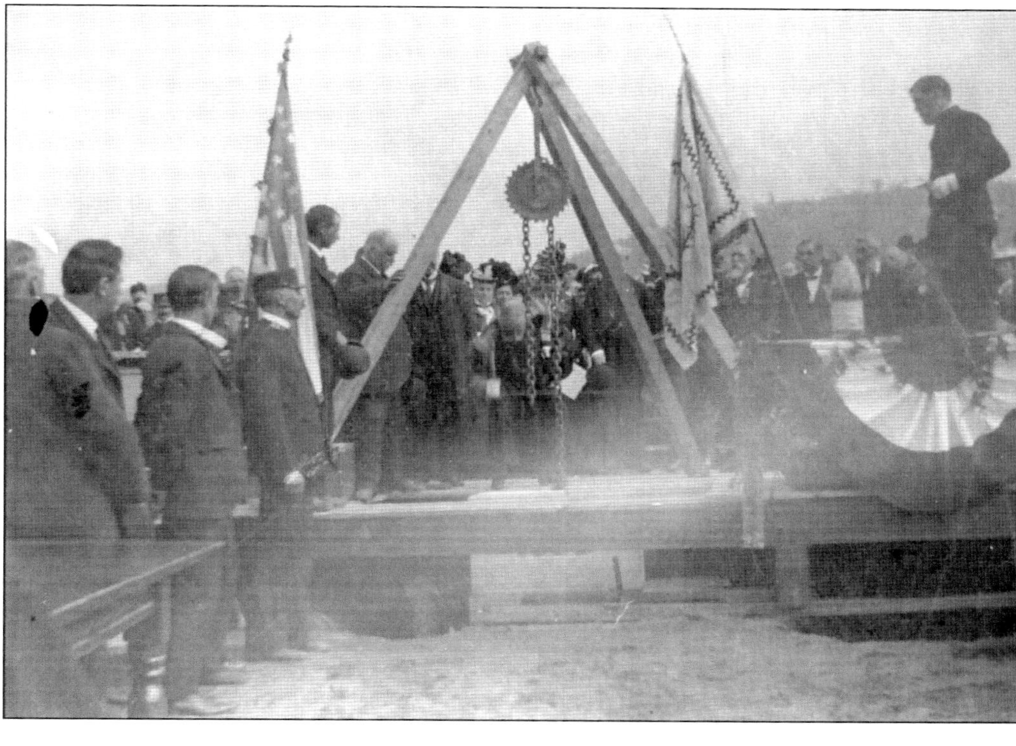

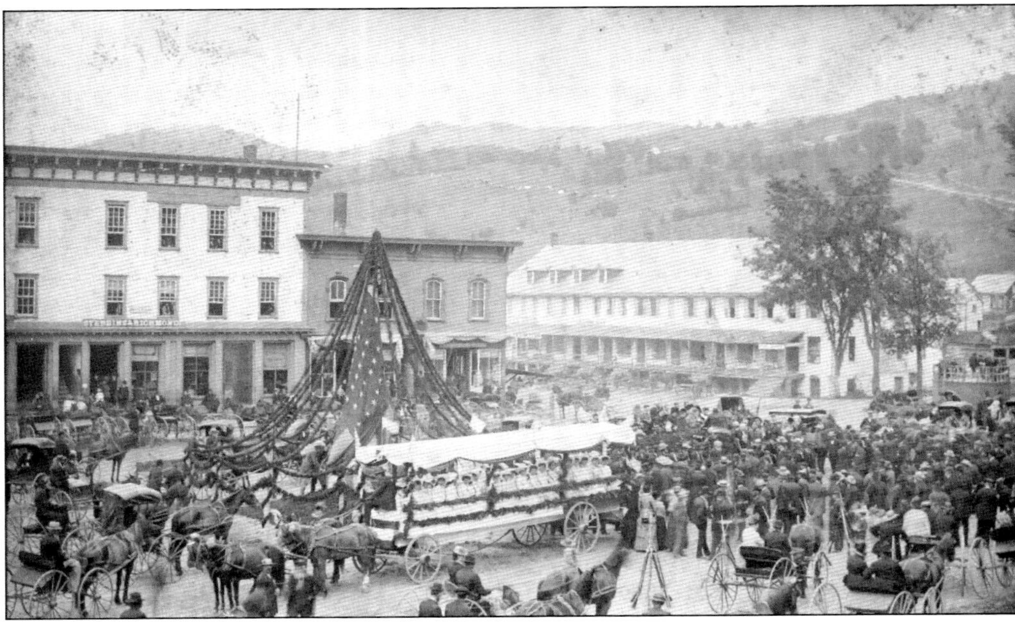

One of the first documented celebrations held on the Village Common in Northfield was the dedication ceremony of the Civil War Monument. The ceremony was held in 1885, and the monument is dedicated to all those from this area who both served and gave their lives in the Civil War. Each young lady dressed in white in the horse-drawn carriage represents a state in the Union at the time of the dedication. The photograph above was taken before the unveiling of the monument, and the image below was taken after. The monument still stands in the same place today.

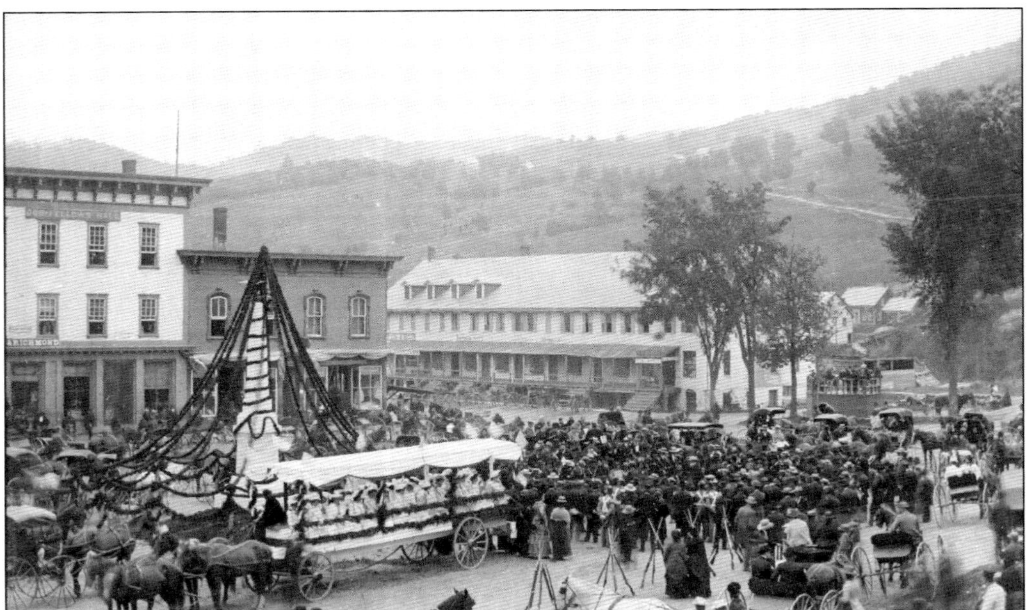

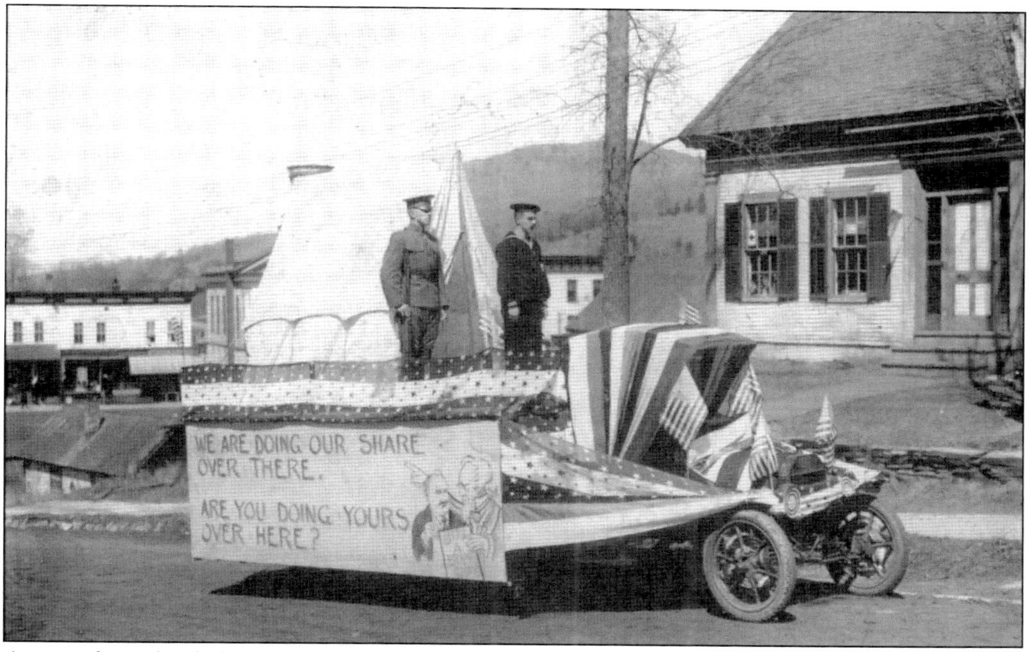

As seen from the dedication of the Civil War Monument, the town of Northfield has always been very supportive of the troops heading off to defend freedom abroad. These two photographs are from during and after World War I. In 1919, the town celebrated the return of these war heroes with a big parade. Many neighboring townspeople also came to join in the festivities and pay respects to the soldiers. The parade consisted of veterans from the Civil War and the Spanish-American War, along with those returning from fighting in World War I, cadets from Norwich University, and numerous organizations from the town.

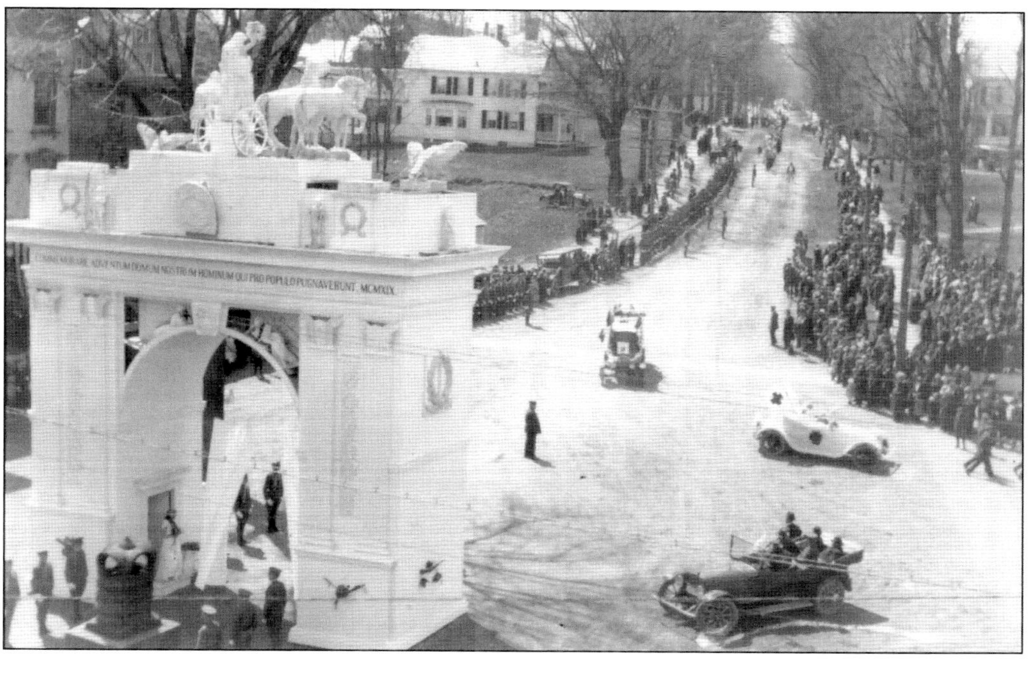

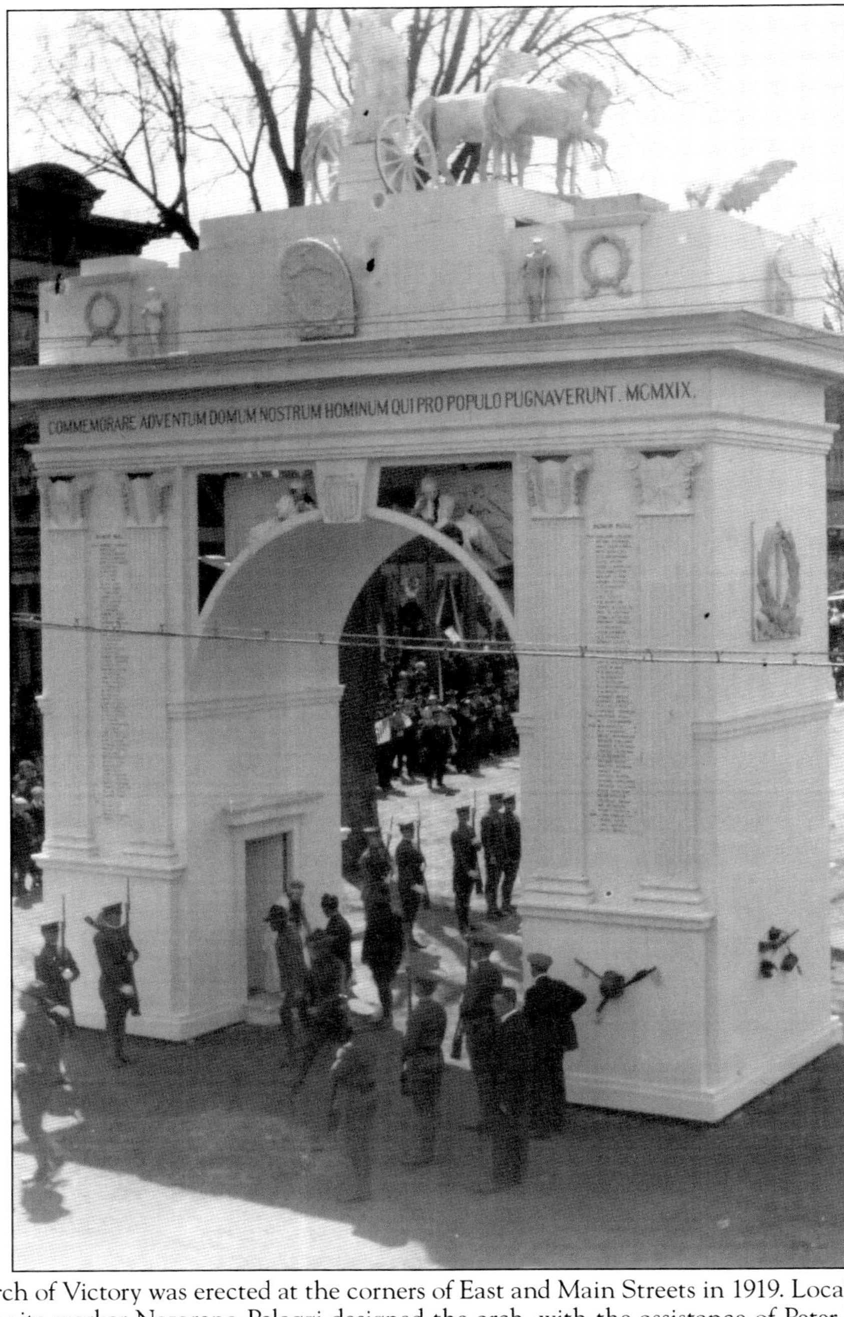

The Arch of Victory was erected at the corners of East and Main Streets in 1919. Local resident and granite worker Nazareno Pelaggi designed the arch, with the assistance of Peter Rabidou, a local construction company owner. This temporary arch was 42 feet high, 29 feet wide, and 11 feet deep and was similar in design and structure to the Arc de Triomphe in Paris. It was a wooden structure made with papier-mâché and only remained standing for a short time before it was taken down. As all the townspeople gathered around the arch, Frank Plumley gave a speech while four ladies, representing statues, lay half-reclining on the arch. After a dinner at Howe's Hall, there was more music and dancing.

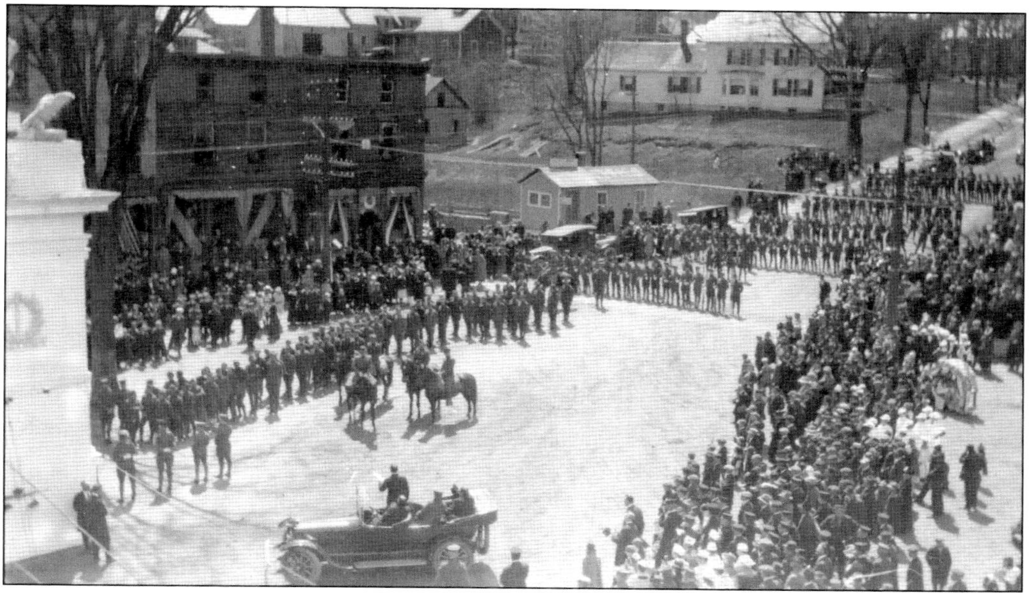

After meeting the returning Northfield men of the 26th Division, who arrived on the morning train, the townspeople had a fun-filled afternoon of excitement. With the Northfield Band playing, the past and current veterans paraded through town. Cadets from Norwich University, schoolchildren, and numerous organizations from the town were also part of the day of celebration.

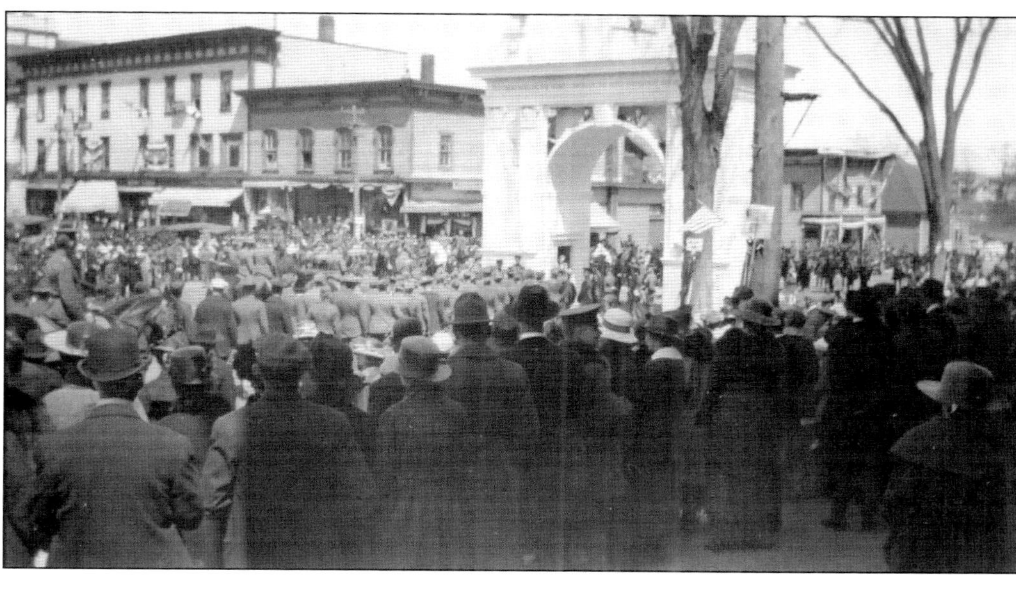

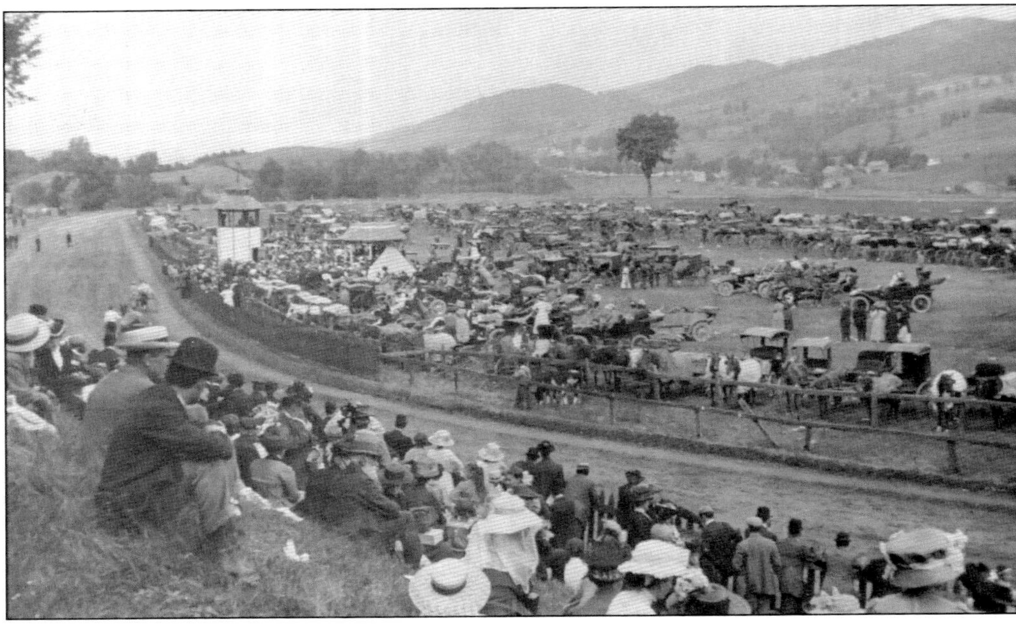

The Northfield fairgrounds was first used in 1873 for the Dog River Valley Fair, held on the Frank Gold's Trotting Park. The fair drew between 8,000 and 10,000 people during the month of September each year. It was so popular that the trains ran special routes every hour, charging 10¢ from Northfield and 15¢ from Northfield Falls. The use of the fairgrounds for the fair continued until 1933. From June 1933 until the start of World War II, the fairgrounds was used for a Civilian Conservation Corps camp, Camp Washington Company No. 198. These two photographs show the fairgrounds around 1910.

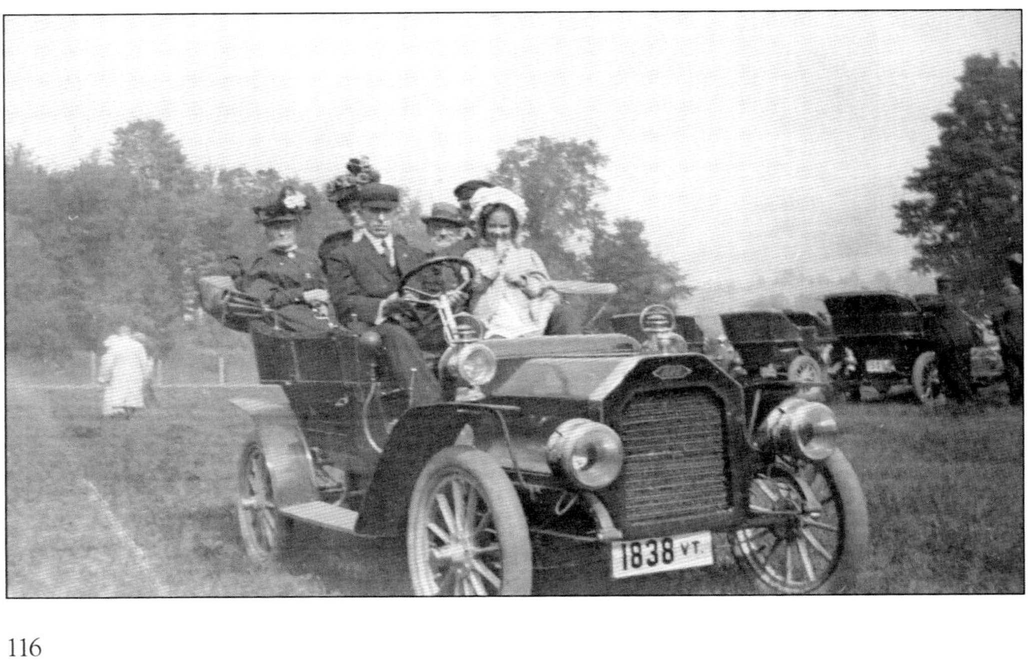

Nine

The Cadets Come Marching In

Norwich Forever

Norwich forever, queen of the hills
When far from thee,
Still memory thrills recalling
Scenes and old friendship,
Songs and old cheers,
Memories that fade not
Through the changing years.

Norwich forever, through rain and shine,
Sunset and dawning,
Still we are thine and in
Defeat or victory we shall acclaim
Thy dauntless spirit and
Thy deathless name.

Norwich forever, hail, hail to thee
Bright is thy glory,
Won in the long years and we
Pledge thee our future,
Thee to adore
Till in the skies the stars
Shall burn no more.

Words by Arthur Wallace Peach

Capt. Alden Partridge founded Norwich University in Norwich, Vermont, in 1819. Since that time, the university has moved to Connecticut and then to Northfield, in 1866. It was the founding school for the Reserve Officers' Training Corps (ROTC). Since it has made its home in Northfield, the university has become a large part of the town and community. Seen here is the university's song, "Norwich Forever."

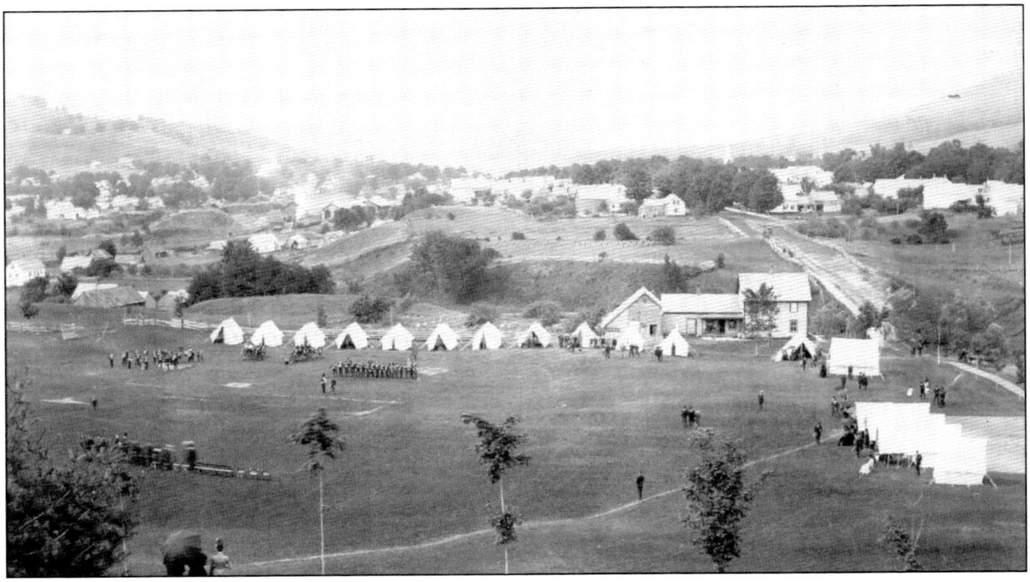

Sabine Field at Norwich University, first dedicated in 1920, has been used for various activities throughout the history of the school. In the late 1800s, the school used the area for drill and parade purposes, as shown in the photograph above. During the winter, the cadets would turn the field into an ice rink by flooding it with water for skating, as seen below. Sabine Field has seen a few renovations over the years. The most recent converted it into a more modern field used for numerous sports like soccer, football, and lacrosse.

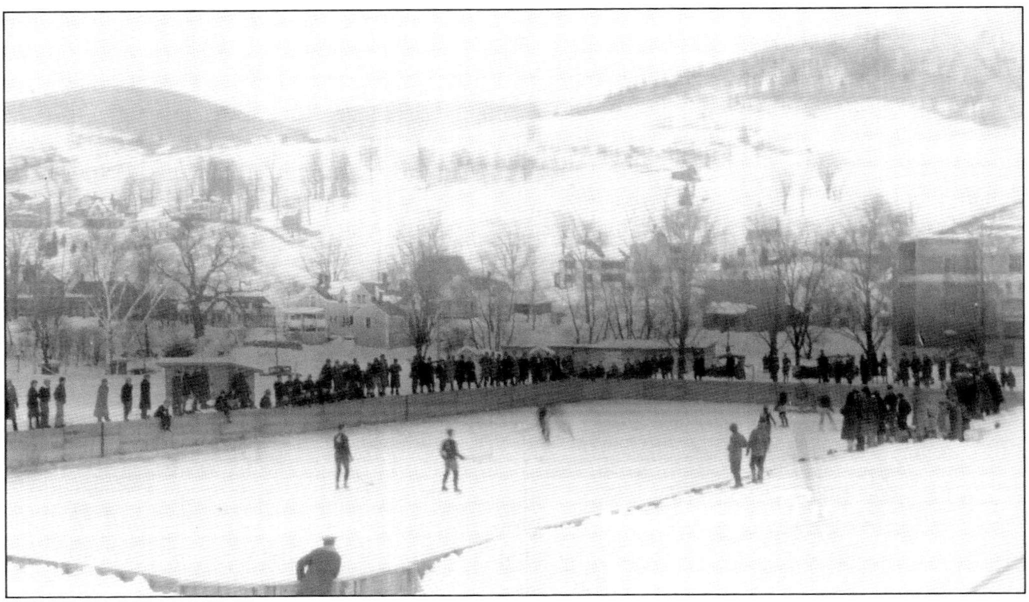

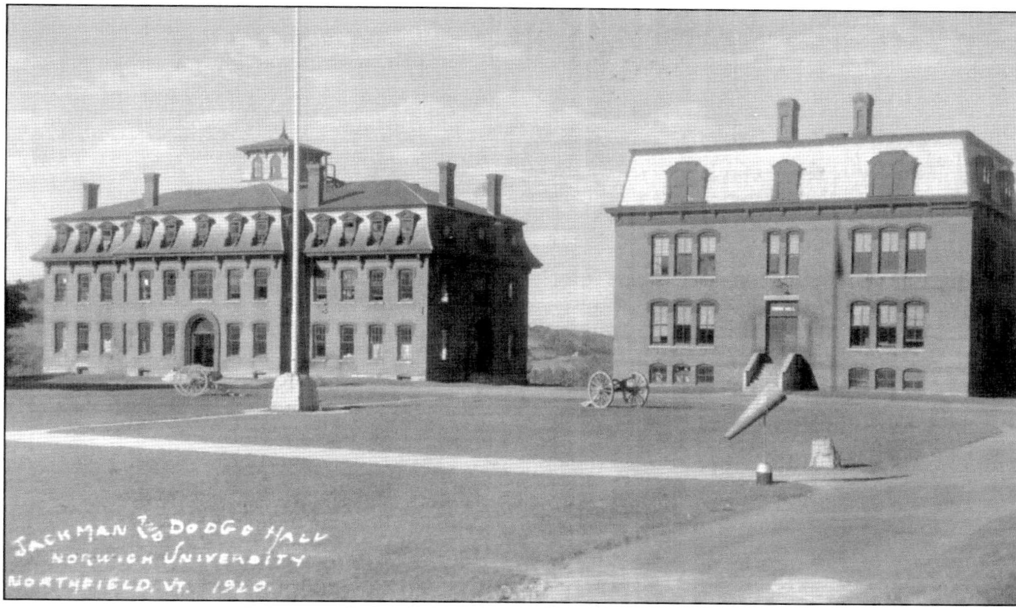

Pictured on this page are Jackman Hall (the "old barracks") and Dodge Hall during two different time periods. The photograph above was taken in 1920. The photograph below is of the cadets during shooting practice. Take note of all of the spectators gathered on the hill in the background. To this day, the town of Northfield and Norwich University have a bond that brings them together through the good and bad times.

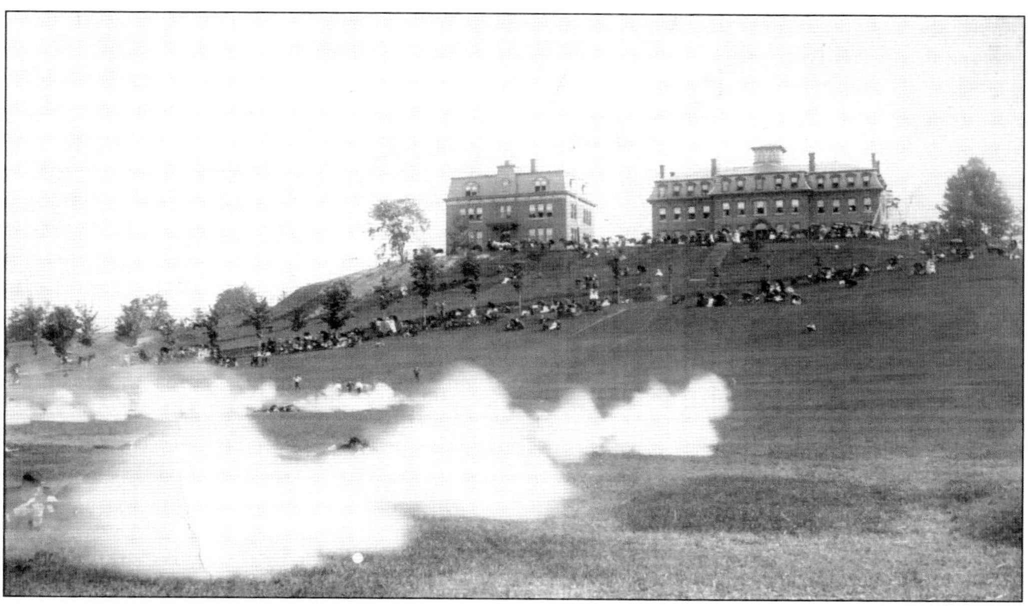

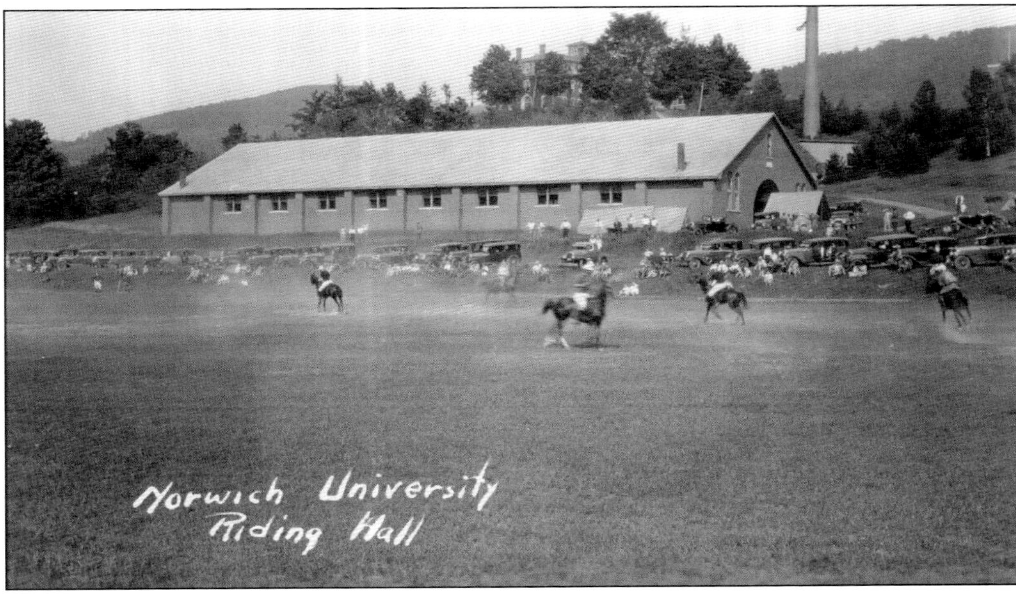

Cavalry has been a part of Norwich University since the early 1900s. By World War I, the cadets were known as "the Horsemen," and they kept that name even after the school shifted toward armor during World War II. The cadets would ride in parades when needed and play polo in their free time. There are many accounts of the cadets riding down to the train depot to escort girls up the hill to big parties. The photographs on this page show the riding hall and the cadets playing polo.

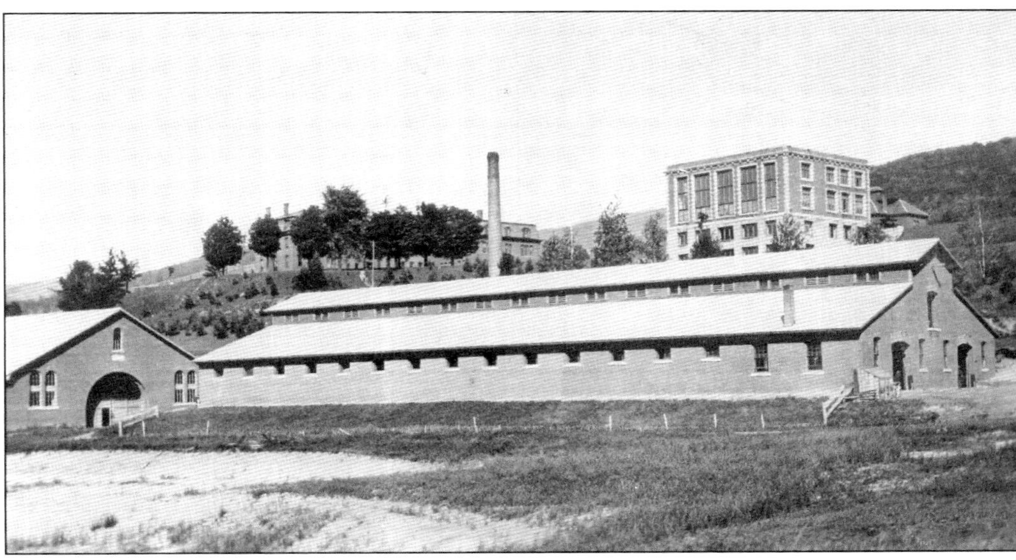

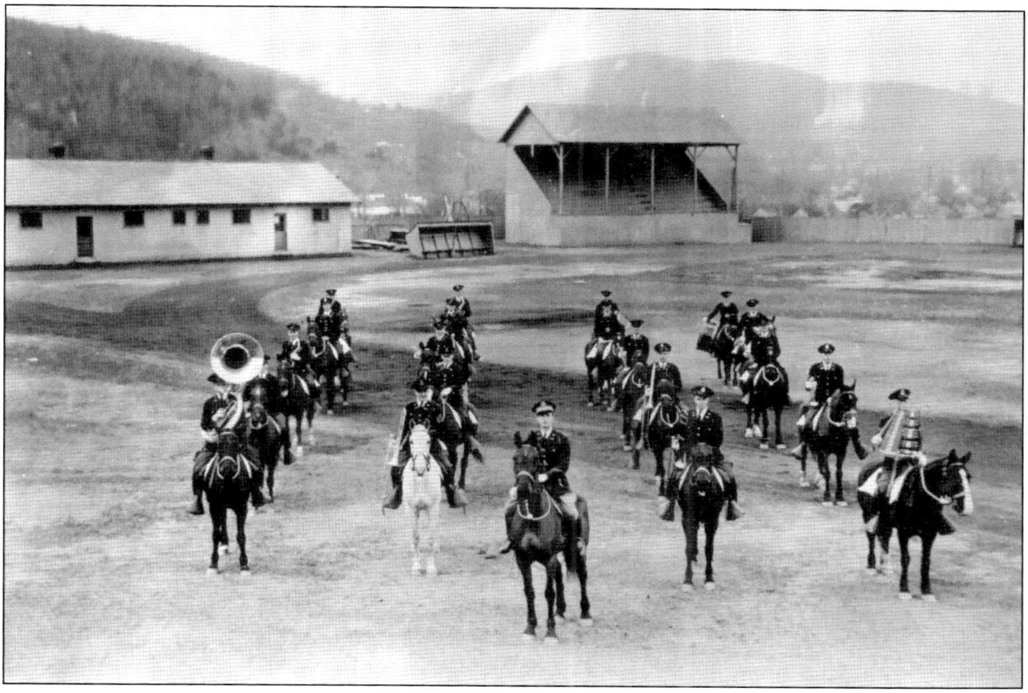

Life as a cavalry cadet was not all fun and games. Some of a cadet's time was spent riding in formations and parades, either as a regular cadet or as part of the cadet band.

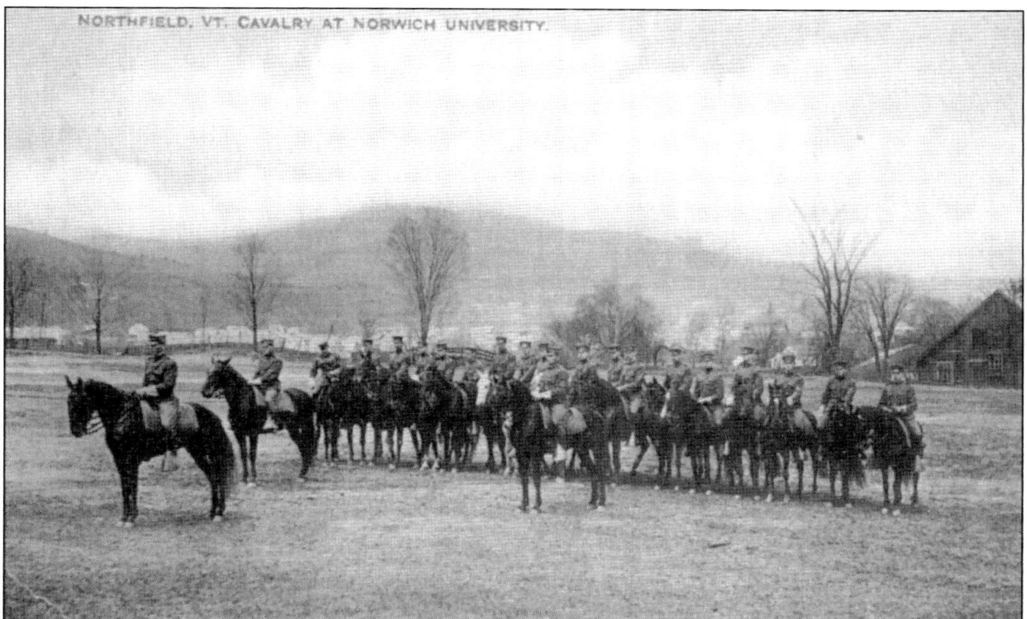

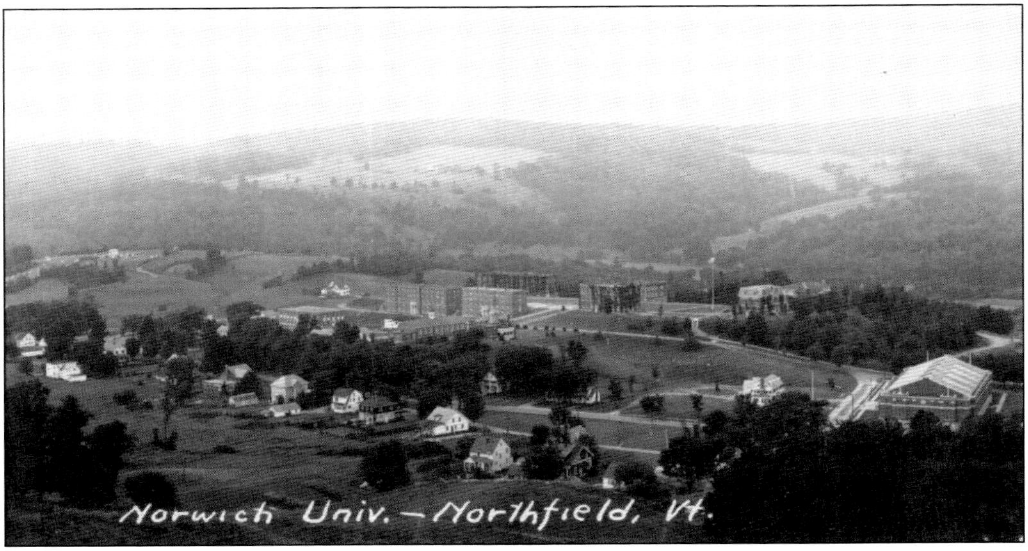

Since Norwich University arrived in Northfield, the university has become an ever-changing backdrop for the town. The old barracks, Jackman Hall, was erected as the first building on campus. Until it was built, the cadets stayed in town at the Northfield House. The campus has grown and changed drastically over the years. As seen in the postcard below, the cadets played football and other games on what is now the upper parade ground.

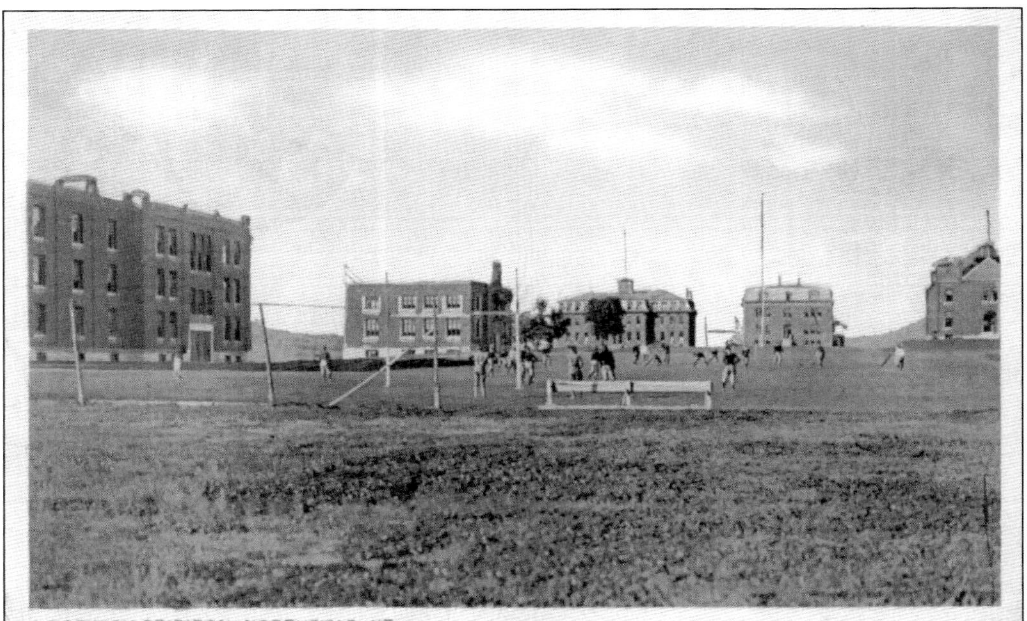

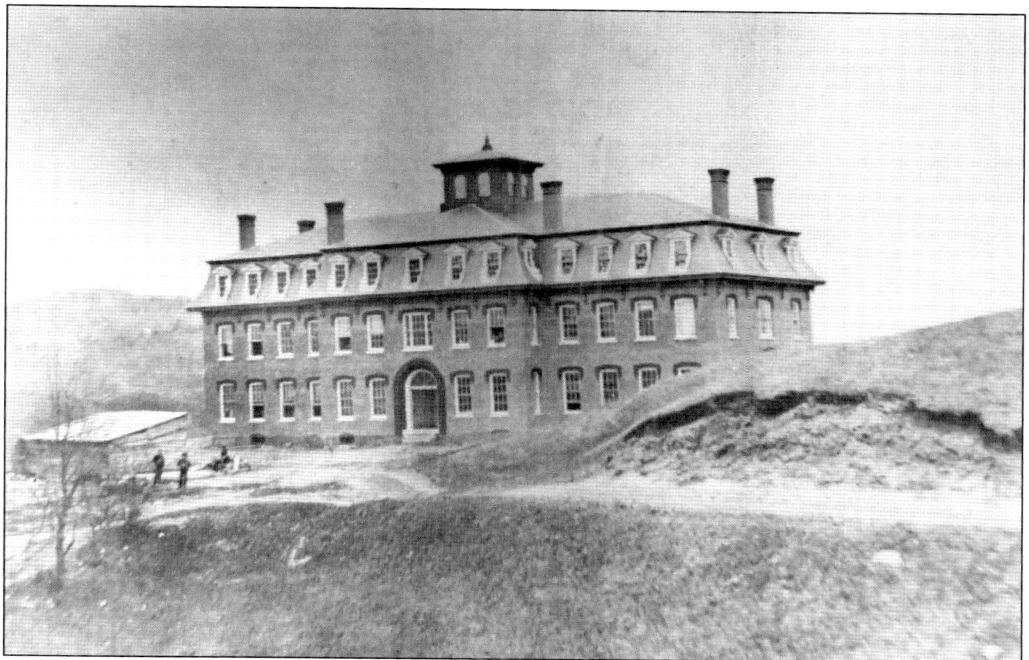

These two images show just a few of the changes made to the university from the first building to the way the campus looked in the 1980s. The old barracks was demolished, and a newer Jackman Hall was erected in its place, as seen on the far right in the picture below.

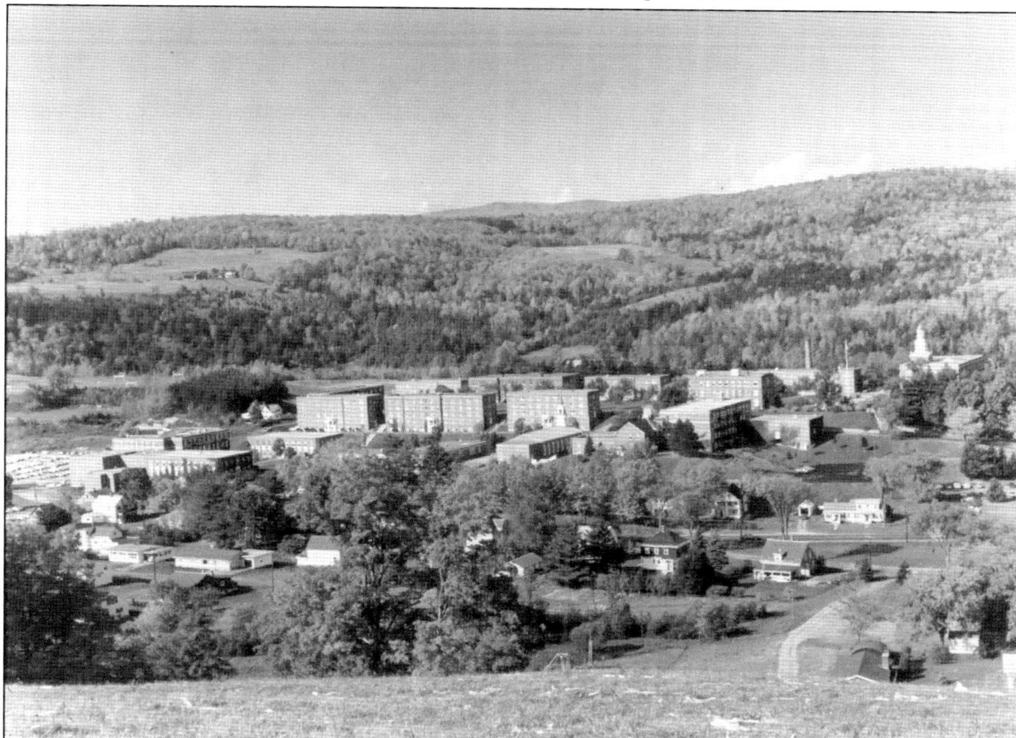

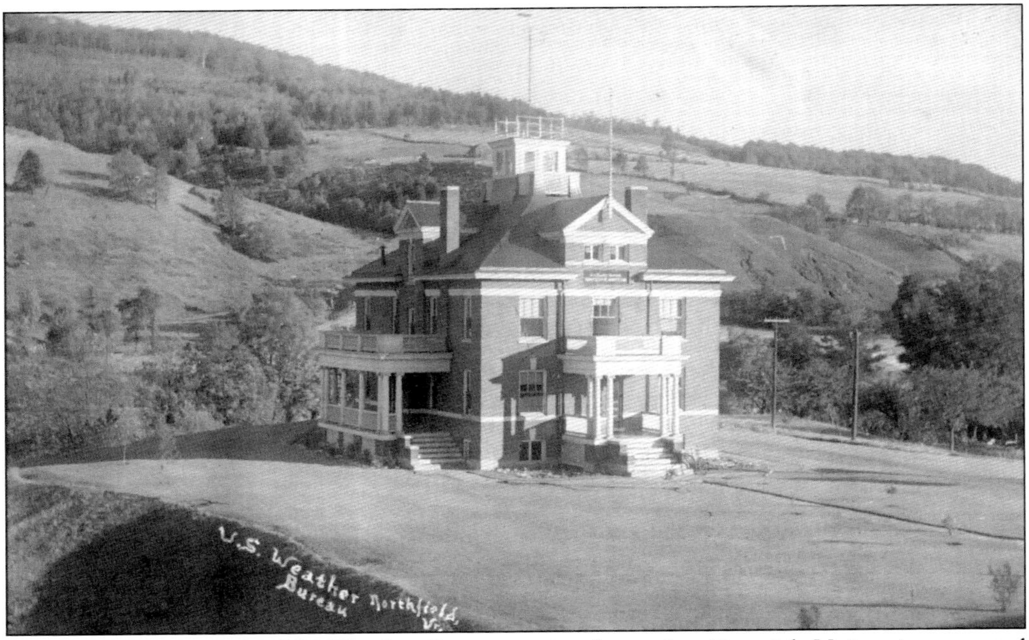

Established in 1888, this US Weather Bureau station located at Norwich University reported Northfield's weather daily to Boston and New York. Prof. Henry J. Cox was hired as the first weather observer. For a long period of time, Northfield was thought to be the coldest spot in New England. In the days of the old telephone system, the Northfield operator would make one long ring at noon to tell people on the line the weather forecast.

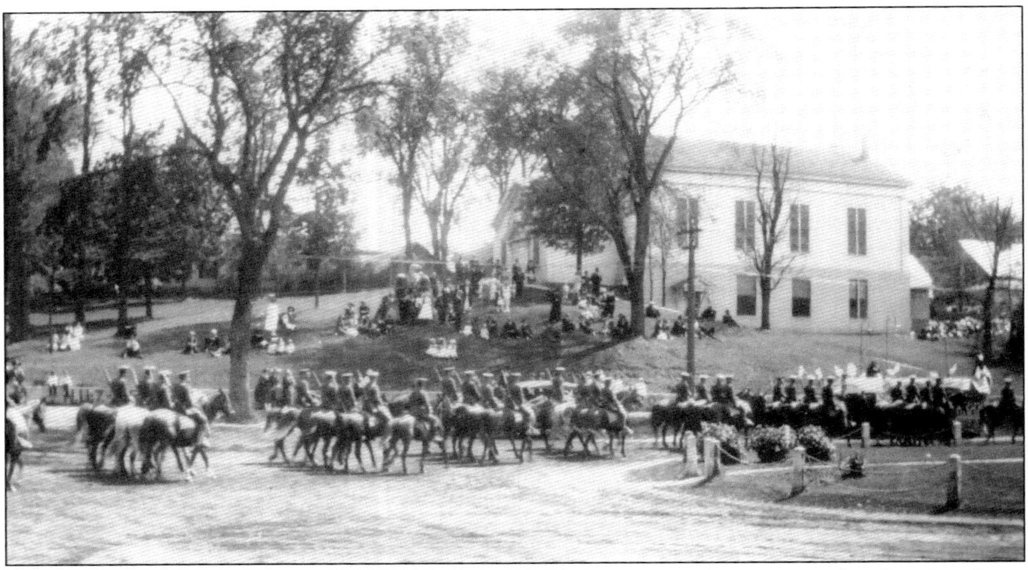

Since coming to the town of Northfield, Norwich University, with its corps of cadets, has been an integral part of the town and its celebrations. The cadets have participated in parades and ceremonies like the dedication of the Civil War Monument in 1885, the Dewey Day festivities in 1899, welcome home celebrations for troops returning from the Spanish-American War, World War I, and World War II, and the modern-day Labor Day parade and festivities.

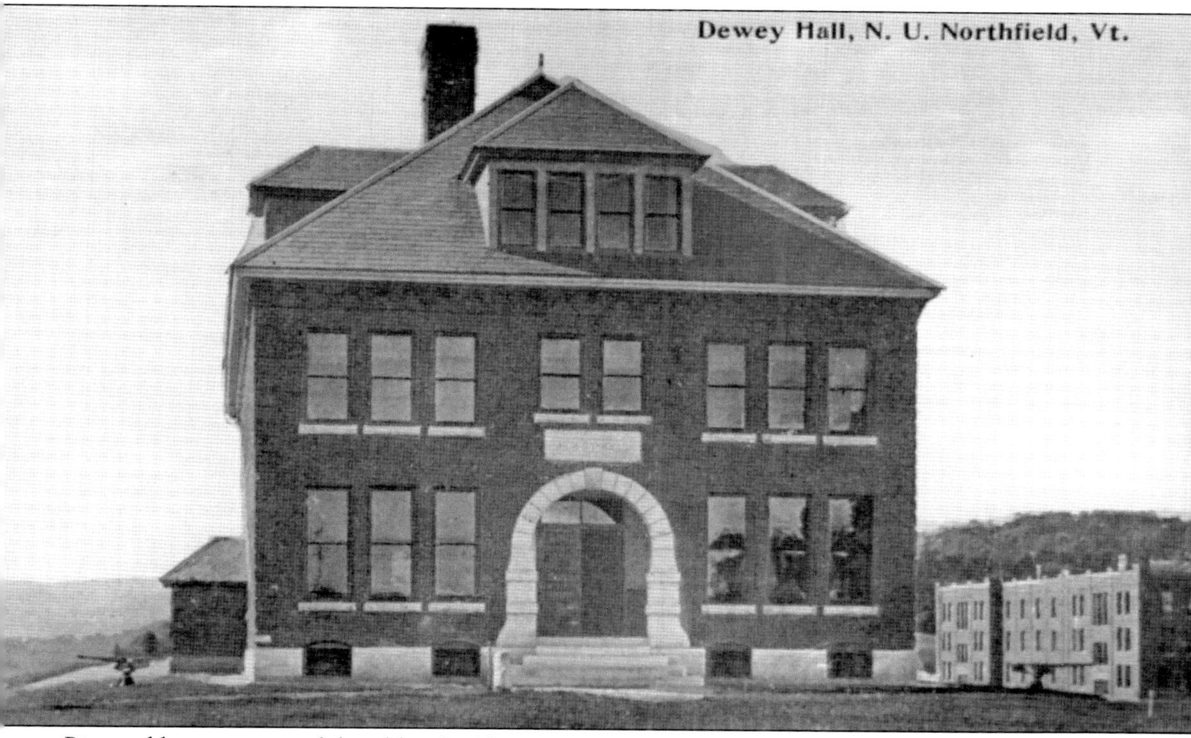

Pictured here are two of the oldest buildings on campus. Dewey Hall, shown in the foreground, was originally designed by Bradford L. Gilbert, a distinguished New York architect and the son of a Norwich alumnus. It was to be grandiose, with an elaborate circular dome adjoined by two wings and a central hall with a large staircase. However, not enough funds could be raised, so the present Dewey Hall was completed and formally opened at commencement in 1902. Alumni Hall is on the right.

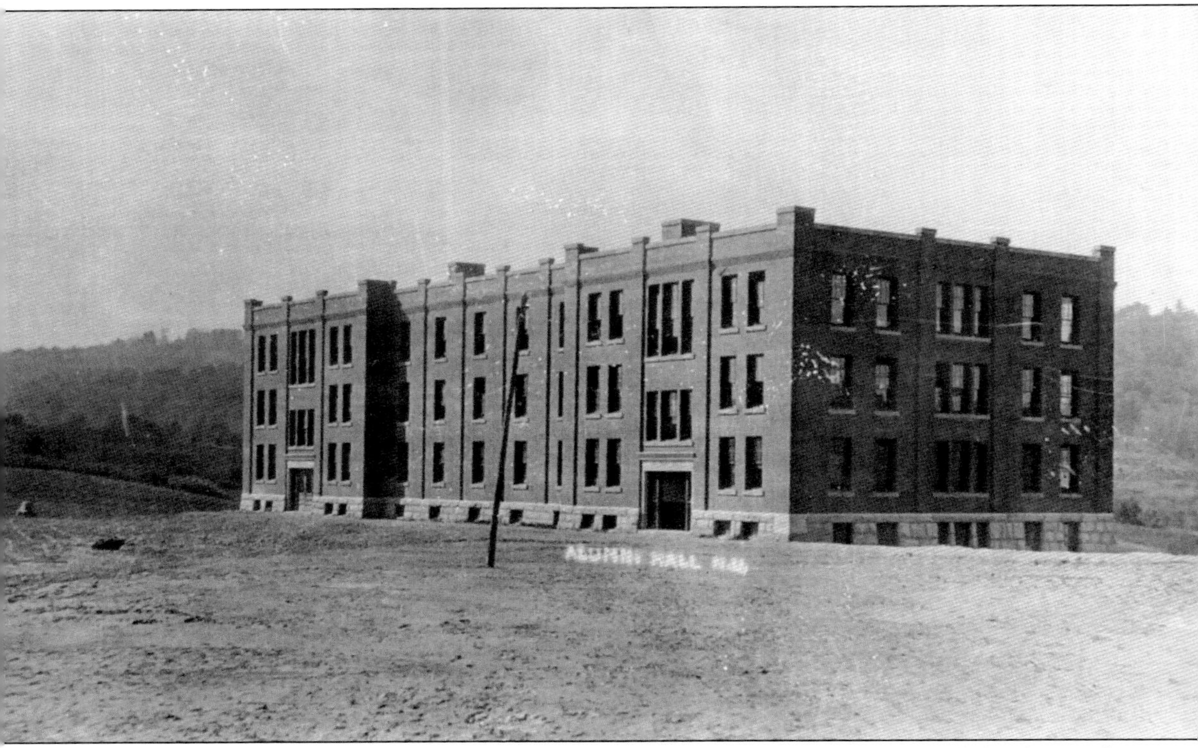

In 1905, attendance at the college was rapidly growing and more space was needed to house the cadets. Alumni Hall, shown here, was to become the second barracks on campus. The building was dedicated to Capt. Alden Partridge, the founder of Norwich, and work was completed in the summer of 1906.

Bibliography

Gregory, John. *Northfield's First Century*. Montpelier, VT: Argus and Patriot Book and Job Printing House, 1878.

McIntire, Julia W. *Green Mountain Heritage: The Chronicle of Northfield, Vermont*. Canaan, NH: Phoenix Publishing, 1974.

McIntire, Julia W. and Richard Cleveland. *Picture Northfield: A Photographic Study*. Northfield, VT: The Northfield Historical Society, 1985.